Colusa County Free Library
3 0738 00099 7865

D1601900

Al-Sahîfat
Al-Sajjâdiyya

Imam Zayn Al ´Âbidin

Translated with an introduction
and annotation by

Dr. William C. Chittick

The Muhammadi Trust
of Great Britain and Northern Ireland

The Psalms of Islam
Al-Ṣaḥīfah Al-Kāmilah Al-Sajjādiyyah

English Version

Translated with Introduction
And Annotation by:
Dr. William C. Chittick

With foreword by S.H.M.Jafri

Re-typesetting by Mrs. Salma Zishan Hussein

Assisted by:
Mohsin S. Khatau – Mahmood G. Dhalla - Ali Musa Amin

Printed and Published on behalf of:
The Muhammadi Trust of
Great Britain and Northern Ireland
131, Walm Lane
London NW2 3AU, England

Printed and published for the Muhammadi Trust by:

Al-Mahdi Institute
532 Moseley Road, Birmingham B12 9AE U.K
Tel: +00 44 870 774 4304 Fax:+00 44 870 774 4305
Email: almahdi@iname.com Web: www.almahdi.edu

Meraj Educational Publishers & Book Distributors
Bilal Muslim Mission of Scandinavia
Tel:/Fax: +46 8 591 198 17
Email: merajbmm@hotmail.com

ISBN 916 315 875-2

2007 (Second Edition)

This book has been published purely to be distributed free of charge on behalf of the donors. The Publishers do not give any permission for it to be distributed at a price in any manner what so ever.

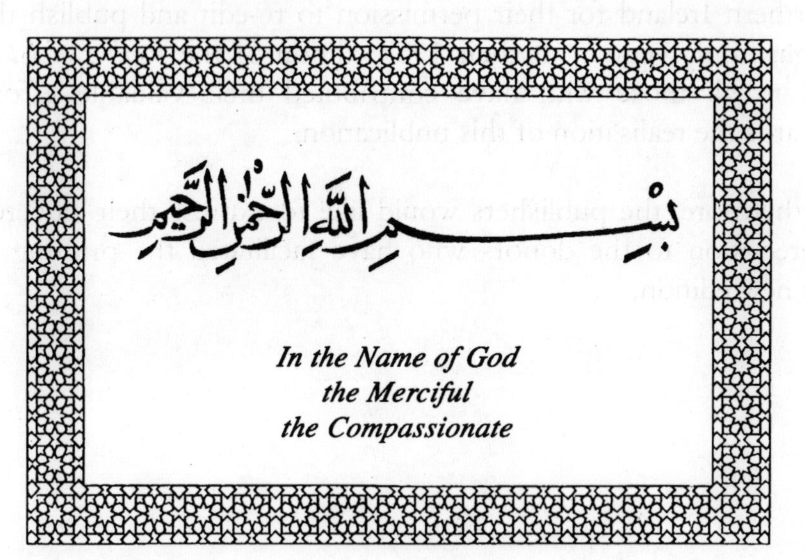
بسم الله الرحمن الرحيم
In the Name of God
the Merciful
the Compassionate

ACKNOWLEDGMENTS

Al-Mahdi Institute of Birmingham, U.K. and Meraj Educational Publishers and Book Distributors of Bilal Muslim Mission of Scandinavia – Sweden, would like to express their deepest gratitude to The Muhammadi Trust of Great Britain and Northern Ireland for their permission to re-edit and publish this English-only version of their 1988 edition of the *Psalms of Islam*, and to all those who have contributed their valuable efforts towards the realisation of this publication.

Furthermore, the publishers would like to express their sincerest appreciation to the donors who have facilitated the printing of this new edition.

CONTENTS

ADDENDA

FOREWORD

The present volume contains the supplications transmitted from one of the most venerated religious authorities of early Islam, 'Alī b. al- Ḥusayn b. 'Alī b. Abī Ṭālib, better known as Zayn al-'Ābidīn ('the ornament of the worshipers'). His grandfather, 'Alī b. Abī Ṭālib, the Prophet's cousin and son-in-law, was adopted by the Prophet in his childhood, and grew up under the personal care and guardianship of the recipient of the divine Revelation, the Founder of Islam. His grandmother, Fāṭima, was not only the most beloved daughter of the Prophet, but also a partner in her father's mission. His father, al-Ḥusayn, and his uncle, al-Ḥasan, the only grandsons that the Prophet had, were brought up by the Prophet, who showered his deepest love and affection upon them. Thus Zayn al-'Ābidīn derived his religious and spiritual authority and his divine knowledge in the closest and most intimate way through his father and grandfather from the Founder of Islam, the Apostle of God.

Zayn al-'Ābidīn was held in special regard not only by the adherents of the Household of the Prophet, who considered him their fourth Imam and the only religious authority of his time, but also by the learned circles of the Muslims in general. His period in Medina was that of a growing interest in the Traditions of the Prophet, especially those which dealt with legal matters. It was the time of the 'seven lawyers of Medina', who were engaged in collecting these Traditions and formulating legal opinions. Among the Medinan scholars, we find that Zayn al-'Ābidīn was considered to be an eminent traditionist. The famous Medinese lawyer of this period Sa'īd b. al-Musayyab, regarded the Imam with the highest esteem. Another great jurist and traditionist of the period, al-Zuhrī though he was attached to the court of the Umayyads, was also a great friend and admirer of the Imam. His honourific, Zayn al-'Ābidīn (the Ornament of the Worshipers), which refers to his devotion to prayer, was given him by al-Zuhrī. Thus, from the overwhelming number of reports recorded by both Shī'a and Sunni authorities, it would seem that Zayn al-'Ābidīn was widely respected by the community in general for his extraordinary qualities, such as the long duration of his prayer, his piety, his forbearance, his learning, and his generosity.

Perhaps the most eloquent testimony to his exalted position is the famous ode composed in his praise by Farazdaq, an eminent poet of his time. In it, Farazdaq refers to the occasion when the Caliph Hishām b. 'Abd al-Malik was overshadowed by the respect which the people showed towards the great-grandson of the Prophet. It was at the time of the *ḥajj* when both of them were trying to reach through the crowds around the Kaʻba to get to the Black Stone. The people gave way to Zayn al-ʻĀbidīn while the Caliph struggled desperately. This deeply offended the Caliph, and, in a sarcastic tone, he enquired who the person had been to whom the people had shown such preference. Farazdaq, who was present at the scene, thereupon composed an ode and recited it, addressing himself to Hishām. It is worth quoting a few lines from this ode, a masterpiece not only of Farazdaq's output but of Arabic literature in general.

It is someone whose footsteps are known by every place,
And it is he who is known to the *bayt*[1] in Mecca,
the most frequented sanctuary;
It is he who is the son of the best of all men of God,[2]
and it is he who is the most pious and devout,
the purest and most unstained,
the chastest and most righteous,
a symbol [for Islam]
This is ʻAlī [b. al- Ḥusayn] whose parent is the Prophet,
This is the son of Fāṭima, if you do not know who he is;
Whosoever recognizes his God knows also
the primacy and superiority of this man,
Because the religion has reached the nations
through his House.

It was this ʻAlī b. al- Ḥusayn, the Zayn al-ʻĀbidīn of Islam, who, as well as through other means, taught the Muslims the essence of Islamic spirituality through his supplications. They are not, however, merely supplications; they embody comforting answers to many questions with which the man of his time and the man of our time are confronted. They deal with the crises through which any Muslim or the follower of any religious persuasion has to pass, which result from a variety of stresses and strains, and which arise from sources both inward and outward.

I do not wish to discuss here the authenticity, validity, textual history, or even the literary beauty of these supplications, as these points have all been dealt with by the translator in his comprehensive introduction. Indeed, there is no space in a foreword such as this in which to conduct such a discussion. Instead, I should like to say a word about the relevance of these

[1] i.e., the Kaʻba
[2] i.e., the Prophet Muhammad

supplications to modern readers, irrespective of their race or religion, or of whether they are from the east or from the west. The author, as has been pointed out, was a man of purity and piety, sincerity and trustworthiness, who was committed to God and the cause of a suffering humanity. He had a bond of pain with the men of his time, as also with those who came after him. So let me start by asking the following question: Do these supplications, composed and taught in the seventh century, have any relevance for those who live in the twentieth century, or indeed those who are yet to be born? To answer this we have to ask a number of other questions. Is man to be regarded only in biological terms as the most cunning of animals? Is he to be seen as an economic beast controlled by the laws of supply and demand and class conflict? Is he to be regarded as a political animal, with a crude and excessive politicism occupying the centre of his mind, displacing all knowledge, religion, and wisdom? Or does he have a spiritual element which requires him to subordinate the temporal and the merely expedient to the Eternal and the True? Are human beings to be understood in terms of biology, politics, or economics, or are we to take into account their sublime nature, the spirit of God infused in them, and the ultimate ideal which they should endeavour to realize?

The essence of every epoch, age, or civilization, whether ancient, medieval, or modern, lies not in any biological unity of race, material achievement, or political order, but in the values that create and sustain that epoch, age, or civilization. Our achievements in perfecting the material aspects of life has led us to exploit matter instead of informing, humanizing, and spiritualising it. Our social life has given us the means, but has denied us the ends. A terrible blindness has afflicted the people of our civilization. The exclusion of the element of spirituality from humanity is the primary cause of the supremacy of matter, which has become so burdensome and oppressive. The defeat of the human by the material is thus the central weakness of the man of today.

Religion is rooted in a sense of wonderment at the eternal mystery of life itself. We feel a sense of awe and amazement at the mystery of the universe (*ghayba*), and move in an endless quest for answers to the perennial riddle with an eager longing to discover the truth of everything, the truth which is universal and absolute in the sense that it is valid for all men in all places and at all times. The experience of the mysterious is the fundamental quality underlying all religions. We must, however, make a clear distinction between religion as a personal concern, as man's encounter with the divine, and religion as a part of history, as a social phenomenon, and as the commitment to a group. Religion at the personal level is a commitment to a belief in the conservation of values and is based on the discovery of the essential worth and dignity of the individual and his relation to a higher world of reality. Thus the crisis comes at a personal level when the forces of evil, hatred, injustice, tyranny, betrayal, and falsehood prevail over love, justice, mercy, loyalty, goodness, and truth.

The supplications of the Imam Zayn al-ʿĀbidīn must be read against this background of man's crisis at the personal and individual level. Seen from this angle, they address themselves, in their essence, to the inner problems of the men of every epoch and age, every region and race, every persuasion and religion. Here was a person, an individual, confronted with hostile forces arising from both within and without, realizing his own limits, crying in the intense passion of devotional prayer, seeking communion with God, and entrusting the secrets of his innermost life to Him. Here was a person who found himself caught up in the din and clamour of life, in the clash of emotions and interests, in the stress and strain of immediate impulses, in the tensions and calamities of existence, and, above all, in the search for spiritual satisfaction, a man who was lonely and helpless, who stood before his Creator in direct communion, and called Him from the very depths of his heart.

Before closing this foreword, something must be said about the translation of something which is untranslatable. Among all the varieties of Arabic literature, supplications, especially those of the Imam Zayn al-ʿĀbidīn, are perhaps the most difficult to translate into an alien tongue. Dr. Chittick must be congratulated on his courage and vision, and on his grasp of the inner meanings of such an emotionally charged and subtle Arabic text. He has admirably rendered into English not only the meaning but also the feelings enshrined in these spontaneous utterances of the heart. The Muḥammadi Trust of Great Britain and Northern Ireland is also to be thanked for presenting this beautiful treasure of Islamic spirituality.

Syed Husain M. Jafri
Karachi
17 January 1988

PUBLISHER'S FOREWORD

As far as the doctrinal tenets are concerned, Islam maintains that it is not enough just to acknowledge them unquestioningly or as a family tradition. It is the duty of every individual to believe in them independently and voluntarily after having been convinced of their truth. From an Islamic point of view worship is not confined to the physical realm of worship alone, such as Prayers and Fasting. There is another 'higher' kind of worship which consists of thinking and pondering. If this kind of worship leads to the awakening of the human being, it is far superior to many years of mere 'physical worship', as can be widely found in the *Aḥadīth*. The spiritual and moral formation of the human being is one stage subsequent to her physical formation. Her body is formed in the womb by the creation factors. But her spiritual and moral systems and the components of her personality have yet to be developed. As such, every individual is the builder and the engineer of his/her own personality. The brush which paints the personality of the human being has been given in her own hand.

Within this noble book are accommodated such issues that nourishes the ever yearning soul of the human being so that she may be awakened and brought to life again. Thus harmonising and aspiring of bringing into perfection the unlimited potentiality from within, by giving a voice to the 'inner', perhaps the same way as prayer and fasting in a way is an expression of the 'outer'. In this way both the 'inner' and the 'outer' become united as one, and the human soul may continue in her striving towards her embellishment.

We have known of communication descending from 'Above to below', contained within this book we could say is demonstrated together with the manner and approach, one of the finest examples of the aspiring soul's communication for perfection, ascending from 'below to Above'.

Gulam Ali Dhalla - Chairman
Meraj Educational Publishers & Book Distributors
Bilal Muslim Mission of Scandinavia

Märsta-Sweden 17th Rabi al-Awwal 1426 / 26th April 2005

TRANSLATOR'S INTRODUCTION

AL-ṢAḤĪFAT AL-SAJJĀDIYYA is the oldest prayer manual in Islamic sources and one of the most seminal works of Islamic spirituality of the early period. It was composed by the Prophet's great grandson, 'Alī ibn al-Ḥusayn, known as Zayn al-'Ābidīn ('the adornment of the worshippers'), and has been cherished in Shi'ite sources from earliest times. Zayn al-'Ābidīn was the fourth of the Shi'ite Imams, after his father Ḥusayn, his uncle Ḥasan, and his grandfather 'Alī, the Prophet's son-in-law. Shi'ite tradition considers the *Ṣaḥīfa* a book worthy of the utmost veneration, ranking it behind only the Qur'ān and 'Alī's *Nahj al-balāgha.*

'ALĪ IBN AL- ḤUSAYN

'Alī ibn al- Ḥusayn was born in Medina, according to most sources in the year 38/658-9.[1] He may have been too small to have remembered his grandfather 'Alī, who was killed in 40/661, but he was brought up in the presence of his uncle Ḥasan and his father Ḥusayn, the Prophet's beloved grandchildren. Many Shī'ite sources state that his mother was Shahrbānū, the daughter of Yazdigird, the last Sasanian king of Persia.[2] Thus he was said to be 'Ibn al-Khiyaratayn', the 'son of the best two', meaning the Quraysh among the Arabs and the Persians among the non-Arabs. According to some accounts, his mother was brought as a captive to Medina during the caliphate of 'Umar, who wanted to sell her. 'Alī suggested instead that she be offered her choice of the Muslim men as husband and that her dower be paid from the public treasury. 'Umar agreed and she chose 'Alī's son of Ḥusayn[3]. She is said to have died shortly after giving birth to her only son 'Alī.

There is no need to recount here the tragedy at Karbalā' in 61/680, when Ḥusayn and many of the male members of his family were killed by the forces of the Umayyad caliph Yazīd, an event which shook the Islamic world and precipitated the nascent Shī'ite movement. Zayn al-'Ābidīn accompanied his father on the march toward Kufa, but he had fallen

[1] Other dates mentioned are 33/653-4, 36/656-7, 37/657-8, 50/670.

[2] Her name has also been given as Shāhzanan, Sulāfa, Ghazāla, and Shahrbānūya, among others.

[3] Mūḥsin al-Amīn al-Amilī, *A'yān al-shi'ā* , Damascus, 1935-, iv, 189.

deathly ill and was lying on a skin in a tent. Once the Umayyad troops had massacred Ḥusayn and his male followers, they looted the tents, stripped the women of their jewellery, and even took the skin upon which Zayn al-'Ābidīn was prostrate. The infamous Shamir (Shimr) ibn Dhī al-Jawshan was about to kill Zayn al-'Ābidīn in spite of his helplessness, but Ḥusayn's sister Zaynab threw herself on top of him to save him, and 'Umar ibn Sa'd, the Umayyad commander, told Shamir to let him be. Zayn al-'Ābidīn was taken along with the women to the caliph in Damascus, and eventually he was allowed to return to Medina.

Several accounts are related concerning his grief over this tragedy. It is said that for twenty years whenever food was placed before him, he would weep. One day a servant said to him, 'O Son of God's Messenger! Is it not time for your sorrow to come to an end?' He replied, 'Woe upon you! Jacob the prophet had twelve sons, and God made one of them disappear. His eyes turned white from constant weeping, his head turned grey out of sorrow, and his back became bent in gloom [cf. 12: 84], though his son was alive in this world. But I watched while my father, my brother, my uncle, and seventeen members of my family were slaughtered all around me. How should my sorrow come to an end?'[4]

Zayn al-'Ābidīn resided in Medina until his death in 95/713-4 (or 94/712-3). He was the object both of great sympathy because of the massacre of his family and of veneration as the great grandson of the Prophet. He dedicated his life to learning and worship and became an authority on prophetic traditions and law, but he was known mostly for his nobility of character and his piety, which earned him his sobriquet already in his lifetime.[5] The details that have reached us about his life in Medina mainly take the form of anecdotes affirming his constant preoccupation with worship and acts of devotion. He fathered fifteen children, eleven boys and four girls.[6]

After Karbalā', there were a number of different factions in the Shī'ite community, not all of which supported Zayn al-'Ābidīn as the rightful

[4] From Shaykh al-Ṣadūq, *Al- khiṣāl*; quoted in al-Amin, *A'yān*, iv *195*. The same is quoted from Ibn Shahrāshūb's *Manāqib* in Biḥār al-anwār, xlvi, 108; cf. similar accounts, ibid., pp. 108-10.

[5] This title is said to have been given bestowed upon him by the great jurist and traditionist Ibn Shihāb al-Zuhrī (S.H.M. Jafri, *The Origins and Early Development of Shi'a Islam,* Beirut, 1979, p. 246), who also called him the best of the Hashmities and narrated many *ḥadīth* from him (W. Madelung, art. "Alī ebn al-Ḥosayn', *Encyclopaedia Iranica,* I, 850).

[6] The most detailed collection of accounts concerning him is found in *Biḥār al-anwār,* XLVI, 2-209. See also al-Mufīd, *Kitāb al-Irshād*, transl. I.K.A. Howard London, 1981, pp.380-92.

Imam of the Muslim community.[7] Many Shīʿites, such as those involved in the 'Tawwābūn' movement, felt that the Umayyads had to be overthrown and that it was the duty of the Imam to lead a revolt. But Zayn al-ʿĀbidīn himself refused to become involved with politics. After his death, a split occurred between his eldest son and designated successor Muhammad al-Bāqir, the fifth Imam, and his second son, al-Bāqir's half brother Zayd, who advocated active resistance to Umayyad oppression and gained a large number of followers as a result. Al-Bāqir continued to pursue his father's policy of rejecting any sort of involvement with political movements until his death (probably in 117/735).[8] Zayd revolted toward the beginning of the imamate of al-Bāqir's son Jaʿfar al- Ṣādiq and was killed in Ṣafar 121/January 739; his son Yaḥyā, who plays an important role in the preface to the *Ṣaḥīfa*, continued in his father's path and was killed three years later at the age of eighteen. The Zaydī Shīʿites, still strong in the Yemen today, trace the lineage of their imams back to Zayd.

AL-SAḤĪFAT AL-SAJJĀDIYYA

The title *Al- Ṣaḥīfat al-Sajjādiyya* means simply 'The Book of al-Sajjād'. Al-Sajjād is one of the titles given to Zayn al-ʿĀbidīn and signifies 'the one who constantly prostrates himself in prayer'. The book is often called *Al- Ṣaḥīfat al-Kāmilat al-Sajjādiyya*, that is, 'The "Perfect", or "Complete", Book of al-Sajjād'. According to its commentator Sayyid ʿAlīkhān Shīrāzī, the word *kāmila* refers to the perfection of the style and content; some sources state that the adjective was added to differentiate it from another, incomplete version of the work, which is known among the Zaydīs, but this seems less likely, given the manner in which the title is employed in the preface (verse 20).[9] The *Ṣaḥīfa* has been called by various honorifics, such as 'Sister of the Qur'ān', 'Gospel of the Folk of the House', and 'Psalms of the Household of Muḥammad'.

According to Shīʿite tradition, Zayn al-ʿĀbidīn had collected his supplications and taught them to his children, especially Muḥammad al-Bāqir and Zayd. In later times the text became widely disseminated among Shīʿites of all persuasions. The specialists in the science of *ḥadīth* maintain

---

[7] Cf. Jafri, *Origins*, pp. 238 ff.

[8] Other dates given range from 112/731-2 to 126/743-4 (Jafri, *Origins*, p. 255).

[9] For the first opinion, cf. Sayyid Alī khan, *Riyāḍ al-sālikīn*, commentary on the prefaces of the *Ṣaḥīfa*, verse 20; for the second, cf. Aqā Najafī in his introduction to the *Ṣaḥīfa* mentioned the following notes.

that the text is *mutawātir*;[10] in other words, it was generally known from earliest times and has been handed down by numerous chains of transmission, while its authenticity has never been questioned. Nevertheless, the arrangement of the text allows us to draw a certain distinction between the fifty-four supplications which make the main body of the text and the additional supplications which make up the fourteen addenda (including the prayers for the days of the week) and the fifteen *munājāt* or 'whispered prayers'. The original fifty-four supplications show an undeniable freshness and unity of theme and style, while the latter, especially the *munājāt*, add a certain orderliness and self-conscious artistry which may suggest the hand of an editor. The addenda are said to have been collected and added to the text by Shams al-Dīn Muḥammad ibn Makkī, known as al-Shahīd al-Awwal (the 'first martyr'), the famous author of *Al-Lum'at al-Dimishqiyya* in jurisprudence (*fiqh*) who was killed in Aleppo in 786/1384.[11] The fifteen *munājāt* have been added to several modern editions of the *Sahīfa* and seem to have been brought to the attention of the main body of Shī'ites by 'Allāma Muḥammad Bāqir Majlisī (d. 1110/1689-9 or a year later), author of the monumental compilation of Shī'ite *ḥadīth*, *Biḥār al-Anwār*.[12]

Many supplications have been handed down from Imam Zayn al-'Ābidīn in addition to those recorded in the text of the *Ṣaḥīfa* as given here, and various scholars have collected these together in a series of works known as the 'second *Ṣaḥīfa*' the 'third *Ṣaḥīfa*' and so on. The second *Ṣaḥīfa* which is about as long as the *Ṣaḥīfa* itself, was compiled as the 'sister' of the *Ṣaḥīfa* by Muḥammad ibn al-Ḥasan al-Ḥurr al-'Āmilī (d. 1104/l692-3), author of the famous *Waṣā'il al-Shī'a* in the year 1053/1643.[13] A third *Ṣaḥīfa* was put together by the author of *Riyāḍ al 'ulamā'* Mirzā 'Abd Allāh ibn Mirzā 'Isā Tabrīzī, known as Afandī and a student of Majlisī. The longest of the published versions is *Al- Ṣaḥīfat al-Sajjādiyyah al-khāmisa* ('The Fifth *Ṣaḥīfa* of al-Sajjād') by Muḥsīn al-Amīn, the well known contemporary author of

---

[10] Cf. the introduction of Sayyid Muhammad Mishkāt and Sayyid Shihāb al-Dīn Mar'ashī (Āqā Najafī) To *al- Ṣaḥīfat al-kāmilat al-Sajjādiyya*, Tehran, 1361/1942; same text with Persian translation of text and introductions by Sadr al Dīn Balāghī Tehran, 1369/1950.

[11] Cf. Majlisī , *Biḥār*, LXXXVII, p. 133-4.

[12] In *Biḥār al-anwār* (xci, 142-53), Majlisī quotes these fifteen *munājāt* from *Al-Kitāb al-'Atīq al-Gharawī*. In his introduction (*Biḥār*, I, i6) he explains that this is a prayer book which he found in Gharī (the district of Najaf where 'Alī is buried) and that it was compiled by one of the ancient authorities in *ḥadīth* (*ba'ḍ qudamā' al-muḥaddithīn*).

[13] Lithographed in Iran as well as in Bombay (1311/1893-4).

A'yan al-shī'a. [14]It includes all the supplications included in the previous *Ṣaḥīfas;* 130 of these are found in the first and second *Ṣaḥīfas* and 52 are added.[15] In her sympathetic study of Islamic prayer manuals, *Muslim Devotions*, Constance Padwick made use of this fifth recension of the text, which fills more than six hundred pages.

Any serious attempt to sort out the relative historical reliability of the individual supplications found in all the versions of the *Ṣaḥīfa* on the basis of modern critical scholarship would be an undertaking of major proportions. The result of such a study - if one can judge by studies of other ancient texts - would probably be that, after years of toil, we would have a series of hypotheses, leaving varying degrees of doubt. This would be of interest to Western scholars and modernized Muslims, both of whom, in any case, have no personal involvement with the contents and teachings of the *Ṣaḥīfa.* But the attitude of most Muslims has been to look at the content of the texts established by the authority of tradition and not be too concerned with who actually wrote the words in 'historical fact'. In this regard the saying of 'Alī is well known: 'Look at what has been said, not at who has said it', since only the truth or untruth of the words is of real concern. From this point of view, if the author of the *Ṣaḥīfat al-kāmila* was not Imam Zayn al-'Ābidīn, he - or they - would in any case have to have been a spiritual authority of equal rank, so the whole exercise leaves us where we started: with a text which expresses the highest aspirations of the Muslim soul.

However this may be, we can be satisfied to have the core text which has been attributed to Zayn al-'Abidin by centuries of Shi'ite tradition. In other words, in the fifty-four basic prayers of the *Ṣaḥīfa* we have the Zayn al-'Ābidīn who has been known to Shī'ites for more than a thousand years and who has helped give to Shī'ism its specific contours down to the present day. Scholars may eventually reach the conclusion that the Zayn al-'Ābidīn of 'historical fact' differs from the Zayn al-'Ābidīn of tradition, but this will remain a hypothesis, since at this distance 'historical facts' are impossible to verify and as open to interpretation as literature. Whether or not historians

---

[14] Damascus, 1330/1912. A fourth *Ṣāḥīfa* was compiled by Mīrza Ḥusayn ibn Muhammad Taqī Nūrī (d. 1330/1902) and was printed in Iran, and a sixth by Muḥammad Ṣāliḥ al-Māzandarānī al-Ḥā'irī 9 for these six, see Āqā Buzurg Ṭihrānī, *Al-Dharī'a ilā taṣānīf al- shi'ā, s.v. Ṣāḥīfat al- sajjādiyya*). Others have been compiled by such contemporary scholars as Ḥājj Shaykh Muḥammad Bāqīr ibn Muḥammad Ḥasan Bīrjandī Qā'inī, Shaykh Hadī ibn 'Abbās Al-i Kāshif al-Ghiṭā' Najafī, and Ḥājj Mīrzā 'Alī Ḥusaynī Mar'ashī Shahristānī Ḥā'irī (cf. Āqā Najafī's introduction to the *Ṣāḥīfa*).

[15] Ṭihrānī, *Al-Dharī'a, s.v. Ṣāḥīfat al-Sajjādiyya.*

accept the text as completely authentic will not change the actual influence which Zayn al-'Ābidīn and the *Ṣaḥīfa* have exercised upon Islam over the centuries, nor is it likely to change the way they continue to influence practising Muslims. The 'real' Zayn al-'Ābidīn is the figure enshrined by the text as it now stands.

The opinion of the writer of these lines concerning the authenticity of the *Ṣaḥīfa* - admittedly based only upon an intimate acquaintance with the text gained through many months spent in translation - is that the original fifty-four prayers go back to Zayn al-'Ābidīn, that the addenda are nearly as trustworthy, and that the *munājāt* may have been worked upon by others. But the *Ṣaḥīfa* in its larger forms probably contains a good deal of material from later authors. It is interesting to note Padwick's comments on the *Ṣaḥīfat al-khāmisa*: 'The great body of devotion attributed to him is characterized by a deep humility and sense of sin, and by an intransigent, undying resentment against the foes of his house.'[16] Only the first half of this statement is true about the present *Ṣaḥīfa*. Though the Imam makes a number of allusions to the injustice suffered by his family and the fact that their rightful heritage has been usurped,[17] no one can call this a major theme of the *Ṣaḥīfa* or an 'intransigent, undying resentment'. In the one instance where Zayn al-'Ābidīn speaks rather explicitly of the injustice suffered by the Imams (48.9-11), this is accompanied by an admission of God's wisdom in His ordainment.

THE ARABIC TEXT

The Arabic text of the *Ṣaḥīfat al-kāmila* which forms the basis for the translation was established by al-Shahīd al-Awwal. The modern Iranian editions are based mainly on the version of this text transmitted by the father of the above-mentioned Muḥammad Bāqir Majlīsi, Mullā Muḥammad Taqī Majlisī (d. 1070/1659-60), also an important scholar of the Safavid period. and another son, Mullā `Abd Allāh (d. c. 1084/1673); but at least one of these editions goes back to the famous Safavid jurist, philosopher, architect, poet, and mathematician Shaykh Bahā'i (d. 1031/1621-2).[18] The elder Majlisī had at his disposal numerous manuscripts of the text, which he had received from the foremost Shi'ite authorities of

[16] *Muslims Devotions*, London, 1961, p. xvi.

[17] For references to the 'right' of the Prophet's Household to the Imamate or to their special role, cf. Supplication 26. I, 4; 42.5.

[18] Note appended to Sha'rānī's edition and translation us that it was copied from a manuscript written, collated, corrected, and signed by Shaykh-i Bahā'ī; the text is identical to that which goes back to Majlisī.

his day. In one of his works he refers to all the chains of transmission by which he had received the *Ṣaḥīfa*, and, we are told, these number more than a million.[19]

The question naturally arises as to why Majlisī chose the particular chain of transmission mentioned in the preface out of the many he had at his disposal, especially since the chain itself is exceedingly weak (as indicated by the commentators and recorded in the notes to the translation). The reason for this seems to be the accuracy of this particular version going back to al-Shahīd al-Awwal, as confirmed by another 'special' route through which Majlisī received the *Ṣaḥīfa*. This special route is worth mentioning in detail, since it provides a good example of the aura which has surrounded the text in Shī'ite circles.

One day, lying in bed half asleep, Majlisī saw himself in the courtyard of the 'Atīq mosque in Isfahan, and before him stood the Mahdī, the Twelfth Imam. Majlisī asked him about a number of scholarly problems which he had not been able to solve, and the Mahdī explained their solutions. Then Majlisī asked him for a book which he could put into practice, and the Mahdī directed him to seek out Mawlāna Muḥammad al-Tāj. In his vision Majlisī found the book, and it appeared to be a book of supplications. Waking up, he saw that his hand was empty, and he wept until morning at his loss. At daybreak it occurred to him that perhaps the Mahdī had meant Shaykh Muḥammad Mudarris, calling him by the title 'Tāj' (the 'crown') because he was so famous among the scholars. Hence he went to see Shaykh Muḥammad, and, entering his circle, saw that he held a copy of the *Ṣaḥīfa* in his hand. He went forward and recounted his vision to Shaykh Muḥammad, who interpreted it to mean that he would reach high levels of gnostic and visionary knowledge. But Majlisī was not satisfied with this explanation, and he wandered around the bazaar in perplexity and sorrow. Upon reaching the melon market, he met a pious old man known as Āqā Ḥasan, whom the people called, Tājā ('Crown'). Majlisī greeted him, and Āqa Ḥasan called to him and said that he had a number of books which were consecrated for religious purpose (*waqfī*) but that he did not trust most of the students to put them to proper use. 'Come', he said, 'and take whichever of these books which you think you can put into practice.'

Entering Aqā Ḥasan's library, Majlisī immediately saw the book he had seen in his dream, so he said: `This is enough for me.' It was a copy of the *Ṣaḥīfa*. He then went back to Shaykh Muḥammad and began collating his newly acquired copy with that of Shaykh Muḥammad; both of them had been made from the manuscript of al-Shahīd al-Awwal. In short, Majlisī

[19] Cf. Mishkāt's introduction to *al- Ṣāḥīfat al-kāmilat al-Sajjādiyya.*

tells us that the authenticity of his copy of the *Ṣaḥīfa* was confirmed by the Mahdī himself.[20]

At least forty commentaries and glosses have been written on the *Ṣaḥīfa* mostly during the period extending from the Safavīd era (907-1125/1502-1722) to the present. Among famous Safavīd scholars who wrote commentaries are Shaykh-i Bahā'i, the philosopher Mir Dāmād (d. c. 1040/1630), and the younger Majlisī. The most well-known of the commentaries is *Riyāḍ al-sālikīn* by al-Sayyīd 'Alīkhān al- Ḥusayn al-Ḥasan al-Shīrāzī (d. 1120/1708-9).

PRAYER IN ISLAM

The *Ṣaḥīfa* has been called a 'prayer manual', but this description may be misleading to Western readers not familiar with the different varieties of prayer in Islam. The best introduction to these - as well as to the contents of the *Ṣaḥīfa* - is provided by Padwick's *Muslim Devotions* which also analyzes the major themes common to all supplications and explains many of the important Arabic terms employed. Given the existence of Padwick's study, we can be excused for providing only a few comments to situate supplication in the larger context of Muslim prayer and to suggest the importance of the *Ṣaḥīfa* for gaining an understanding of Islam as a religion.

'Prayer' in Islam can be divided into obligatory and voluntary. The obligatory prayer includes the daily ritual or canonical prayer (*ṣalāt*) which the Prophet called the 'pillar of Islam', and various occasional prayers such as the Friday congregational prayer (according to most opinions), which need not concern us here. Nothing is more basic than the daily prayers to Muslim practice except the testimony of faith or *shahāda*: "There is no god but God and Muḥammad is His Messenger." Every Muslim must perform the *ṣalāt* five times a day, exceptions being made only for children and for women during periods when they cannot fulfil the requirements of ritual purity. Even the bedridden must pray the *ṣalāt* if they are conscious and coherent, though they are excused from the physical movements which normally accompany it. 'Perform the *ṣalāt*!' is one of the most common injunctions in the Qur'ān.

Most of the many forms of recommended prayer can be classified either as *ṣalāt*, *dhikr* or *du'ā'*. The recommended *ṣalāt* involves the same movements and recitations that are contained in the obligatory *ṣalāt* while the Prophet's *sunna* sets down various times during the day or occasions

---

[20] Ibid. The Mishkāt edition was collated with Majlisī's autograph.

when various specific *ṣalāts* may be performed. In addition, the worshiper is free to perform *ṣalāt* as he desires, and thus it is related that Imam Zayn al-ʿĀbidīn used to perform one thousand supererogatory cycles of *ṣalāt* every night, in imitation of his grandfather ʿAlī.

Dhikr - which means literally 'remembrance' or 'mention' and which is frequently translated as 'invocation' - is the mention of a name or names of God, often in the form of the repetition of a Qur'ānic formula such as *There is no god but God, Praise belongs to God, Glory be to God,* or *God is great.* Most Muslims recite such formulas a set number of times after completing an obligatory ritual prayer. Fifteen Qur'ānic verses command *dhikr* of Allāh or the 'name of Allāh', emphasizing the fact that this practice involves a verbal mention of a divine name. If the *Sharīʿa* does not make *dhikr* an incumbent act, this has to do with the fact that the Qur'ānic command to remember God was not given a single, specific form by the Prophet's *sunna*, in contrast to the command to perform the *ṣalāt.* In other words, everyone agrees that it is important to perform *dhikr* and that the Prophet practiced it constantly. But the Prophet never made any specific form of *dhikr* mandatory for the faithful; on the contrary, he practiced many different forms and seems to have suggested a great variety of forms to his Companions in keeping with their needs.

From earliest times the sources confirm the power of *dhikr* to provide for human psychological and spiritual needs and to influence activity. It is not difficult to understand that reciting *yā raḥmān yā raḥīm* ('O All-merciful, O All-compassionate') will have a different effect upon the believer than reciting, *la hawla wa-lā quwwata illā bi-llāh al- ʿAlī al-ʿaẓīm* ('There is no power and no strength save in God, the All-high, the All-mighty'). Spiritual teachers eventually developed a science of different *adhkār* (plural of *dhikr*) appropriate for all the states of the soul.[21]

Duʿā' or 'supplication' is closely connected to *dhikr*, such that it is often difficult to make a distinction between the two. [22]The term means literally 'to call upon' and it is commanded by the Qur'ān in several suggestive verses, including the following:

Supplicate your Lord humbly and secretly; He loves not transgressors. (7:55)

Supplicate Allāh or supplicate the All-merciful. Whichever you supplicate - to Him belong the most beautiful names. (17:110)

Supplicate God, making your religion His sincerely, though the unbelievers be averse. (40:14)

---

[21] Cf. Chittick, art. 'Dhikr', *Encyclopaedia of religion*, New York, 1987, iv, 341-4.

[22] Cf. Al-Ghazālī's 'Book of invocations and supplications,' in his *Iḥyā' ʿulūm al-dīn*, translation by Nakamura, *Ghazāli on prayer*, Tokyo, 1973.

Your Lord has said: 'Supplicate Me and I will respond to you. Surely those who wax too proud to worship Me shall enter Gehenna utterly abject.' (40:60)

And when My servants question thee concerning Me - I am near to respond to the supplication of the supplicator when he supplicates Me. (2:186)

Collections of *hadīth*, both Sunni and Shī'ite, devote chapters to the benefits of supplication; the following sayings of the Prophet from Sunni sources are typical:

Supplication is the pith of worship. (TIRMIDHĪ)

When one of you supplicates, he should not say, 'O God, forgive me if Thou wilt', but he should be firm in his asking and make his desire great, for what God gives is nothing great for him. (MUSLIM)

God will respond to the servant as long as he does not supplicate for anything sinful or for breaking the ties of the womb, and as long as he does not ask for an immediate response. (MUSLIM)

Each of you should ask your Lord for all your needs; he should even ask Him for the thong of his sandal when it breaks. (TIRMIDHĪ)[23]

Shī'ite sources provide some of the same sayings while adding many more. For example:

The Prophet related that God says: 'O My servants, all of you are misguided except him whom I guide, so ask Me for guidance, and I will guide you. All of you are poor except him whom I enrich, so ask Me for riches, and I will provide for you. All of you are sinners except him whom I release, so ask Me to forgive you, and I will forgive you.'

The Prophet said: 'Supplication is the weapon of the man of faith, the centre-pole of religion, and the light of the heavens and the earth.'

'Alī was asked: 'Which speech is best in God's eyes?' He replied: 'A great amount of *dhikr*, pleading (*taḍarru'*), and supplication.'

'Alī said: 'Four things work to a man's benefit and not against him: faith and thanksgiving, for God says: *What would God do with chastising you, if you are thankful and have faith?* (4:147); asking forgiveness, for He says: *God would never chastise them with thee among them; God would never chastise them while*

[23] From *Mishkāt al-maṣābīḥ*; cf. the translation of this work by J. Robson, Lahore, 1963-3, pp.471-5.

they prayed forgiveness (8:33); and supplication, for He says: *My Lord esteems you not at all were it not for your supplication* (25:77).

Ḥusayn said: 'The Prophet used to raise his hands when he implored and supplicated, like a man in misery begging for food.'

Imām Muḥammad al-Bāqir said: 'God loves nothing better than that His servants ask from Him.'[24]

In short, supplicating or calling upon God is to address Him with one's praise, thanksgiving, hopes, and needs. It is 'prayer' in the personal sense commonly understood from the term by contemporary Christians. It forms a basic part of the religious life, but like *dhikr*, though commanded by the Qur'ān in general terms, it does not take a specific form in the injunctions of the *Sharī'a* because of its personal and inward nature. Everyone must remember God and supplicate Him, but this can hardly be legislated, since it pertains to the secret relationship between a human being and his or her Lord. The *ṣalāt*, however, is the absolute minimum which God will accept from the faithful as the mark of their faith and their membership in the community. Its public side is emphasized by the physical movements which accompany it and the fact that its form and contents are basically the same for all worshipers, even if its private side is shown by the fact that it can be performed wherever a person happens to find himself. In contrast *dhikr* and supplication are totally personal.

But the private devotional lives of the great exemplars of religion often become public, since they act as models for other human beings. The '*sunna*' of the Prophet is precisely the practices of the highest exemplification of human goodness made into an ideal which everyone should emulate, and the supplications which the Prophet used to make are part of his *sunna*. When he recited them aloud, his Companions would remember and memorize them. They also used to come to him and ask him for supplications which they could recite on various occasions and for different purposes.[25]

To the Prophet's supplications, the Shī'ites add the supplications of the Imams, beginning with 'Alī. Nowadays the most widely employed of the comprehensive prayer manuals, which contain a wide variety of supplications from all the Imams and for every occasion, is probably

[24] Majlisī, *Biḥār al-anwār*, xc, 288-94

[25] For a good cross section of the prophetic supplications provided in the most authentic Sunni source, cf. *Mishkāt al- maṣābīḥ*, pp. 486-534.

Mafātīḥ al-Jinān ('Keys to the Gardens of Paradise') by 'Abbās Qumī (d. 1359/1940).[26]

THE ROLE OF SUPPLICATION

Though many of the supplications which have been handed down from the Prophet and the Imams were certainly spontaneous utterances of the heart, others must have been composed with the express purpose of reciting them on specific occasions or passing them on to the pious. Most of the prophetic supplications are short and could easily have been recited on the spur of the moment, but some of the prayers of the Imams - such as Zayn al-'Ābidīn's supplication for the Day of 'Arafa (no. 47) - are long and elaborate compositions. Even if they began as spontaneous prayers, the very fact that they have been designated as prayers for special occasions suggests that they were noted down and then repeated by the Imam or his followers when the same occasion came around again.

Naturally it is not possible to know the circumstances in which supplications were composed, but we do know a good deal about early Islam's general environment which can help suggest the role that supplication played in the community. Many Muslims, no doubt much more so than today, devoted a great deal of their waking lives to recitation of the Qur'ān, remembrance of God, and prayer. Even those who left Mecca and Medina to take part in the campaigns through which Islam was spread or participate in the governing of the new empire did not necessarily neglect spiritual practices. And for those who devoted themselves to worship, supplication was the flesh and blood of the imagination. It provided a means whereby people could think about God and keep the thought of Him present throughout their daily activities. It was an intimate expression of *tawḥīd* or the 'profession of God's Unity' which shaped their sensibilities, emotions, thoughts, and concepts.

In the Islamic context, supplication appears as one of the primary frameworks within which the soul can be moulded in accordance with the Divine Will and through which all thoughts and concepts centered upon the ego can be discarded. The overwhelming emphasis in the *Ṣaḥīfa* upon doing the will of God – 'Thy will be done', as Christians pray - illustrates clearly a God-centeredness which negates all personal ambitions and individual desires opposed in any way to the divine Will, a Will which is given concrete form by the *Sharī'a* and the *Sunna.* For Muslims then as

[26] Published in many editions. For a good cross section of the Shi'ite supplication, excluding the main prayer of the *Ṣāḥīfa* , cf. *Biḥār*, XL-XLII

today, obeying God depended upon imitating those who had already been shaped by God's mercy and guidance, beginning with the Prophet, and followed by the great Companions. For the Shī'ites, the words and acts of the Imams play such a basic role in this respect that they sometimes seem - at least to non-Shī'ites - to push the *Sunna* of the Prophet into the background.

The companions of the Imams constantly referred to them for guidance, while the Imams themselves followed the Prophet's practice of spending long hours of the day and night in *ṣalāt*, *dhikr*, and supplication. Though much of this devotional life was inward and personal, the Imams had the duty of guiding the community and enriching their religious life. As Imam Zayn al-'Ābidīn emphasizes in the 'Treatise on Rights', translated in the appendix, it is the duty of every possessor of knowledge to pass it on to others, and the Imams were acknowledged as great authorities of Islam by their contemporaries, Sunni and Shī'ite alike. Hence it was only natural that they would compose prayers in which their knowledge of man's relationship with God was expressed in the most personal terms and which could be passed around and become communal property. Many if not most of the supplications recorded in the *Ṣaḥīfa* seem to be of this sort. A few of them, such as 'His supplication for the Day of Fast-Breaking' (46) or 'for the Day of Sacrifice' (48) seem to have been composed for public occasions. One of them provides internal evidence to suggest that the Imam had in mind his followers rather than himself: in the supplication for parents (24), he speaks as if his parents were still alive, whereas this could hardly have been the case, unless we suppose that he composed it in his youth before the events at Karbalā'.

TAWḤĪD IN DEVOTIONAL MODE

No one with any sensitivity toward human weakness and God's love can fail to be moved at least by some of the supplications contained in the *Ṣaḥīfa*. Here we have one of the greatest spiritual luminaries of Islam so overawed by the sense of God's goodness, mercy, and majesty as to express his utter nothingness before the Creator in terms that may seen surprisingly explicit for one deemed by his followers to be the possessor of such holiness. In the *Ṣaḥīfa* we see Islamic spirituality - or that dimension of the religion of Islam which deals with the practical and lived reality of the personal relationship between man and God - expressed in the most universal of languages, that of the concrete and intimate yearning of the soul for completion and perfection.

Muslim ideas and attitudes go back to *tawhīd* or the 'profession of God's Unity' as expressed in the first half of the *shahāda*: 'There is no god but God.' This is the essence of the Qur'ānic message, as Muslim authorities have affirmed and reaffirmed throughout Islamic history. The *Ṣaḥīfa* provides a particularly striking example of what this means in personal, practical terms, not in the abstract language of theology or metaphysics. The basic theme of the *Ṣaḥīfa* can be put into a series of formulas simply by taking every positive human attribute and placing it within the context of the *shahāda*: 'There is no goodness but in God', 'There is no repentance but by God's grace', 'There is no gratitude but through God', 'There is no patience without God's help', 'There is no knowledge but in God', 'There is no love except through God's initiative'. The complement of this perspective is that every negative attribute belongs to the human self: 'There is no evil but in me', 'There is no pride but in myself', 'There is no impatience but in my own ego', 'There is none ignorant but me', 'There is no hate but in myself.'

Later authorities frequently cite the first prophet and his wife, Ādam and Eve, as Qur'ānic examples of this attitude of self-deprecation demanded by the *shahāda*. When Ādam and Eve had disobeyed their Lord's commandment, they said: '*Our Lord, we have wronged ourselves*' (7:23). In contrast, Iblīs - who personifies the tendency in the human soul to pride, self-centredness, and heedlessness said to God: '*Now, because Thou hast led me astray...*' (7:16). The prophetic attitude is to ascribe any evil, sin, error, stumble, slip, fall, inadvertence, negligence, and so on to oneself, while the satanic attitude is to ascribe these to God or to others. To suggest that God is responsible - certainly a temptation in the Islamic context where the stress on the Divine Unity tends to negate secondary forces - is the epitome of discourtesy and ignorance, since it is to deny one's own self precisely where it has a real affect upon the nature of things: where evil enters into the cosmos.

In short, the *shahāda* means in practice that the worshiper is nothing and God is all. Everything positive that the servant possesses has been given to him by God, while every fault and imperfection goes back to the servant's own specific attributes. If he has patience in adversity, this was given by God, but if he lacks it, this is his own shortcoming. If he knows anything at all, the knowledge was bestowed by God's guidance and mercy, but if he is ignorant, that is his own limitation. If he possesses a spark of love in his heart, God has granted it, but every coldness and hardness belongs to himself. Every good and praiseworthy quality - life, knowledge, will, power, hearing, sight, speech, generosity, justice, and so on - is God-given. Only when this fact shapes a person's imagination and awareness can he begin to see things in their right proportions and be delivered from his own self-deceptions.

From the beginning of Islam, supplication has been one of the fundamental modes through which Muslims actualised the awareness of correct proportions and trained themselves to see God as the source of all good. In its great examples, as typified by the *Ṣaḥīfa*, supplication is the constant exercise of discernment by attributing what belongs to God to God and what belongs to man to man. Once this discernment is made, man is left with his own sinfulness and inadequacy, so he can only abase himself before his Lord, asking for His generosity and forgiveness.

Those familiar with the writings of the later spiritual authorities may object that the perspective of supplication as just described deals with only one-half of Islamic spirituality, leaving out the theomorphic perfections which the friends of God (*awliya'*) actualise by following the spiritual path. Granted, on the one hand man is the humble and poor slave of God, possessing nothing of his own. But is he not - at least in the persons of the prophets and friends – God's vicegerent (*khalīfa*) and image (*ṣūra*)? In fact, this second perspective is implicit in the first, since the more one negates positive attributes from the servant, the more one affirms that they belong to the Lord. By denying that the creature possesses any good of his own, we affirm that everything positive which appears within him belongs only to God. To the extent that the servant dwells in his own nothingness, he manifests God's perfections. This point of view is made rather explicit in the famous *ḥadīth qudsī* in which God says: 'My servant continues drawing near to Me through supererogatory works [such as supplication], until I love him, and when I love him, I am the hearing through which he hears, the sight through which he sees, the hand through which he grasps, and the foot through which he walks.'[27] But the early Islamic texts leave the mystery of 'union with God' or 'supreme identity' largely unvoiced, since it is far too subtle to be expressed in the relatively straightforward terms which characterize these texts.[28] In any case, identity is alien to the perspective of supplication, which keeps in view the dichotomy between Lord and servant, a dichotomy which remains valid on one level at least in all circumstances and for all human beings, even in the next world.[29]

---

[27] Bukhārī, Riqāq.38.

[28] One of the reason for Islam's avoiding explicit expressions of this point of view is the danger of *shirk* or associating others with God, which it perceives in Christianity's divinisation of Christ or in some of its own sectarian movements, such as the *ghulāt* among the Shī'ites.

[29] As Ibn al-'Arabī often reminds us: 'It is impossible for realities to change, so the servant is always servant, and the Lord always Lord. God remains God, and the creature creature' (*Al-Futuḥāt al-makkiyya,* Beirut, n.d., II, 371.5). No one has ever suggested that the Prophet Muḥammad, because he has attained to the greatest perfection possible for any human being, ceases by that fact to be God's

ASKING FORGIVENESS

As is well known, the Shī'ites hold that the Imams are 'inerrant' or 'sinless' (*ma'ṣūm*, from the verb *'isma*, which means to be preserved by God from sins). The reader of the *Ṣaḥīfa* will be struck by how often Zayn al-'Ābidīn asks God to forgive his sins, employing all the standard terms (*ithm*, *dhanb*, *ma'ṣiyya*, etc.).[30] To be surprised at this or to suggest that therefore the Shī'ites are wrong to call the Imams sinless is to miss the points which have just been made about the *shahāda* as the root of Islamic spirituality. It is not my concern to defend the dogma of *'isma*, but I should at least point out that one cannot object to it on this level.

According to various *ḥadīth*s, the Prophet used to pray for forgiveness seventy or one hundred times a day by repeating the formula 'I pray forgiveness from God' (*astaghfir Allāh*), a formula which is pronounced universally by practicing Muslims. Muslims hold that all prophets are sinless, and the Prophet Muḥammad is the greatest of the prophets, yet no one has ever seen any contradiction between his asking forgiveness and his lack of sins. One easy but shallow way of explaining this is to say that the Prophet was the model for the whole community, so he had to pray as if he were a sinner, since all those who followed his *sunna* and recited the prayers which he taught would be sinners. But to say this is to suggest that he was a hypocrite of sorts and to lose sight of the meaning of the *shahāda.*

Christians have never doubted Christ's divinity because he said: 'Why do you call me good? No one is good but God alone' (Mark 10:18). Here, in Christian terms, is a concise statement of the *shahāda* as applied to the lives of God's creatures. In as much as anything can be called created, it is 'other than God' and less than absolutely good. God is possessor of mercy, knowledge, love, life, power, will, patience, and so on - the 'ninety-nine names of God' provide a basic list of the divine attributes. If something 'other than God' possesses any of these attributes, it clearly does not possess them in the same way that God possesses them. They belong to God by the fact that He is God, but if they belong to the creatures in any sense, it is by His bestowal, just as the creatures have received their existence through His creation.

This basic teaching of the *shahāda* means that nothing and no one - not even the greatest of the prophets - stand on a par with God. Since goodness is a divine attribute, 'None is good but God alone', and everything other

---

'servant'. He will always be so inasmuch as he is Muḥammad, even if he dwells in the supreme identity at the same time.

[30] For a catalogue of these terms, cf. Padwick, *Muslim Devotions,* pp. 189-97.

than God is evil at least in respect of being 'other'. 'Evil' here may be another name for 'lesser good', and no one in the Islamic context would dream of attributing evil to the prophets. Nevertheless, the prophets in as much as they are human beings cannot be placed on the same level as God. The respect in which human beings differ from God is all-important for the spiritual life. It is man's clinging to the difference his own servant-hood, his own createdness, his own inadequacy, his own sinfulness - which allows him to fulfil what is required of him as the creature of his Lord.[31] Just as the Prophet is first '*abduhu*, 'His servant', and only then *raslūhu,* 'His messenger' so also every human being must first actualise the fullness of his own servant-hood before he can hope to manifest anything on behalf of his Lord.

The greater a person's awareness and knowledge of God, the greater his awareness of the gulf between the 'I' and the Divine Reality. As the Qur'ān says: *Only those of His servants fear God who have knowledge* (35:28). The greater the knowledge of God and self, the greater the understanding of the claims of independence and pride that are involved with saying 'I', and so also the greater the fear of the consequences. Those nearest to God fear Him more than others because they have grasped the infinite distance that separates their created nature from their Creator; hence also they are the most intense in devotion to Him, since they see that only through devotion and worship can they fulfil His claims upon them. No Muslim can think that he has reached a point where he no longer has need for God's forgiveness, so no Muslim can stop praying for it. Moreover, the overriding goodness of God and the nothingness of the creatures demands that a pious act can never belong to the servant. To the extent that a human being is able to do what God wants from him, this is because God has granted him the power to do so. The well-known formula *wa mā tawfiqī illā bi-llāh*, 'I have no success except through God', is of universal application. In the last analysis, no good act can be attributed to the servant - the merit is always God's (for example, Supplication 74.2). It is here that the mystery of God's ever-present and immanent reality manifests itself, such that there is nothing left of the creature but a face of God turned toward creation.

If the Prophet and the Imams constantly prayed for forgiveness with the utmost sincerity, this does not contradict the idea that they were 'sinless', since the sins envisaged here entail a wilful disobedience to the divine command, not the 'creaturely sin' of being other than God. Later authorities invariably distinguish among levels of sinfulness as also among

[31] Only after full actualization of the difference can there be any hope for the realization of identity. The more intense the affirmation of the ego's otherness and sinfulness, the more fully the divine attributes are reflected in the purified mirror of the soul.

levels of virtue, a doctrine epitomized in the oft-quoted saying, 'The good qualities of the pious are the bad qualities of those brought near to God' (*Ḥasanāt al-abrār say'iyyāt al-muqarrabīn*). At least three basic levels are distinguished for every positive human quality, though these levels are not exclusive and may coexist in various degrees within a single person depending upon his spiritual maturity. The examples of 'repentance' (*tawba*) and 'asking forgiveness' (*istighfār*) can illustrate these points.

In the *Ṣaḥīfa* the Imam often asks God for success in repentance, which may be defined as turning toward God through acts of obedience and avoiding disobedience. The later authorities speak of a first level of repentance belonging to the faithful in general, who sin by breaking the commands of the *Sharī'a* and who repent by asking God to forgive their sins and trying their best not to repeat the sin. In other words, their repentance pertains basically to the level of the activities governed by the *Sharī'a* while the forgiveness they seek means that they ask God to pardon any act of commission or omission which is contrary to the *Sharī'a*.

On the second level of repentance there are those who have dedicated their lives to God and spend their waking moments in careful observance of the details of the *Sharī'a* and following the recommended acts of the *sunna*. Such people, who might be called the 'pious' in keeping with the above saying, have no difficulty following the practical commands and prohibitions of the *Sharī'a*, so they turn their attention toward the inward attitudes which should accompany the outward activities. They repent of the heedlessness (*ghafla*) of their own souls, which are unable to remember God with perfect presence. They see their acts of obedience as falling short of the ideal because of their inward weaknesses and the various forms of blindness and hypocrisy which Satan is able to instil into their hearts, such as the temptation to ascribe their piety and diligence in observing the *Sharī'a* to themselves. They repent not of sinful acts, since they observe the *Sharī'a* with exactitude and do not `sin' according to the Shari'ite definitions. Rather, they repent of inappropriate thoughts and intentions and ask God to forgive these whenever they occur.

The third level is that of 'those brought near to God'. They have passed beyond outward and inward sins, since they see nothing but God's will, guidance, and mercy in every act and every thought, but they are still faced with the greatest of all barriers, that of their own self, the 'supreme veil' between man and God. God has given them knowledge of Himself and of themselves, so they have come to understand that the 'I' can never be totally innocent or sinless. They repent of their own inadequacies as creatures and ask forgiveness for their own existence as separate beings.[32]

---

[32] A three-fold division of virtues is found in many classical Sufi texts which discuss the stations of the travellers on the path to God, such as Anṣārī's *Manāzil*

Western readers may object that there is something artificial about this division of 'repentance' into levels. How can one 'repent' of one's own existence? How can one ask forgiveness for something which is not one's own fault? These objections might be valid if the texts had originally been written in English, but in fact the objection arises because of the difficulty of translating the concepts of one religious universe into another. The original Arabic words translated as 'repentance' and 'forgiveness' convey meanings far broader than the English terms, both of which are connected with a sentimental and moralistic sense of guilt. (Similar problems, it should be remarked, exist with much of the terminology which is normally used to translate Islamic texts and which has also been employed - because there is no other real choice - in the present translation of the *Ṣaḥīfa*.)

The word *tawba* or 'repentance' means literally to 'turn' or 'return' from one thing to another. One of God's Qur'ānic names is *al-Tawwāb*, 'He who turns', and the verb from this root is used both for God's turning toward man and man's turning toward God. Man's 'repentance' refers to every level of turning away from self and towards God; it makes no difference whether the self is conceived of as a tissue woven of sins or as the veil of ignorance and heedlessness that pertains to one's creaturely situation. There may be a moralistic sense attached to the word in a particular context, and there may not.

In a similar way, *maghfira* in Arabic is far richer than the term 'forgiveness' in English. To begin with, the Qur'ān attributes three different divine names to God from this root, *al-ghafūr*, *al-ghāfir*, and *al-ghaffār*, and subtle distinctions are often drawn to differentiate the different modes of 'forgiveness' which they imply. More importantly the root meaning of *maghfira* is 'to cover over', 'to veil', 'to conceal'. Hence the 'Forgiver' is He who veils human sins and inadequacies. In Arabic the literal sense of saying 'I pray forgiveness from God' is 'I ask God for concealment.' Most people may understand that they are asking God to conceal their 'sins', but 'those brought near to God' will see that they have need for the concealment of something much deeper and more radical since it is inherent to every created thing.

When the Prophet or Imam Zayn al-'Ābidīn ask God to 'forgive their sins, they are perfectly sincere in this request, but this does not necessarily imply that their sins lie at the same level as our own. As Islamic texts frequently remind us, *qiyās bi al-nafs*, 'judging others by one's own self', is

---

al-sā'irīn (cf. the text and translation by S. de Laugier de Beaurecueil, *Les étapes des itinérants vers Dieu,* Cairo, 1962). For a selection of classical texts in which virtues are frequently analyzed in this manner, see Jawad Nurbaksh, *Sufism IV: Repentance, Abstinence, Renunciation, Wariness, Humility, Humbleness, Sincerity, Constancy, Courtesy,* London, 1987.

always misleading, especially if the others happen to have been the recipients of God's special favours.

SPIRITUAL ATTITUDES AND NAMES OF GOD

Muslim thinkers have often divided the names of God into two broad categories by contrasting attributes such as wrath (*ghaḍab*) and mercy (*raḥma*), justice (*'adl*) and bounty (*faḍl*), severity (*qahr*) and gentleness (*luṭf*), majesty (*jalāl*) and beauty (*jamāl*), or majesty and munificence (*ikrām*). The 'names of wrath' are connected to God's distance and transcendence, while the 'names of mercy' are connected to His nearness and immanence. The *Sharī'a* and *kalām* (dogmatic theology) tend to emphasize God's severity and incomparability (*tanzīh*), while Islamic spirituality and the devotional literature put more stress on His gentleness and similarity (*tashbīh*).

The *Sharī'a* is not particularly concerned with speaking about God, since its function is to set down guidelines for the domain of activity. To the extent that God is taken into account, He is conceived of primarily as the Commander and the Lawgiver. In respect of laying down the Law, He is a monarch who must be obeyed. A monarch - and especially the Eternal King - stands far above his subjects, who are in fact his slaves, and he enforces his edicts by means of scourges, dungeons, and executions. Hence the *Sharī'a* naturally calls to mind the God of transcendence and justice, and the 'jurists' (*fuqahā'*), generally speaking, present Islam with a stern and severe countenance.

The God of the jurists shares many of the attributes of the God described by the proponents of *kalām*, who concerned themselves mainly with bolstering the authority of the *Sharī'a* while employing the tools of rational thought. Moreover, *kalām* has never played the same important role in Islam that theology plays in Christianity, since its concerns are far overshadowed by the dedication of all Muslims to the *Sharī'a*. *Kalām* sets out to defend the *Sharī'a* and the tenets of the faith against rational criticisms, so the theologians have approached their subject by employing reason (*'aql* or *al-naẓar al-'aqlī*). As a result, they singled out for their consideration certain subjects which were of no interest to the community at large. For most people, it makes no difference if the Qur'ān is eternal or created, so long as God speaks to them through it. Though *kalām* performs a necessary function in the Islamic universe, the vast majority of the faithful had no knowledge of the rational criticisms against which *kalām* was defending them, so they had no use for *kalām*. It was simply irrelevant to the religious life of most people.[33]

[33] Padwick sometimes alludes to this point in *Muslim Devotions*, e.g., p. 178.

Since the theologians called upon reason to bear witness to their endeavours, they affirmed God's transcendence with great fervour. Reason cannot accept the literal sense of many details of the Qur'ān and the *ḥadith*, such as God's face, eyes, hand, feet, sitting, laughter, smiling, wavering, yearning, joy at man's repentance, surprise at the lack of sensual desire in a young man of piety, and so on. Hence the theologians felt compelled to explain such descriptions in terms of abstract qualities. Thus, for example, God's 'hand' is interpreted as a reference to an impersonal quality such as power. This is not to question the validity of these interpretations, only to point out that the relatively concrete words and images found in the Qur'ān and the *ḥadīth* provide food for the imagination; through them human beings gain the ability to think about God in personal terms and establish an intimate, inward relationship with their Lord. An inconceivable God - or a God who can only be known through abstract creedal statements - is of no use to the vast majority of people.

Imagination feeds upon the concrete, not the abstract. When God speaks in a language that appeals to the imagination, He thereby addresses all the faithful, bypassing reason and appealing to something far more universal in human hearts. But when the theologians employ a disciplined rational methodology, they are addressing intellectuals like themselves. As a result, the faithful found spiritual nourishment not in the dry and abstract depictions of a far-away God provided by *kalām* but in the warm and concrete imagery of the Qur'ān , the *ḥadith*, and the spiritual authorities. No one could love the God of the theologians.[34]

In short, by the nature of their disciplines, the jurists and the theologians lay stress on the God of remoteness and transcendence. In contrast, the spiritual authorities speak of the God described in the Qur'ān and the *ḥadīth* as He describes Himself, not neglecting His nearness to all creatures. Since the God of the Qur'ān is pre-dominantly a God of mercy and tenderness, a God of intimacy and concern, the spiritual authorities emphasize the personal dimension of the human/divine relationship. They stress God's nearness and immanence, and they often remind us of Qur'ānic verses such as, *Whithersoever you turn - there is the face of God* (2:115); *He is with you wherever*

[34] Cf. the words of Ibn al-'Arabī: 'If mankind had been left with rational proofs-which, in the opinion of the rational thinkers [i.e., the theologians], establishknowledge of God's Essence, showing that "He is not like this" and "not like that"-no one would ever have loved God. But the divine reports came on the tongues of the revealed religions that "He is like this" and "He is like that", mentioning affairs which outwardly contradict rational proofs. He made us love Him through these affirmative attributes' (*Al-Futūḥāt al-makkiyya,* II, 326.13). this work develops the theme of the contrast between the rational approach of the theologians and the imaginative approach of revelation in great detail. Cf. my forthcoming book on Ibn al-'Arabī.

you are (57:3); *We indeed created man; We know what his soul whispers within him; and We are nearer to him than the jugular vein* (50:16).

Since the *Sharī'a* concerns itself basically with activity, it is directed toward the outward affairs which are governed by the laws of the remote King. *Kalām* is polemical and rational, concerning itself mainly with the divine attributes of the transcendent God, not with the human dimensions of the relationship with a God who is also immanent. The Qur'ān and the *ḥadīth* provide the seeds from which the *Sharī'a* and *kalām* grew up, but they also provide the seeds for the subsequent attention that was paid by the spiritual authorities to all the dimensions of the soul. Devotional literature addresses this inward domain in an eminently practical way, attempting to shape the soul according to the revealed models.[35]

There is, of course, no contradiction between thinking of God as transcendent and perceiving Him as immanent, any more than there is a contradiction between perceiving Him as Merciful and as Wrathful. God reveals Himself under a variety of guises, and these in turn demand different rational perceptions and psychological responses. One cannot think in exactly the same terms about the Glorified (*al-subbūḥ*), who transcends everything that man can conceive, and the Near (*al-qarīb*), who is closer than the jugular vein; nor can one feel the same toward the Gentle, the Kind, and the Compassionate as one feels toward the Vengeful and the Severe in Punishment. Once codified and institutionalized, the human responses to God's self-revelations in the Qur'ān came to emphasize certain divine attributes rather than others. One response was called 'jurisprudence', another '*kalām*', another 'Sufism', and so on. All of these points of view coexist in the great representatives of Islam, just as they coexist in the Qur'ān and in the soul of the Prophet. But in the early period, it is difficult to disentangle the different strands, since the institutional forms which highlight them have not yet come into existence. However, it is easy to see that certain manifestations of early Islam tend in one direction or another. The particular characteristic of the devotional literature such as the *Ṣaḥīfa* is to emphasize the personal quality of God's relationship with His servants and His all-pervading love.

[35] Other early forms of literature written by spiritual authorities also demonstrate a practical concern with the soul's growth and development. Not all of this literature emphasizes God's mercy: many of the early figures known as 'ascetics' were far more concerned with His wrath and emphasized the awe and the fear which is the proper response of the human soul to the divine majesty. But these works share with the devotional literature a fundamental concern with inwardness.

THE PREDOMINANCE OF MERCY

Some modern day Muslims and many Western scholars have looked at the Qur'ān wearing the eyeglasses of the jurists and theologians. As a result, they see a God who is a just and stern Commander, concerned only with beating His servants into shape so that they will follow His Law. They tend to ignore the fact that practically every chapter of the Qur'ān begins with the words, *In the name of God, the All-merciful, the All-compassionate*, and that the Qur'ān mentions God's names of mercy, compassion, kindness, generosity, forgiveness, and love about ten times as often as it mentions His names of wrath and severity. The overwhelming Qur'ānic picture is that of a God deeply concerned with the well-being of His creatures and ready to forgive almost anything, if only they will repent and acknowledge His sovereignty.

Faced with the reality of both mercy and wrath, the worshiper seeks out the one and does everything he can to avoid the other. This is a constant theme in the devotional literature in general and the *Ṣaḥīfa* in particular. The Prophet set the pattern in his well-known supplication: 'I seek refuge in Thy good pleasure from Thy displeasure and in Thy pardon from Thy punishment. I seek refuge in Thee from Thee.'[36] God is both: He who becomes pleased and He who becomes displeased, He who pardons and He who punishes. Hence the worshiper prays to God for protection against God Himself, since there is no other significant threat. Moreover, the servant can be confident that God's mercy will in fact overcome His wrath, since God is essentially merciful and only accidentally wrathful. The Qur'ān tells us in two verses that God's mercy *embraces all things* (7:156, 40:7), but it never suggests that His wrath is so universal. According to a famous *ḥadīth qudsī*, God says: 'My mercy precedes My wrath', or 'has precedence over My wrath', or 'predominates over My wrath.'[37] God appears to His creatures as harsh and domineering only in certain circumstances and for specific purposes - purposes which themselves are defined by mercy. The Prophet expressed this point with his remark: 'Hellfire is a whip with which God drives His servants to Paradise.' God's mercy is so overwhelmingly real that He will certainly overlook the sins of those who open themselves up to it.[38]

---

[36] Found in most of the standard sources, e.g. Muslim Ṣalāt 222; Dārimī, Ṣalāt 148; Tirmidhī, Da'awāt 75, 112. Cf. Padwick, *Muslim Devotions*, pp. 90-3. for allusions to it in the *Ṣaḥīfa,* see 10.1-2, 48.13,60.1,73.1; part of it is quoted in 60.5.

[37] The *ḥadīth* is found in several versions, in Bukhārī, Muslim, and other standard sources. Cf. Wensinck, *Concordance*, IV, 526.3; Graham, *Divine Word,* 184-5.

[38] God's precedent mercy explains why even most theologians agreed that the torment of hell cannot be everlasting. 'In general...the non-eternity of the Fire has prevailed in the understanding of the Muslim community, supported by al-Ash'arī's opinion that punishment is not of unlimited duration.' J.I. Smith and

Padwick refers to the 'mosaic' quality of Muslim supplications. She writes: 'While the prayers of some of the great saints show a spiritual individuality, the great mass of these devotions is built up of well-tried small items arranged in ever new patterns - traditional prayers of the Prophet, Qur'ān verses, blessings of the Prophet, forgiveness-seekings, cries of praise, all on known and authorized forms.'[39] The *Ṣaḥīfa* is strongly marked by the individuality of the Imam, while also displaying this mosaic quality. But this quality itself reflects the Qur'ān , which is a mosaic of God's names and activities, stories of the prophets, legal injunctions, and promises and warnings about the Last Day.

It was said above that one of the purposes of supplication is to shape the imagination of the worshiper in accordance with Islamic norms. A well-known *ḥadīth* tells us that Muslims can know the 'character' (*khuluq*) of the Prophet through studying the Qur'ān . By following the Prophet's *sunna* the worshiper absorbs the Qur'ān on all levels of his being, and in turn he is absorbed by the Qur'ān , the Divine Word and the divine model of his own soul. If some early authorities referred to the *Ṣaḥīfa* as the 'Sister of the Qur'ān', part of the reason for this may lie in the fact that its mosaic quality expresses a variety of spiritual attitudes that reflect accurately the Qur'ānic and prophetic model for human perfection. Every element in the *Ṣaḥīfa's* mosaic corresponds to elements of the Qur'ānic text and the Prophet's soul.

The connection between the spiritual attitudes expressed in the *Ṣaḥīfa* and the Qur'ānic statements about God and His relationship to His servants can most clearly be perceived in the Imam's constant recourse to God's names and his always appropriate expression of the corresponding human attitude. On the one hand the Imam places great emphasis upon his own inadequacy and sinfulness, acknowledging that he deserves nothing but God's wrath. On the other, he repeatedly takes refuge in God's mercy and in God's own Qur'ānic statements concerning the primacy of forgiveness, asking God to do with him as is worthy of such a merciful Being, not as he himself deserves.

> Act toward me with the forgiveness and mercy of which Thou art worthy! Act not toward me with the chastisement and vengeance of which I am worthy! (73.3)

In short, through the mosaic of the supplication, the worshiper moves from viewpoint to viewpoint in keeping with the different relationships which exist between himself and God as described in the Qur'ān. Man's

Y.Y. Haddad, *The Islamic Understanding of Death and Resurrection,* Albany, 1981, p. 95.

[39] *Muslim Devotions*, p. xxviii.

point of view changes because each of the divine names points to a different face of God turned toward him. Yet all are faces of God, and 'There is no god but God', so the apparent multiplicity of names and faces dissolves into the divine Unity.

Human inadequacy and sin are real enough on their own level, and the *Ṣaḥīfa* among others shows a remarkable awareness of the depth of human imperfection. But the great spiritual authorities of Islam hold that in responding to human weakness, God's overwhelming mercy takes charge and the divine wrath pales by comparison. The more that human beings admit to their own inadequacy, the more they call down upon themselves God's pity and commiseration. Supplication and pleading are the natural human response to the *shahāda* the fact that man is nothing compared to God, and that God - who is fundamentally mercy - is the only true reality. Supplication responds to God's command, *Despair not of God's mercy! Surely God forgives all sins* (39:53).

A *ḥadīth* is related concerning Imam Zayn al-'Ābidīn which is worth recounting because it is so completely in character with the *Ṣaḥīfa*'s emphasis upon God's mercy and forgiveness. One day he was told that Ḥasan al-Baṣrī (d. 110/728), the famous ascetic, had said: 'It is not strange if a person perishes as he perishes. It is only strange that a person is saved as he is saved.' The Imam replied, 'But I say that it is not strange if a person is saved as he is saved; it is only strange that a person perishes as he perishes, given the scope of God's mercy.'[40]

The supplicant who responds to the God of the Qur'ān never forgets the wrath of God, but he remains confident that God's essential nature will show itself, in spite of his own weaknesses. Padwick was so struck with the devaluation of human sins that seems to result from this attitude that she displays a rare instance of Christian bias, objecting that it 'leads to a certain moral shallowness in some forgiveness-seeking prayers' and is unable `to attribute any moral cost to God's forgiveness', alluding here and in the rest of the passage to the Christian doctrine of atonement. Among three examples of 'moral shallowness' she cites the following lines from Imam Zayn al-'Ābidīn, found in *Al-Ṣaḥīfat al-khāmisa*:

> My God my sins do not harm Thee and Thy pardon does not impoverish Thee. Then forgive me what does not harm Thee and give me what Thou wilt not miss.[41]

In order to understand the attitude expressed here, one needs to put it into its larger context. The specific attitude expressed by the Imam corresponds

[40] *Biḥār,* LXXV, 153

[41] *Muslim Devotions,* p. 204. CF. Supplication 32.10, 39.6, 63.9

precisely to the reality of God's infinite mercy and forgiveness as revealed in various Qur'ānic verses. Many passages from the *Ṣaḥīfa* present the same point of view. Moreover, when the Imam says: 'Thou art the Generous Lord for whom the forgiveness of great sins is nothing great' (31.10), or 'Pardoning great sin is nothing great for Thee, overlooking enormous misdeeds is not difficult for Thee, putting up with indecent crimes does not trouble Thee' (12.13), he is merely echoing the command of the Prophet mentioned above: The worshiper 'should be firm and make his desire great, for what God gives is nothing great for Him.'

In any case, the context of these prayers shows that the accompanying moral attitude is hardly shallow, since it demands 'refraining from arrogance, pulling aside from persistence [in sin], and holding fast to praying forgiveness' (12.13). Moral shallowness could only follow if the worshiper remembered God's mercy and forgot His wrath, but both are always kept in view.

THE *SAḤĪFA* AND ISLAMIC SPIRITUALITY

In spite of studies that have rejected the idea, many people in the West still believe that 'true Islam' lies in simplicity, austerity, legalism, formalism, and a God perceived as Just and Transcendent. Hence those elements of Islamic civilization which demonstrate complexity, subtlety, warmth, love, inwardness, spirituality, and a God of mercy, compassion, and immanence are seen as largely extraneous to or reactions against Qur'ānic Islam. Scholars such as Massignon have pointed out that a person of spiritual sensitivity only needs to read the Qur'ān for such ideas to be dissolved. But few people who have adopted the old stereotypes possess this sort of sensitivity or would be interested in changing their preconceived ideas, lest sympathy be stirred up in their hearts. It is not my aim here to reject, as so many have done before me, these common biases concerning the nature of 'true Islam', but I would like to point out that a work like the *Ṣaḥīfa* brings out an inward dimension of Islam which may be much more difficult to perceive in other early texts.

When scholars and other outsiders look at Islam, they naturally perceive what can be seen at first glance, that is, events, written reports and records, social relationships, and so on. It is not easy to look into people's hearts or to investigate their personal relationship with God, nor are most people interested in doing so. If there is a way into hearts, it must come by studying the most inward concerns of individuals as reflected in their outward activities and writings. But those dimensions of Islam which have caught the most attention of outside observers are external and obvious, and they also happen to be relatively devoid of the love and warmth normally associated in the West with spirituality.

Islamic civilization as a whole is much like a traditional Muslim city: The outer walls make it appear dull and sombre, and it is not easy to gain access to the world behind the walls. But if one becomes an intimate with the city's inhabitants, one is shown into delightful courtyards and gardens, full of fragrant flowers, fruit trees, and sparkling fountains. Those who write about Islamic history, political events, and institutions deal with the walls, since they have no way into the gardens. Some of the gardens are opened up through the study of Sufism, art and architecture, poetry, and music, but since all of these have appeared in specific historical forms influenced by the surrounding environment, their deep Islamic roots can easily be lost to sight. The most traditional and authentic gardens of the city, and the most difficult of access, are the hearts of the greatest representatives of the civilization. It is here that the supplications handed down from the pillars of early Islam can open up a whole new vision of Islam's animating spirit, since they provide direct access to the types of human attitudes that are the prerequisite for a full flowering of the Islamic ideal.

OTHER DIMENSIONS

This introduction may seem to be suggesting that the *Ṣaḥīfa* deals exclusively with Islamic spirituality. But the *Ṣaḥīfa* deals with other domains as well. As was pointed out above, the great representatives of Islam bring together all levels of Islamic teachings, just as these are brought together by the Qur'ān and the *ḥadith*. If spirituality has been emphasized in discussing the *Ṣaḥīfa*, this has to do with the fact that the work is a collection of supplications, and these presuppose certain attitudes toward the Divine Reality which cannot be understood outside spirituality's context.

But the *Ṣaḥīfa* also provides teachings that are applicable on many different levels, from the theological (in the broadest sense of the term) to the social. A thorough analysis of these would demand a book far longer than the *Ṣaḥīfa* itself. It is hoped that the publication of this translation will encourage scholars to study the content of the prayers contained in the *Ṣaḥīfa* (as well as the prayers left by other pillars of early Islam, the Shī'ite Imams in particular) to bring out the whole range of teachings they contain. The most that can be done here is to allude to some of the other important topics touched upon by the *Ṣaḥīfa* and mention a few of the significant questions which these bring up.

Islam is an organic reality possessing three basic dimensions: practice or the Sharī'a (*al-islām*) faith (*al-imān* which includes doctrine and intellectual teachings), and spirituality (*al-iḥsān*). In the lived experience of the community, these dimensions are intimately interrelated, even if various institutional forms tend to deal with them separately. The earliest sources, such as the prophetic *ḥadith* or 'Alī's *Nahj al-balāgha* deal with all three of these dimensions, though different passages can be isolated which stress one specific epic rather than another. But a work like the *Nahj al-balāgha* converges profoundly from the *Ṣaḥīfa* in that it brings together sayings on all sorts of matters, from metaphysics, to the nature of correct government, to the personal flaws of some of 'Alī's contemporaries. There is no stress on spirituality, since this is clearly one dimension of Islam among others, though a deep spirituality and holiness underly everything that 'Alī says.

In contrast, the *Ṣaḥīfa* by its supplicatory form and content stresses the innermost dimension of Islam. But at the same time, it also touches upon Islam's other dimensions. For example, the traditional category of 'faith' is concerned with God, the angels, the prophets, the scriptures, the Last Day, and the 'measuring' (*qadar*) of both good and evil. These objects of faith form the basic subject matter of most of Islamic thought as developed in *kalām* philosophy, and theoretical Sufism. Imam Zayn al-'Ābidīn discusses all of these in the *Ṣaḥīfa* sometimes briefly and sometimes in detail. Thus he often mentions the angels, while his 'Blessing upon the Bearers of the Throne' (3) provides the best available summary of Muslim beliefs concerning them.

The Imam also refers frequently to the domain of Islamic practices, or the *Sharī'a* in the wide sense. He emphasizes the absolute necessity of following God's guidelines as set down in the Qur'ān and the *ḥadīth* in both individual and social life. Hence the *Ṣaḥīfa* provides many specific social teachings as well as general injunctions, such as the necessity of establishing justice in society. But since the social teachings deal with the domain of practice, the outermost dimension of Islam, they need to be viewed within the context of the Imam's doctrinal and spiritual teachings. As he makes eminently clear in his 'Treatise on Rights', a hierarchy of priorities must always be observed: The individual comes before the social, the spiritual before the practical, and knowledge before action. Each human being has a long series of social duties, but these depend upon his more essential duties, which are first, faith in God, and second, placing one's own person into the proper relationship with the Divine Reality.

THE TRANSLATION

The present translation of the *Ṣaḥīfa* follows the Arabic original with as much literal accuracy as could be contrived while maintaining a readable and understandable English text. I have kept Arberry's *Koran Interpreted* in view as the model of how this might be done. I have been particularly concerned with maintaining consistency in rendering terms and preserving the concreteness of the original terminology, feeling that the 'meaning' of the text cannot be grasped without due regard for its form.[42] It has already been suggested that one of the virtues of the early devotional literature is its ability to speak in a relatively concrete, pre-theological language of great universality. As a result, any move in the direction of rendering concrete terms abstractly, by paying attention to the rational meaning rather than the images conjured up by the linguistic form, will take us in the direction of *kalām* and away from the universe of the Qur'ān, the *ḥadīth* and the intimacy of the supplications themselves. This explains why I have usually preferred more literal terms such as 'Garden' to relatively abstract terms such as 'Paradise'.

Where difficulties arose in interpreting the meaning of the text, I have followed the commentary of Sayyid 'Alīkhan Shīrāzī. I have also profited from the excellent Persian translation and commentary by 'Alī Naqī Fayḍ al-Islām and the less useful Persian translation of Mirzā Abū l-Qāsim Sha'rānī. I have not tried to be exhaustive in the notes, aiming only to identify proper names, clarify obscurities, and point to a few of the Qur'ānic references in order to suggest how thoroughly the text is grounded in the revealed book. In a few cases I have mentioned relevant *ḥadīth* or discussed the different interpretations offered by the commentators.

The translation of the *Ṣaḥīfa* is followed by a translation of Imam Zayn al-'Ābidīn's 'Treatise on Rights', which is the only work attributed to him other than supplications or relatively short sayings and letters. This treatise is especially important for the manner in which it deals with many of the same themes as the *Ṣaḥīfa* in a different style and language.

The Arabic text printed here was copied from the Sha'rānī edition by Tehzib Ḥusayn Naqvī. It was proof-read by the dedicated and diligent efforts of S. Aṭā Muḥammad Ābidī Amrohvī. Āghā Aḥsān 'Abbās is also to be thanked for his efforts in coordinating the production of the Arabic text.

I owe a debt of gratitude to my dear friend Wing Commander (ret'd) Qasim Ḥusain, the moving spirit behind the Muḥammadi Trust. He caught me in a weak moment and pushed me into accepting a project which I never would have undertaken otherwise. His gentle but always firm and forceful pressure has made it possible for me to complete the translation practically on schedule. Without his intervention I would have been deprived of the opportunity to gain an intimate acquaintance with one of the deepest veins of Islamic spirituality. Anyone who comes to appreciate

---

[42] It is particularly in this respect that the translation differs from that of Syed Ahmad Ali Mohani (*The Sahifat=ul=Kamilah,* originally published in Lucknow in 1929-31; second edition, revised by M.A.H. Khan, Lucknow, 1969-70. Several other editions have also appeared).

the contents of the *Ṣaḥīfa* through the present work would do well to offer a prayer of thanks for the sake of Commander Ḥusain. I also thank Sayyid 'Alī Moḥammad Naqavī, who read the translation and offered a number of useful suggestions for its improvement, and Sayyid Muḥammad Ḥusain al-Ḥusaini al-Jalālī, who placed at my disposal a useful bibliography of works concerning the *Ṣaḥīfa*.

الصَّحِيفَةُ الكَامِلَةُ السَّجَّادِيَّةُ

The Psalms of Islam

Al-Sahîfat Al-Kâmilat Al-Sajjâdiyya

This is

Al- Ṣaḥīfat al-Kāmilat al-Sajjādiyya

(The Perfect Book of al-Sajjād)

In the Name of God,
the All-merciful, the All-compassionate

[Preface:
Concerning the Chain of Authorities of the *Ṣaḥīfa*]

1 The greatest sayyid, Najm al-Dīn Bahā' al-Sharaf Abū l-Ḥasan Muḥammad ibn Aḥmad ibn 'Alī ibn Muḥammad ibn 'Umar ibn Yaḥyā al-'Alawī al Ḥasanī[1] (God have mercy upon him) related to us:[2]

2 He said: The felicitous shaykh, Abū 'Abd Allāh Muḥammad ibn Aḥmad ibn Shahriyār[3], the treasurer of the treasure-house of our master, the Commander of the Faithful, 'Alī ibn Abī Ṭālib (upon him be peace) told us in the month of Rabi' I in the year 516 [May-June 1122 CE] while [the *Ṣaḥīfa*] was being read before him and I was listening.

3 He said: I heard it [being read] before the truthful shaykh Abū Manṣūr Muḥammad ibn Muḥammad ibn Aḥmad ibn 'Abd al-'Azīz al-'Ukbarī the Just[4] (God have mercy upon him) by Abū l-Mufaḍḍal Muḥammad ibn 'Abd Allāh ibn al-Muṭṭalib al-Shaybānī.[5]

4 He said: Al-Sharīf Abū 'Abd Allāh Ja'far ibn Muḥammad ibn Ja'far ibn al-Ḥasan ibn Ja'far ibn al-Ḥasan ibn al-Ḥasan ibn Amīr al-Mu'minīn 'Alī ibn Abī Ṭālib[6] (upon them be peace) related to us.

5 He said: 'Abd Allāh ibn 'Umar ibn Khaṭṭāb al-Zayyāt[7] related to us in the year 265 [878-9].

6 He said: My maternal uncle 'Alī ibn al-Nu'mān al-A'lam[8] related to me.

7 He said: 'Umayr ibn Mutawakkil al-Thaqafī al-Balkhī related to us from his

father Mutawakkil ibn Hārūn.[9]

8 He said: I met Yaḥyā ibn Zayd ibn ʻAlī (upon him be peace) when he was going to Khurasan after his father was slain and I greeted him.[10]

9 He said to me: From whence are you coming? I said: From the *ḥajj*.

10 He asked me about his household and the sons of his paternal uncle in Medina and he pressed me urgently about [Imam] Jaʻfar ibn Muḥammad (upon him be peace), so I gave him news of him and of them and of their sorrow over his father Zayd ibn ʻAlī (upon him be peace).

11 He said to me: My paternal uncle [Imam] Muḥammad [al-Bāqir] ibn ʻAlī (upon him be peace) advised my father not to revolt and he let him know what would be the outcome of his affair if he revolted and left Medina. Have you met the son of my paternal uncle, Jaʻfar ibn Muḥammad (upon him be peace)?

I said: Yes.

12 He said: Did you hear him mention anything about my affair?

I said: Yes.

13 He said: What did he say about me? Tell me!

I said: May I be made your sacrifice! I do not want to confront you with what I heard from him.

14 So he said: Will you frighten me with death? Tell me what you heard!

I said: I heard him saying that you would be slain and crucified as your father was slain and crucified.

15 His face changed colour and he said: *God erases whatsoever He will, and He establishes, and with Him is the Mother of the Book!*[11] O Mutawakkil! God has supported this affair through us and appointed for us knowledge and the sword. These two are combined in us, while the sons of our paternal uncle have been singled out only for knowledge.

16 I said: May I be made your sacrifice! Surely I see people inclining more to the son of your paternal uncle, Jaʻfar (upon him be peace) than to you and

your father.

17 He said: Surely my paternal uncle Muḥammad ibn ʿAlī and his son Jaʿfar (upon them both be peace) summon people to life, but we summon them to death.

18 I said: O son of the Messenger of God! Have they more knowledge, or have you?

He looked toward the ground for a time. Then he lifted his head and said: All of us have knowledge, but they know everything we know, and we do not know everything they know.

19 Then he said to me: Have you written anything from the son of my paternal uncle?

I said: Yes.

20 He said: Show it to me. So I brought out various kinds of knowledge, and I brought out for him a supplication which had been dictated to me by Abū ʿAbd Allāh (upon him be peace). He had related to me that his father, Muḥammad ibn ʿAlī (upon them both be peace) had dictated it to him and had told him that it was one of the supplications of his father, ʿAlī ibn al-Ḥusayn (upon them both be peace), from *Al- Ṣaḥīfat al-Kāmila.*[12]

21 Yaḥyā looked at it until he came to its end. He said to me: Will you permit me to copy it?

I said: O son of the Messenger of God! Do you ask permission for that which belongs to all of you?

22 He said: Truly I will bring out for you a *Ṣaḥīfa* with the Perfect Supplications, which my father had in safekeeping from his father. My father counselled me to safeguard it and to withhold it from those unworthy of it.

23 ʿUmayr said: My father [Mutawakkil] said: So I stood up before him, kissed him on the head, and said to him: By God, O son of the Messenger of God! I profess the religion of God through love for you and obedience toward you! I hope that He will favour me in my life and my death with your friendship.

24 So he tossed the page of mine which I had given to him to a servant who was with him and said: Write this supplication with a beautiful, clear script, and give it to me. Perhaps I will memorize it, for I had been seeking it from Jaʿfar (God safeguard him) and he withheld it from me.

25 Mutawakkil said: So I regretted what I had done and did not know what I should do. Abū ʻAbd Allāh had not ordered me not to hand it over to anyone.

26 Then he called for a box and brought out from it a *Ṣaḥīfa* locked and sealed.[13] He looked at the seal, kissed it, and wept. Then he broke it and undid the lock. He opened the *Ṣaḥīfa*, placed it upon his eyes, and passed it across his face.

27 He said: By God, O Mutawakkil, were it not for the words you mentioned from the son of my paternal uncle - that I will be slain and crucified - I would not hand this over to you and would be niggardly with it.

28 But I know that his word is the truth which he has taken from his fathers and that it will be verified. So I fear lest knowledge like this fall to the Umayyads and they hide it and store it in their treasuries for themselves.

29 So take it, guard it for me, and wait with it. Then, when God has accomplished in my affair and the affair of those people what He will accomplish, it will be a trust from me with you to be taken to the sons of my paternal uncle, Muḥammad and Ibrāhīm,[14] the two sons of ʻAbd Allāh ibn al-Ḥasan ibn al-Ḥasan ibn ʻAlī (upon the [last] two of them be peace). They will undertake this affair after me.

30 Mutawakkil said: So I took the *Ṣaḥīfa.* when Yaḥyā ibn Zayd was slain, I went to Medina and met [Imam] Abu ʻAbd Allāh [Jaʻfar al-Ṣādiq] (upon him be peace). I related to him the news of Yaḥyā. He wept and his feeling for him was intense.

31 He said: God have mercy on the son of my paternal uncle and join him to his fathers and grandfathers!

32 By God, O Mutawakkil, the only thing that prevented me from handing the supplication over to him was what he feared for the *Ṣaḥīfa* of his father. Where is the *Ṣaḥīfa*?

I said: Here it is. He opened it and said: This, by God, is the handwriting of my paternal uncle Zayd and the supplications of my grandfather ʻAlī ibn al-Ḥusayn (upon both of them be peace).

33 Then he said to his son: Stand up, O Ismāʻīl,[15] and bring out the supplications which I commanded you to memorize and safeguard!

34 So Ismāʿīl stood up, and he brought out a *Ṣaḥīfa* just like the *Ṣaḥīfa* which Yaḥyā ibn Zayd had handed over to me. Abū ʿAbd Allāh kissed it and placed it upon his eyes. He said: This is the handwriting of my father and the dictation of my grandfather (upon both of them be peace), while I was a witness.

35 I said: O son of the Messenger of God! Would it be proper for me to compare it to the *Ṣaḥīfa* of Zayd and Yaḥyā?

He gave me permission to do that and said: I consider you worthy of that.

36 I looked, and I found the two to be a single thing. I did not find a single letter to differ from what was in the other *Ṣaḥīfa.*

37 Then I asked permission from Abū ʿAbd Allāh to hand over the *Ṣaḥīfa* to the two sons of ʿAbd Allāh ibn al-Ḥasan.

He said: *God commands you to deliver trusts back to their owners.*[16] Yes, hand it over to them.

38 When I rose to go and meet them, he said to me: Stay in your place.

39 Then he sent for Muḥammad and Ibrāhīm, and they came. He said: This is the inheritance of the son of your paternal uncle, Yaḥyā, from his father. He has singled you out for it instead of his own brothers. But we place upon you a condition concerning it.

40 They said: God have mercy upon you! Tell us, for your word is accepted.

41 He said: Leave not Medina with this *Ṣaḥīfa*!

42 They said: And why is that?

43 He said: The son of your paternal uncle feared for it what I fear for you.

44 They said: He only feared for it when he came to know he would be slain.

45 Abū ʿAbd Allāh (upon him be peace) said: As for you - feel not secure! By God, I know that you will revolt as he revolted, and you will be slain as he was slain!

46 They arose, while they were saying: "There is no force and no strength save in God, the All-high, the All-mighty!"[17]

47 When they revolted Abū ʿAbd Allāh (upon him be peace) said to me: O

Mutawakkil! What did Yaḥyā say to you? 'Surely my paternal uncle Muḥammad ibn 'Alī and his son Ja'far summon the people to life, but we summon them to death."

48 I said: Yes, God set you right! The son of your paternal uncle Yaḥyā said that to me.

49 He said: God have mercy upon Yaḥyā! My father related from his father from his grandfather from 'Alī (upon him be peace) that the Messenger of God (God bless him and his Household) was seized from his senses for an instant while he was on the pulpit.

50 He saw in a vision some men leaping upon his pulpit like monkeys and making the people retrace their steps.

51 So the Messenger of God sat down (God bless him and his Household), and sorrow was apparent on his face.

52 Then Gabriel (upon him be peace) came to him with this verse: *And We made the vision that We showed thee and the tree cursed in the Qur'ān, that is, the Umayyads, to be only a trial for men; and We frighten them, but it only increases them in great insolence.*[18]

53 He said: O Gabriel! Will they be in my period and my time?

54 He said: No, but the mill of Islam will turn from your migration, and it will come to a halt ten [years] after that. Then it will begin turning exactly thirty-five years after your migration, and come to a halt five [years] after that. Then there is no avoiding a mill at whose axis stands error. Then there will be the kingdom of the pharaohs.

55 He said: God sent down concerning that: *Surely We sent it down on the Night of Decree. And what will teach thee what is the Night of Decree? The Night of Decree is better than a thousand months*[19] in which the Umayyads rule, during which time there will be no Night of Decree.

56 He said: So God gave news to His Prophet (upon him be peace) that the Umayyads would own sovereignty over this community and that their kingdom would last this period of time.

57 Were the mountains to vie with them, they would tower over the mountains until God (exalted is He) gave permission for the disappearance of their kingdom; and during this time they have made their banner enmity and hatred

for us, the Folk of the House.

58 God gave news to His Prophet concerning what the Folk of the House of Muḥammad, the people of love for them, and their partisans would meet from the Umayyads during their days and their kingdom.

59 He said: God sent down concerning them: *Hast thou not seen those who exchanged the favour of God for unbelief, and caused the people to dwell in the abode of ruin? Gehenna, wherein they are roasted; an evil resting place!*[20]

60 The 'favour of God' is Muḥammad and the People of his House. Love for them is a faith that takes into the Garden, and hate for them is an unbelief and a hypocrisy that takes into the Fire.

61 So the Messenger of God (God bless him and his Household) confided that to 'Alī and the Folk of his House.

62 He said: Then Abū 'Abd Allāh said (upon him be peace): Before the rise of our Qā'im[21] not one of us Folk of the House has revolted or will revolt to repel an injustice or to raise up a right, without affliction uprooting him and without his uprising increasing the adversity of us and our partisans.

63 Al-Mutawakkil ibn Hārūn said: Then Abū 'Abd Allāh dictated to me the supplications, which are seventy-five chapters. Of them eleven chapters have escaped me, while I have safeguarded sixty-some.

64 Abū l-Mufaḍḍal related to us.[22] He said: Muḥammad ibn al-Ḥasan ibn Rūzbih Abū Bakr al-Madā'īnī[23] the scribe, who lived in Rahba, related to us in his house.

65 He said: Muḥammad ibn Aḥmad ibn Muslim al-Muṭahharī[24] related to me.

66 He said: My father related to me from 'Umayr ibn Mutawakkil al-Balkhī from his father al-Mutawakkil ibn Hārūn.

67 He said: I met Yaḥyā ibn Zayd ibn 'Alī (upon them both be peace). Then he mentioned the whole *ḥadīth* including the vision of the Prophet (God bless him and his Household) which was mentioned by Ja'far ibn Muḥammad from his fathers (God's blessings be upon them).

68 In al-Muṭahharī's version, the chapter headings are mentioned. They are:

69 The remaining chapter headings are in the words of Abū ʿAbd Allāh al- Ḥa have mercy upon him).[25]

70 Abū ʿAbd Allāh Jaʿfar ibn Muḥammad al-Ḥasanī related to us.[26]

71 He said: 'Abd Allāh ibn ʿUmar ibn Khaṭṭāb al-Zayyāt related to us.

72 He said: Khālī ibn al-Nuʿmān al-Aʿlam related to us.

73 He said: ʿUmayr ibn Mutawakkil al-Thaqafī al-Balkhī related to us from his father Mutawakkil ibn Hārūn.

74 He said: My truthful master, Abū ʿAbd Allāh Jaʿfar ibn Muḥammad dictated to me.

75 He said: My grandfather ʿAlī ibn al-Ḥusayn dictated to my father Muḥammad ibn ʿAlī (upon them all be peace) while I was witness:

1

When he (upon him be peace) began to supplicate, he would begin with praise and laudation of God (Mighty and Majestic is He).

He would say:

1 Praise belongs to God,
the First, without a first before Him,
the Last, without a last behind Him.

2 Beholders' eyes fall short of seeing Him,
describers' imaginations are not able to depict Him.

3 He originated the creatures through His power with an origination,
He devised them in accordance with His will with a devising.

4 Then He made them walk on the path of His desire,
He sent them out on the way of His love.
They cannot keep back
from that to which He has sent them forward,
nor can they go forward
to that from which He has kept them back.

5 He assigned from His provision to each of their spirits
a nourishment known and apportioned.
No decreaser decreases those whom He increases,
no increaser increases those of them whom He decreases.

6 Then for each spirit He strikes a fixed term in life,
for each He sets up a determined end;
he walks toward it through the days of his span,
he overtakes it through the years of his time.
Then, when he takes his final step
and embraces the reckoning of his span,
God seizes him to the abundant reward
or the feared punishment
to which He has called him,
That He may repay those who do evil for what they have done
and repay those who do good with goodness,[27]

7 as justice from Him
(holy are His names,
and manifest His boons).
He shall not be questioned as to what He does,
but they shall be questioned.[28]

8 Praise belongs to God, for,
had He withheld from His servants the knowledge
to praise Him
for the uninterrupted kindnesses
with which He has tried them[29]
and the manifest favours
which He has lavished upon them,
they would have moved about in His kindnesses
without praising Him,
and spread themselves out in His provision
without thanking Him.

9 Had such been the case,
they would have left the bounds of humanity
for that of beastliness
and become as He has described in the firm text
of His Book:
They are but as the cattle—nay, but they are further astray
from the way!.[30]

10 Praise belongs to God, for
the true knowledge of Himself He has given to us,
the thanksgiving He has inspired us to offer Him,
the doors to knowing His Lordship He has opened
for us,
the sincerity towards Him in professing His Unity
to which He has led us,
and the deviation and doubt in His Command
from which He has turned us aside;

11 a praise through which
we may be given long life
among those of His creatures who praise Him,
and overtake those who have gone ahead
toward His good pleasure and pardon;

12 a praise through which
He will illuminate for us the shadows of the interworld,[31]
ease for us the path of the Resurrection,
and raise up our stations
at the standing places of the Witnesses[32]
on the day *when every soul will be repaid*
for what it has earned –
they shall not be wronged;[33]
the day a master shall avail nothing a client,
and they shall not be helped;[34]

13 a praise
which will rise up from us to the highest of the 'Illiyun[35]
in *a book inscribed,*
witnessed by those brought nigh,[36]

14 a praise whereby
our eyes may be at rest when sight is dazzled,[37]
our faces whitened when skins are blackened,[38]

15 a praise through which
we may be released from God's painful Fire
and enter God's generous neighbourhood,

16 a praise by which
we may jostle the angels brought nigh
and join the prophets, the envoys,
in a House of Permanence that does not remove,
the Place of His Generosity that does not change.

17 Praise belongs to God,
who chose for us the good qualities of creation,
granted us the agreeable things of provision,

18 and appointed for us excellence
through domination over all creation;
every one of His creatures submits to us
through His power
and comes to obey us
through His might.[39]

19 Praise belongs to God,
who locked for us the gate of need

except toward Him.
So how can we praise Him?
When can we thank Him?
Indeed, when?

20 Praise belongs to God,
who placed within us the organs of expansion,
assigned for us the agents of contraction,
gave us to enjoy the spirits of life,
fixed within us the limbs of works,
nourished us with the agreeable things of provision,
freed us from need through His bounty,
and gave us possessions through His kindness.

21 Then He commanded us that He might test our obedience
and prohibited us that He might try our thanksgiving.
So we turned against the path of His commandments
and mounted the backs of His warnings.
Yet He hurried us not to His punishment,
nor hastened us on to His vengeance.
No, He went slowly with us through His mercy,
in generosity,
and awaited our return through His clemency,
in mildness.

22 Praise belongs to God,
who showed us the way to repentance,
which we would not have won save through His bounty.
Had we nothing to count as His bounty but this,
His trial of us would have been good,
His beneficence toward us great,
His bounty upon us immense.

23 For such was not His wont in repentance
with those who went before us.[40]
He has lifted up from us
what we have not the strength to bear,[41]
charged us only to our capacity,[42]
imposed upon us nothing but ease,
and left none of us with an argument or excuse.

24 So the perisher among us is he who perishes in spite of Him

and the felicitous among us he who beseeches Him.

25 And praise belongs to God
with all the praises of
His angels closest to Him,
His creatures most noble in His eyes,
and His praisers most pleasing to Him;

26 a praise that may surpass other praises
as our Lord surpasses all His creatures.

27 Then to Him belongs praise,
in place of His every favour upon us
and upon all His servants, past and still remaining,
to the number of all things His knowledge encompasses,
and in place of each of His favours,
their number doubling and redoubling always and forever,
to the Day of Resurrection;

28 a praise whose bound has no utmost end,
whose number has no reckoning,
whose limit cannot be reached,
whose period cannot be cut off;

29 a praise which will become
a link to His obedience and pardon,
a tie to His good pleasure,
a means to His forgiveness,
a path to His Garden,
a protector against His vengeance,
a security against His wrath,
an aid to obeying Him,
a barrier against disobeying Him,
a help in fulfilling His right and His duties;

30 a praise that will make us felicitous
among His felicitous friends,
and bring us into the ranks
of those martyred by the swords of His enemies.
He is a Friend, Praiseworthy!

2

After this praise of God he (upon him be peace) would supplicate by calling down blessings upon God's Messenger (God bless him and his Household)

1 Praise belongs to God
who was kind to us through Muḥammad
(God bless him and his Household)
to the exclusion of past communities and bygone generations,
displaying thereby His power,
which nothing can render incapable,
though it be great,
and nothing can escape,
though it be subtle.

2 He sealed through us all He created,
appointed us witnesses over those who deny,
and increased us by His kindness over those who are few.

3 O God,
bless Muḥammad,
entrusted by Thee with Thy revelation,
distinguished by Thee among Thy creatures,
devoted to Thee among Thy servants,
the imam of mercy,
the leader of good,
the key to blessing,

4 who wearied his soul
for Thy affairs,

5 exposed his body to detested things
for Thy sake,

6 showed open enmity toward his next of kin
by summoning to Thee,

7 fought against his family

for Thy good pleasure,

8 cut the ties of the womb
in giving life to Thy religion,

9 sent far those close
because of their denial,

10 Brought near those far
because of their response to Thee,

11 showed friendship to the most distant for
Thy sake,

12 Displayed enmity toward the nearest
for Thy sake,

13 Made his soul persevere
in delivering Thy message,

14 Tired it in summoning
to Thy creed,

15 busied it in counselling
those worthy of Thy summons,

16 migrated to the land of exile and the place of remoteness from
the home of his saddlebags,
the walkway of his feet,
the ground of his birth,
and the intimate abode of his soul,
desiring to exalt Thy religion
and seeking help
against those who disbelieved in Thee,

17 until what he attempted against Thy enemies
went well with him

18 and what he arranged for Thy friends
was accomplished.

19 He rose up against them seeking victory
through Thine aid,

becoming strong in spite of his weakness
with Thy help.

20 He fought against them
in the centre of their cities

21 and attacked them
in the midst of their dwellings,

22 Until Thy command prevailed,
and Thy word rose up,
though the idolaters were averse.[43]

23 O God,
so raise him, because of his labours for Thy sake,
to the highest degree of Thy Garden,[44]

24 that none may equal him in station,
none may match him in level,
and no angel brought nigh or prophet sent out
may parallel him in Thy sight.

25 And inform him concerning his Household the pure
and his community the faithful
of an excellent intercession,
greater than what Thou hast promised him![45]

26 O Keeper of promises!
O Faithful to Thy word!
O He who changes evil deeds into manifold good deeds![46]
Thou art of bounty abounding!

3

A Supplication in Calling down Blessings upon the Bearers of the Throne and Every Angel Brought Nigh

1 O God,
as for the Bearers of Thy Throne,[47] who
never flag in glorifying Thee,
never become weary of calling Thee holy,
never tire of worshipping Thee,
never prefer curtailment over diligence in Thy command,
and are never heedless of passionate love for Thee;

2 Seraphiel,
the Owner of the Trumpet,
fixed in his gaze,
awaiting Thy permission
and the descent of the Command,
that he may arouse through the Blast
the hostages thrown down in the graves;

3 Michael,
possessor of standing with Thee
and a raised up place in Thy obedience;

4 Gabriel,
entrusted with Thy revelation,
obeyed by the inhabitants of Thy heavens,
distinguished in Thy Presence,[48]
brought nigh to Thee;

5 the spirit who is over the angels of the veils;[49]

6 And the spirit
who is of Thy command[50] –
bless them and the angels below them:
the residents in Thy heavens,
entrusted with Thy messages,

7 those who become not wearied by perseverance,
or exhausted and flagged by toil,

whom passions distract not from glorifying Thee,
and whose magnification of Thee is never cut off
by the inattention of heedless moments;

8 their eyes lowered,
they do not attempt to look at Thee;
their chins bowed,
they have long desired what is with Thee;
unrestrained in mentioning Thy boons,
they remain humble before Thy mightiness
and the majesty of Thy magnificence;

9 and those who say when they look upon Gehenna
roaring over the people who disobeyed Thee:
'Glory be to Thee,
we have not worshipped Thee
with the worship Thou deservest!'

10 Bless them,
and Thy angels who are the Reposeful,
those of proximity to Thee,
those who carry the unseen to Thy messengers,
Those entrusted with Thy revelation,

11 the tribes of angels
whom Thou hast singled out for Thyself,
freed from need for food and drink by their calling Thee holy,
and made to dwell inside Thy heavens' layers,

12 those who will stand upon the heavens' borders[51]
when the Command descends to complete Thy promise,

13 the keepers of the rain,
the drivers of the clouds,

14 Him at whose driving's sound is heard the rolling of thunder,
and when the reverberating clouds swim before his driving,
bolts of lightning flash;

15 the escorts of snow and hail,
the descenders with the drops of rain when they fall,
the watchers over the treasuries of the winds,
those charged with the mountains lest they disappear,

16 those whom Thou hast taught the weights of the waters
and the measures contained by torrents and masses of rain;

17 the angels who are Thy messengers to the people of the earth
with the disliked affliction that comes down
and the beloved ease;

18 the devoted, noble scribes,[52]
the watchers, noble writers,[53]
the angel of death and his helpers,
Munkar and Nakīr,[54]
Rūmān, the tester in the graves,[55]
the circlers of the Inhabited House,[56]
Mālik[57] and the guardians,
Riḍwān[58] and the gatekeepers of the gardens,

19 those who *disobey not God in What He commands them*
and do What they are commanded;[59]

20 those who say, *Peace be upon you, for that you were patient*
- and fair is the Ultimate Abode;[60]

21 The Zabāniya, who, when it is said to them,
take him, and fetter him,
then roast him in hell,[61]
hasten to accomplish it,
nor do they give him any respite;[62]

22 Him whom we have failed to mention,
not knowing his place with Thee,
nor with which command Thou hast charged him;

23 And the residents in the air, the earth, and the water,
and those of them charged over the creatures;

24 bless them on the day when *every soul will come,*
with it a driver and a witness,[63]

25 and bless them with a blessing that will add
honour to their honour
and purity to their purity.

26 O God,
and when Thou blessest Thy angels and Thy messengers
and Thou extendest our blessings to them,
bless us through the good words about them
which Thou hast opened up for us!
Thou art Munificent, Generous.

4

His Supplication in Calling down Blessings upon the Followers of, and Attesters to, the Messengers

1 O God,
as for the followers of the messengers
and those of the people of the earth
who attested to them unseen
(while the obstinate resisted them through crying lies) –
they yearned for the emissaries through the realities of faith,

2 in every era and time in which Thou didst send a messenger
and set up for the people a director
from the period of Adam down to Muḥammad
(God bless him and his Household)
from among the imams of guidance
and the leaders of the god fearing
(upon them all be peace) –
remember them with forgiveness and good pleasure!

3 O God,
and as for the Companions of Muḥammad specifically,
those who did well in companionship,
who stood the good test in helping him,
responded to him
when he made them hear his messages' argument,

4 separated from mates and children
in manifesting his word,
fought against fathers and sons
in strengthening his prophecy,
and through him gained victory;

5 those who were wrapped in affection for him,
hoping for a commerce
that comes not to naught[64] in love for him;

6 Those who were left by their clans

when they clung to his handhold
and denied by their kinsfolk
when they rested in the shadow of his kinship;

7 forget not, O God,
what they abandoned for Thee and in Thee,
and make them pleased with Thy good pleasure
for the sake of the creatures they drove to Thee
while they were with Thy Messenger,
summoners to Thee for Thee.

8 Show gratitude to them for leaving the abodes of their people
for Thy sake
and going out from a plentiful livelihood
to a narrow one,
and [show gratitude to] those of them who became
objects of wrongdoing
and whom Thou multiplied in exalting Thy religion.

9 O God,
and give to those
who have done well in following the Companions,
who say, *Our Lord, forgive us and our brothers*
who went before us in faith,[65]
Thy best reward;

10 Those who went straight to the Companions' road,
sought out their course,
and proceeded in their manner.

11 No doubt concerning their sure insight diverted them
and no uncertainty shook them
from following in their tracks
and being led by the guidance of their light.

12 As their assistants and supporters,
they professed their religion,
gained guidance through their guidance,
came to agreement with them,
and never accused them in what they passed on to them.

13 O God,
and bless the Followers,
from this day of ours to the Day of Doom,
their wives,
their offspring,
and those among them who obey Thee,

14 With a blessing through which
Thou wilt preserve them from disobeying Thee,
make room for them in the plots of Thy Garden,
defend them from the trickery of Satan,
help them in the piety in which they seek help from Thee,
protect them from sudden events that come
by night and day
- except the events which come with good -

15 and incite them to
tie firmly the knot of good hope in Thee,
what is with Thee,
and refrain from ill thoughts [toward Thee]
because of what the hands of Thy servants'
hold.

16 Thus Thou mayest
restore them to beseeching Thee and fearing Thee,
induce them to renounce the plenty of the immediate,
make them love to
work for the sake of the deferred
and prepare for what comes after death,

17 make easy for them every distress that comes to them
on the day when souls take leave from bodies,

18 release them from
that which brings about the perils of temptation
and being thrown down in the Fire
and staying forever within it,

19 and take them to security,
the resting place of the god fearing.

5

His Supplication for himself and the People under his Guardianship

1 O He the wonders of whose mightiness will never end!
Bless Muḥammad and his Household
and prevent us from deviation concerning Thy mightiness!

2 O He the term of whose kingdom will never cease!
Bless Muḥammad and his Household
and release our necks from Thy vengeance!

3 O He the treasuries of whose mercy will never be exhausted!
Bless Muḥammad and his Household
and appoint for us a portion of Thy mercy!

4 O He whom eyes fall short of seeing!
Bless Muḥammad and his Household
and bring us close to Thy nearness!

5 O He before whose greatness all great things are small!
Bless Muḥammad and his Household
and give us honour with Thee!

6 O He to whom all hidden tidings are manifest!
Bless Muḥammad and his Household
and expose us not before Thee!

7 O God,
remove our need for the gifts of the givers
through Thy gift,
spare us the loneliness of those who break off
through Thy joining,
that we may beseech no one
along with Thy free giving,
that we may feel lonely at no one's absence
along with Thy bounty!

8 O God,
bless Muḥammad and his Household,

scheme for us, not against us,
devise to our benefit, not to our loss,[66]
give the turn to prevail to us, not to others!

9 O God,
bless Muḥammad and his Household,
protect us from Thyself,
safeguard us through Thyself,
guide us to Thyself,
and take us not far from Thyself![67]
He whom Thou protectest stays safe,
he whom Thou guidest knows,
and he whom Thou bringest near Thyself
takes the spoils.

10 O God,
bless Muḥammad and his Household
and spare us the cutting edge of time's turning changes,
the evil of Satan's snares,
and the bitterness of the sovereign's aggression!

11 O God,
the spared are spared only through the bounty
of Thy strength,
so bless Muḥammad and his Household
and spare us!
The givers give only through the bounty of Thy wealth,
so bless Muḥammad and his Household
and give to us!
The guided are guided only by the light of Thy face,
so bless Muḥammad and his Household
and guide us!

12 O God,
he whom Thou befriendest will not be injured
by the abandonment of the abandoners,
he to whom Thou givest will not be diminished
by the withholding of the withholders,
he whom Thou guidest will not be misled
by the misguidance of the misguiders.

13 So bless Muḥammad and his Household,
defend us from Thy servants
through Thy might,
free us from need for other than Thee
through Thy support,
and make us travel the path of the Truth
through Thy right guidance!

14 O God,
bless Muḥammad and his Household
and put
the soundness of our hearts
into the remembrance of Thy mightiness,
the idleness of our bodies
into giving thanks for Thy favour,
and the flow of our tongues
into the description of Thy kindness!

15 O God,
bless Muḥammad and his Household
and make us one of
Thy summoners who summon to Thee,
Thy guiders who direct to Thee,
and Thy special friends whom Thou hast singled out!
O Most Merciful of the merciful!

6

His Supplication in the Morning and Evening

1 Praise belongs to God,
who created night and day
through His strength,

2 set them apart
through His power,

3 and appointed for each
a determined limit
and a drawn-out period.

4 He makes each of the two enter into its companion,
and makes its companion enter into it,
as an ordainment from Him for His servants
in that through which He feeds them
and with which He makes them grow.

5 He created for them the night,
that they might rest in it[68]
from tiring movements
and wearisome exertions
and He made it a garment for them
that they might be clothed
in its ease and its sleep,
that it might be for them refreshment and strength,
that they might reach therein pleasure and passion.

6 He created for them *the daytime, giving sight,*
that they might seek within it of His *bounty,*[69]
find the means to His provision,
and roam freely in His earth,
searching for that through which
to attain the immediate in their life in this world
and to achieve the deferred in their life to come.

7 Through all of this He sets right their situation,
tries their records,[70]
and watches their state in
the times for obeying Him,

the waystations of His obligations,
and the places of His ordinances,
that He may repay those who do evil with what they have done
and repay those who do good with goodness.[71]

8 O God,
to Thee belongs praise
for the sky Thou hast split into dawn for us,[72]
giving us to enjoy thereby the brightness of daytime,
showing us sought-after nourishments,
and protecting us from the striking of blights.

9 In the morning we and all things, every one, rise for Thee,
the heaven and the earth
and what Thou hast scattered in each,
the still and the moving,
the resident and the journeying,
what towers up in the air and what hides under the ground.

10 We rise in the morning in Thy grasp:
Thy kingdom and authority contain us
and Thy will embraces us.
We move about by Thy command
and turn this way and that through Thy governing.

11 We own nothing of the affair
except what Thou hast decreed
and nothing of the good
except what Thou hast given.

12 This is a fresh, new day,
over us a ready witness.
If we do good,
it will take leave from us with praise,
and if we do evil,
it will part from us in blame.

13 O God,
bless Muḥammad and his Household,
provide us with the day's good companionship
and preserve us against parting from it badly
by doing a misdeed

or committing a sin, whether small or great!

14 Make our good deeds within it plentiful
empty us therein of evil deeds,
and fill what lies between its two sides for us
with praise and thanksgiving,
wages and stores,
bounty and beneficence!

15 O God,
ease our burden on the Noble Writers,[73]
fill our pages for us
with our good deeds,
and degrade us not before them
with our evil works!

16 O God,
appoint for us in each of the day's hours
a share from Thy servants,
a portion of giving thanks to Thee,
and a truthful witness among Thy angels!

17 O God,
bless Muḥammad and his Household
and safeguard us from before us and behind us,
from our right hands and our left hands
and from all our directions,[74]
a safeguarding that will preserve from disobeying Thee,
guide to obeying Thee,
and be employed for Thy love!

18 O God,
bless Muḥammad and his Household
and give us success in this day of ours,
this night of ours,
and in all our days,
to employ the good,
stay away from the evil,
give thanks for favours,
follow the *Sunna's* norms,
avoid innovations,
enjoin good behaviour,

forbid the disapproved,
defend Islam,
diminish falsehood and abase it,
help the truth and exalt it,
guide the misguided,
assist the weak,
and reach out to the troubled!

19 O God,
bless Muḥammad and his Household
and make this
the most fortunate day we have known,
the most excellent companion we have accompanied,
and the best time in which we have lingered!

20 Place us among
the most satisfied of all Thy creatures
whom night and day have passed by,
the most thankful of them
for the favours Thou hast done,
the firmest of them
in the laws Thou hast set down in the *Sharī'a,*
and the most unyielding of them
toward the prohibited acts
against which Thou hast cautioned!

21 O God,
I call Thee to witness
- and Thou art sufficient witness -
and I call Thy heaven and Thy earth to witness
and Thy angels and Thy other creatures who inhabit them
in this my day,
this my hour,
this my night,
and this my resting place,
that I bear witness
that Thou art God,
other than whom there is no god,
Upholding justice,
Equitable in judgement,
Clement to the servants,[75]

Master of the kingdom,[76]
Compassionate to the creatures,

22 and that Muḥammad is Thy servant and Thy messenger,
Thy chosen from among Thy creatures.
Thou didst charge him with Thy message
and he delivered it;
Thou didst command him to counsel his community
and he counselled it.

23 O God,
so bless Muḥammad and his Household
more than Thou hast blessed any of Thy creatures!
Give him for our sake the best Thou hast given any of
Thy servants,
and repay him on our behalf better and more generously
than Thou hast repaid any of Thy prophets
on behalf of his community!

24 Thou art All-kind with immensity,
the Forgiver of the great,
and Thou art more merciful
than every possessor of mercy!
So bless Muḥammad and his Household,
the good, the pure, the chosen, the most distinguished!

7

His Supplication when Faced with a Worrisome Task Or when Misfortune Descended and at the Time of Distress

1 O He through whom the knots of detested things are untied!
O He through whom the cutting edge of hardships is blunted!
O He from whom is begged the outlet to the freshness of relief!

2 Intractable affairs yield to Thy power,
means are made ready by Thy gentleness,
the decree goes into effect through Thy power,
and all things proceed according to Thy desire.

3 By Thy desire they follow Thy command
without Thy word
and by Thy will they obey Thy bans
without Thy prohibition.

4 Thou art the supplicated in worries
and the place of flight in misfortunes;
none of them is repelled unless Thou repellest,
none is removed unless Thou removest.

5 Upon me has come down, My Lord,
something whose weight burdens me
and upon me has fallen
something whose carrying oppresses me.

6 Through Thy power
Thou hast brought it down upon me
and through Thy authority
Thou hast turned it toward me.

7 None can send away what Thou hast brought,
none can deflect what Thou hast turned,
none can open what Thou hast closed,
none can close what Thou hast opened,
none can make easy what Thou hast made difficult,
none can help him whom Thou hast abandoned.

8 So bless Muḥammad and his Household,

open for me, my Lord, the door of relief through
Thy graciousness,
break from me the authority of worry by Thy strength,
confer the beauty of Thy gaze upon my complaint,
let me taste the sweetness of benefaction in what I ask,
give me from Thyself mercy and wholesome relief,
and appoint for me from Thyself a quick way out!

9 Distract me not through worry
from observing Thy obligations
and acting in accordance with Thy prescriptions.

10 My capacity has been straitened, my Lord,
by what has come down on me,
and I am filled with worry
by carrying what has happened to me,
while Thou hast power to remove what has afflicted me
and to repel that into which I have fallen.
So do that for me
though I merit it not from Thee,
O Possessor of the Mighty Throne!

8

His Supplication in Seeking Refuge from Hateful Things, Bad Moral Qualities, and Blameworthy Acts

1 O God, I seek refuge in Thee from
the agitation of craving,
the violence of wrath,
the domination of envy,
the frailty of patience,
the lack of contentment,
surliness of character,
urgency of passion,
the disposition to vehemence,

2 following caprice,[77]
opposing guidance,
the sleep of heedlessness,
undertaking the toilsome,
preferring falsehood over truth,
persisting in sin,
making little of disobedience,
making much of obedience,

3 vying with the wealthy,
disparaging the poor,
guarding badly over those in our hands,
failing to thank those who have done good to us,

4 aiding a wrongdoer,
abandoning someone troubled,
wanting what is not rightfully ours,
and speaking about knowledge without knowing.

5 We seek refuge in Thee from
harbouring dishonesty toward anyone,
being pleased with our works,
and stretching out our expectations.

6 We seek refuge in Thee from
ill-mindedness,
looking down on the small,

Satan's gaining mastery over us,
time's afflicting us,
and the sovereign's oppressing us.

7 We seek refuge in Thee from
acting with prodigality
and not having sufficiency.

8 We seek refuge in Thee from
the gloating of enemies,
indigent need for equals,
living in hardship,
and dying without readiness.

9 We seek refuge in Thee from
the most dreadful remorse,
the greatest affliction,
the most wretched wretchedness,
the evil end to the journey,
the deprivation of reward,
and the advent of punishment.

10 O God,
bless Muḥammad and his Household
and through Thy mercy, give to me refuge from all of that,
and to all the faithful, both men and women!
O Most Merciful of the merciful!

9

His Supplication in Yearning to Ask Forgiveness from God

1 God, bless Muḥammad and his Household,
make us go to the repentance that Thou lovest
and make us leave the persistence that Thou hatest!

2 O God,
when we halt before two decreases,
in religion or in this world,
let the decrease fall upon that which passes quickly
and relent in that which lasts the longer!

3 When we set out after two concerns,
one of which makes Thee pleased with us
and the other of which displeases Thee,
incline us toward that which makes Thee pleased
and weaken our strength in that which displeases Thee!

4 Leave not our souls alone to choose in that,
for they choose falsehood
except inasmuch as Thou givest success,
and they command to evil
except inasmuch as Thou hast mercy![78]

5 O God,
thou created us from frailty,[79]
built us up from feebleness,
and began us from *a mean water;*[80]
we have no force except through Thy strength
and no strength except through Thy help.

6 So confirm us
by giving us success,
point us the right way
by Thy pointing,
blind the eyes of our hearts
toward everything opposed to Thy love,
and set not in any of our limbs
passage to disobeying Thee!

7 O God,
bless Muḥammad and his Household
and assign
the whisperings of our hearts,
the movements of our members,
the glances of our eyes,
and the idioms of our tongues,
to that which makes incumbent Thy reward, lest
a good deed slip by us,
through which we might deserve Thy repayment,
or an evil deed remain with us,
by which we might merit Thy punishment!

10

His Supplication in Seeking Asylum with God

1 O God,
if Thou willest,
Thou wilt pardon us through Thy bounty
and if Thou willest,
Thou wilt chastise us through Thy justice.

2 So make our ways smooth to Thy pardon
through Thy kindness
and grant us sanctuary from Thy chastisement
through Thy forbearance,
for none of us has the endurance for Thy justice
and none of us can reach deliverance without
Thy pardon!

3 O Richest of the rich!
Here we are, Thy servants, before Thee.
I am the neediest of the needy toward Thee,
so redress our neediness
through Thy plenty
and cut us not off from our hopes
through Thy withholding,
lest Thou makest wretched him who seeks felicity
through Thee
and deprivest him who seeks help from Thy
bounty!

4 Then to whom would we return after Thee?
Where would we go from Thy gate?
Glory be to Thee!
We are the distressed,
the response to whom
Thou hast made incumbent,
the people from whom
Thou hast promised to remove the evil.[81]

5 That thing most resembling Thy will
and that affair most worthy for Thee in Thy mightiness

is showing mercy to him who asks Thee for mercy
and helping him who seeks help from Thee.
So show mercy upon our pleading with Thee
and free us from need when we throw ourselves before Thee!

6 O God,
Satan will gloat over us if we follow him
in disobeying Thee,
so bless Muḥammad and his Household
and let him not gloat over us
after we have renounced him for Thee
and beseeched Thee against him!

11

His Supplication for Good Outcomes

1 O He remembering whom brings honour
to those who remember!
O He thanking whom brings triumph
to those who give thanks!
O He obeying whom brings deliverance
to those who obey!
Bless Muḥammad and his Household,
and divert our hearts through remembering Thee
from every act of remembrance,
our tongues through thanking Thee
from every act of thanksgiving,
our limbs through obeying Thee
from every act of obedience!

2 If Thou hast ordained for us idleness from these occupations,
make it an idleness of safety, within which
no ill consequence visits us
or weariness overtakes us!
Then the writers of evil deeds may depart from us
with a page empty of the mention of our evil deeds,
and the writers of good deeds may turn away from us
happy with the good deeds of ours which they have written.

3 And when the days of our life have passed by,
the terms of our lifetimes have elapsed,
and Thy call, which must come and be answered,
summons us forth,
then bless Muḥammad and his Household
and make the outcome of what the writers of our works
count against us
an accepted repentance,
which afterwards gave us no rest
in a sin that we committed
or an act of disobedience that we performed!

4 Remove not from us any covering
with which Thou hast covered over the heads of the

witnesses
on the day when the records of Thy servants are tried!

5 Verily Thou art compassionate to him who supplicates Thee,
the responder to him who calls upon Thee!

12

His Supplication in Confession and in Seeking Repentance toward God

1 O God,
three traits have prevented me from asking Thee
and one trait has urged me on:

2 I am prevented by
a command Thou hast commanded
in which I have been slow,
a prohibition Thou hast prohibited
toward which I have hurried,
and a favour through which Thou hast favoured
for which I have not given sufficient thanks.

3 I am urged to ask Thee
by Thy gratuitous bounty upon him who
turns his face toward Thee
and comes to Thee with a good opinion,
since all Thy beneficence is gratuitous bounty
and every one of Thy favours a new beginning!

4 So here I am, my God,
standing at the gate of Thy might,
the standing of the lowly, the surrendered,
asking Thee in my shame,
the asking of the destitute, the pitiful,

5 admitting to Thee that
at the time of Thy beneficence I surrendered not
save through abstaining from disobedience toward Thee
and in none of my states was I ever without
Thy Kindness.

6 Will it profit me, my God,
to admit to Thee the evil of what I have earned?
Will it save me from Thee
to confess the ugliness of what I have done?
Or wilt Thou impose upon me in this my station

Thy displeasure?
Will Thy hate hold fast to me in the time of
my supplication?

7 Glory be to Thee!
I do not despair of Thee,
for Thou hast opened the door of repentance toward
Thyself.
Rather, I say,
the words of a lowly servant,
having wronged himself
and made light of his Lord's inviolability,

8 and whose sins are dreadful, great,
whose days have parted, fled,
until, when he sees the term of his works expired
and the limit of his lifetime reached
and knows with certainty that he has no escape from Thee,
no place to flee from Thee,
he turns his face toward Thee in repeated turning,
makes his repentance toward Thee sincere,
stands before Thee with a pure and purified heart,
then supplicates Thee with a feeble, quiet voice.

9 He is bowed before Thee, bent,
his head lowered, thrown down,
his legs shaking in fear,
his tears flooding his cheeks.
He supplicates Thee:
O Most Merciful of the merciful!
O Most Merciful of those toward whom seekers of mercy
keep on turning!
O Tenderest of those around whom run
seekers of forgiveness!
O He whose pardon is greater
than His vengeance!
O He whose good pleasure is more abundant
than His anger![82]

10 O He who seeks His creatures' praise
with excellent forbearance!

O He who has accustomed His servants
to the acceptance of their repeated turning![83]
O He who seeks to heal their corruption
through repentance!
O He who is pleased with the easy
of their acts!
O He who recompenses with the much
their little!
O He who has made himself accountable to them
to respond to supplication![84]
O He who pledged Himself by His gratuitous bounty
to give them excellent repayment!

11 I am not the most disobedient of those who have disobeyed Thee
and whom Thou hast forgiven,
nor am I the most blameworthy to offer excuses
which Thou hast accepted,
nor am I the most wrongdoing of those who have repented to Thee,
and to whom Thou hast returned

12 I repent to Thee in this my station,
the repentance of one
remorseful over what preceded from him hastily,
apprehensive of what has gathered around him,
pure in shame for that into which he has fallen,

13 knowing that
pardoning great sins is nothing great for Thee.[85]
overlooking enormous misdeeds is not difficult for Thee,
putting up with indecent crimes does not trouble Thee,
and the most beloved of Thy servants to Thee is he who
refrains from arrogance before Thee,
pulls aside from persistence,
and holds fast to praying forgiveness!

14 I am clear before Thee of arrogance,
I seek refuge in Thee from persistence,

I pray forgiveness from Thee for shortcomings,
I seek help from Thee in incapacity!

15 O God,
bless Muḥammad and his Household,
dispense with what is incumbent upon me toward Thee,
release me from what I merit from Thee,
and grant me sanctuary from what the evildoers fear!
For Thou art full of pardon,
the hoped-for source of forgiveness,
well known for Thy forbearance.
My need has no object but Thee,
my sin no forgiver other than Thee
- could that be possible?

16 I have no fear for myself except from Thee;
Thou art *worthy of reverential fear,*
and worthy to forgive![86]
Bless Muḥammad and his Household,
grant my need,
answer my request favourably,
forgive my sin,
and give me security from fear for myself!
Thou art powerful over everything,[87]
and that is easy for Thee.
Amen, Lord of the worlds!

13

His Supplication in Seeking Needs from God

1 O God,
O ultimate object of needs!

2 O He through whom requests
are attained!

3 O He whose favours are not bought
by prices!

4 O He who does not muddy His gifts
by the imposition of obligations!

5 O He along with whom nothing is needed
and without whom nothing can be done!

6 O He toward whom desire is ever directed
and never turned away!

7 O He whose treasuries cannot be exhausted
by demands!

8 O He whose wisdom cannot be altered
by any means!

9 O He from whom the needs of the needy
are never cut off!

10 O He who is not distressed
by the supplications of the supplicators!

11 Thou hast lauded Thyself for having no need for Thy creatures,
and it suits Thee to have no need for them,

12 and Thou hast attributed to them poverty,
and it suits them to be poor toward Thee.[88]

13 So he who strives to remedy his lack through what is with Thee
and wishes to turn poverty away from himself through Thee
has sought his need in the most likely place

and come to his request from the right quarter.

14 But he who turns in his need toward one of Thy creatures
or assigns the cause of its being granted to other than Thee,
has exposed himself to deprivation
and deserves to miss Thy beneficence.

15 O God,
I have a need of Thee:
My exertion has fallen short of it
and my stratagems have been cut back before reaching it.
My soul induced me to present it to him who
presents his needs to Thee
and can do nothing without Thee in his requests,
but this is one of the slips of the offenders,
one of the stumbles of the sinners!

16 Then through Thy reminding me,
I was aroused from my heedlessness,
through Thy giving success,
I stood up from my slip,
and through Thy pointing the way,
I returned and withdrew from my stumble.

17 I said:
Glory to my Lord!
How can the needy ask from the needy?
How can the destitute beseech the destitute?

18 So I went straight to Thee, my God, in beseeching,
and I sent Thee my hope with trust in Thee.

19 I came to know that
the many I request from Thee are few before Thy wealth,
the weighty I ask from Thee is vile before Thy plenty;
Thy generosity is not constrained by anyone's asking,
Thy hand is higher in bestowing gifts than every hand!

20 O God,
so bless Muḥammad and his Household,

take me through Thy generosity
to Thy gratuitous bounty
and take me not through Thy justice
to what I deserve!
I am not the first beseecher to beseech Thee
and Thou bestowed upon him
while he deserved withholding,
nor am I the first to ask from Thee
and Thou wast bounteous toward him
while he merited deprivation.

21 O God,
bless Muḥammad and his Household,
respond to my supplication,
come near my call,
have mercy on my pleading,
listen to my voice,

22 cut not short my hope for Thee,
sever not my thread to Thee,
turn not my face in this my need,
and other needs,
away from Thee,

23 attend for my sake to
the fulfilment of my request,
the granting of my need,
and the attainment of what I have asked
before I leave this place
through Thy making easy for me the difficult
and Thy excellent ordainment for me in all affairs!

24 Bless Muḥammad and his Household
with a permanent, ever-growing blessing,
whose perpetuity has no cutting off
and whose term knows no limit,
and make that a help to me
and a cause for the granting of my request!
Thou art Boundless, Generous!

25 And of my needs, My Lord, are such and such.

HERE YOU SHOULD STATE YOUR NEEDS,
THEN PROSTRATE YOURSELF,
AND SAY IN YOUR PROSTRATION

26 Thy bounty has comforted me
and Thy beneficence has shown the way,
So I ask Thee by Thee
and by Muḥammad and his Household
(Thy blessings be upon them)
that Thou send me not back in disappointment!

14

His Supplication when Hostility was Shown to Him or when he Saw what he did not Like in Wrongdoers[89]

1 O He from whom is not concealed
news of the aggrieved!

2 O He who has no need to be told about them
by the witnessing of the witnesses!

3 O He who whose help is near to the wronged!

4 O He whose aid is far from the wrongdoers!

5 Thou knowest, my God,
how so-and-so, son of so-and-so, has harmed me
in that which Thou hast forbidden,
and how he has violated me
in that which Thou hast prohibited,
showing thereby ingratitude toward Thy favour upon him
and delusion concerning what Thou hast denied him.

6 O God,
so bless Muḥammad and his Household,
keep my wrongdoing enemy from wronging me through Thy strength,
blunt his blade toward me through Thy power,
and assign to him
a diversion in that which is close to him
and the inability to reach his enemy!

7 O God,
bless Muḥammad and his Household,
let the wrongdoer not find it easy to wrong me,
give me good help against him,
preserve me from the like of his acts,
and place me not in the like of his situation!

8 O God,
bless Muḥammad and his Household,
and assist me with an immediate assistance

that will heal my rage toward him
and redeem my fury toward him!

9 O God,
bless Muḥammad and his Household,
compensate me for his wronging me with Thy pardon
and replace his evil action toward me with Thy mercy,
for every detested thing less than Thy anger is slight
and every disaster next to Thy rancour indifferent!

10 O God,
just as Thou hast made me detest being wronged,
so also protect me from doing wrong!

11 O God,
I complain to no one but Thee,
and I seek help from no ruler other than Thee -
how could I?
So bless Muḥammad and his Household,
join my supplication to response,
and unite my complaint with change!

12 O God,
tempt me not with despair of Thy just treatment
and tempt him not with feeling secure from Thy disapproval,
lest he persist in wronging me
and constrain me in my rights.[90]
Let him soon recognize
what Thou hast promised the wrongdoers[91]
and let me recognize
Thy promised response to the distressed![92]

13 O God,
bless Muḥammad and his Household,
give me success in accepting Thy decrees
for me and against me,
make me pleased with what Thou takest
for me and from me,
guide me to that which is most upright
and employ me in that which is safest!

14 O God,
if the best for me with Thee lies
in delaying the taking to task for my sake
of him who has wronged me
and in refraining from vengeance toward him
until the Day of Decision and
the Gathering of Disputants,
then bless Muḥammad and his Household,
strengthen me from Thee
with true intention
and lasting patience,

15 give me refuge
from evil desire
and the impatience of the greedy,
and form in my heart the image of
Thy reward
which Thou hast stored away for me
and the repayment and punishment
which Thou has prepared for my disputant!
Make this a cause of my contentment
with what Thou hast decreed
and my trust
in what Thou hast chosen!

16 Amen, Lord of the worlds!
Thou art of bounty abounding
and Thou art powerful over everything.

15

His Supplication when Sick or Visited by Distress or an Affliction

1 O God, to Thee belongs praise
for the good health of my body
which lets me move about,
and to Thee belongs praise,
for the ailments
which Thou cause to arise in my flesh!

2 For I know not, my God,
which of the two states deserves more my thanking Thee
and which of the two times is more worthy for my praise of Thee:

3 the time of health,
within which Thou makest me delight
in the agreeable things of Thy provision,
through which Thou givest me the joy to seek
the means to Thy good pleasure and bounty,
and by which Thou strengthenest me
for the acts of obedience
which Thou hast given me success to accomplish;

4 or the time of illness
through which Thou puttest me to the test
and bestowest upon me favours:
lightening of the offences
that weigh down my back,
purification of the evil deeds
into which I have plunged,
incitement to reach
for repentance,
reminder of the erasure of misdeeds
through ancient favour;

5 and, through all that, what the two writers write for me:
blameless acts,
which no heart had thought,

no tongue had uttered,
and no limb had undertaken,
rather, as Thy bestowal of bounty upon me
and the beneficence of Thy benefaction toward me.[93]

6 O God,
bless Muḥammad and his Household,
make me love
what Thou hast approved for me,
make easy for me
what Thou hast sent down upon me,
purify me of the defilement
of what I have sent ahead,
erase the evil
of what I have done beforehand,
let me find the sweetness
of well-being,
let me taste the coolness
of safety,
and appoint for me
a way out from my illness to Thy pardon,
transformation of my infirmity into Thy forbearance,
escape from my distress to Thy refreshment,
and safety from this hardship in Thy relief!

7 Thou art gratuitously bountiful in beneficence,
ever gracious in kindness,
the Generous, the Giver,
Possessor of majesty and munificence!

16

His Supplication when he Asked Release from his Sins or Pleaded in Seeking Pardon for his Defects

1 O God,
O He through whose Mercy sinners seek aid!

2 O He to the remembrance of whose beneficence the distressed flee!

3 O He in fear of whom the offenders weep!

4 O Comfort of every lonely stranger!
O Relief of all who are downcast and distressed!
O Aid of everyone abandoned and alone!
O Support of every needy outcast!

5 Thou art He
who *embracest everything in mercy and knowledge!*[94]

6 Thou art He
who hast appointed for each creature a share of Thy favours!

7 Thou art He
whose pardon is higher than His punishment!

8 Thou art He
whose mercy runs before His wrath!

9 Thou art He
whose bestowal is greater than His withholding!

10 Thou art He
by whose mercy all creatures are embraced!

11 Thou art He
who desires no repayment by him upon whom He bestows!

12 Thou art He
who does not overdo the punishment of him who disobeys Thee!

13 And I, my God, am Thy servant
whom Thou commanded to supplicate
and who said:
I am at Thy service and disposal!
Here am I, my Lord,
thrown down before Thee.

14 I am he
whose back offences have weighed down!
I am he
whose lifetime sins have consumed!
I am he
who was disobedient in his ignorance,
while Thou didst not deserve that from him!

15 Wilt Thou, my God,
be merciful toward him who supplicates Thee,
that I should bring my supplication before Thee?
Wilt Thou forgive him who weeps to Thee
that I should hurry to weep?
Wilt Thou show forbearance toward
him who puts his face in the dust before Thee in lowliness?
Wilt Thou free from need
him who complains to Thee of his indigent need with confidence?

16 My God,
disappoint not him who finds no bestower
other than Thee,
and abandon not him who cannot be freed from his need for Thee
through less than Thee!

17 My God,
so bless Muḥammad and his Household,
turn not away from me
when I have turned my face toward Thee,
deprive me not
when 1 have besought Thee,
and slap not my brow with rejection
when I have stood before Thee!

18 Thou art He who has described Himself by mercy,
so bless Muḥammad and his Household
and have mercy upon me!
Thou art He who has named Himself by pardon,
so pardon me!

19 Thou hast seen, my God,
the flow of my tears
in fear of Thee,
the throbbing of my heart
in dread of Thee,
and the infirmity of my limbs
in awe of Thee.

20 All this from my shame before Thee
because of my evil works!
So my voice has become silent,
no longer crying to Thee,
and my tongue has gone dumb,
no longer whispering in prayer.

21 My God,
so to Thee belongs praise!
How many of my haws Thou hast covered over
without exposing me!
How many of my sins Thou hast cloaked
without making me notorious!
How many faults I have committed, yet Thou didst not
tear away from me their covering,
collar me with their detested disgrace,
or make their dishonour plain
to those of my neighbours who search for my
defects
and to those who envy Thy favour toward me!

22 But that did not prevent me from passing on
to the evil that Thou knowest from me!

23 So who is more ignorant than I, my God,
of his own right conduct?
Who is more heedless than I
of his own good fortune?

Who is further than I
from seeking to set himself right?
For I spend the provision Thou deliverest to me
in the disobedience Thou hast prohibited to me!
Who sinks more deeply into falsehood
and is more intensely audacious in evil than I?
For I hesitate between Thy call and the call of Satan
and then follow his call
without being blind in my knowledge of him
or forgetful in my memory of him,

24 while I am certain that Thy call takes to the Garden
and his call takes to the Fire!

25 Glory be to Thee!
How marvellous the witness I bear against my own soul
and the enumeration of my own hidden affairs!

26 And more marvellous than that is Thy lack of haste with me,
Thy slowness in attending to me!
That is not because I possess honour with Thee,
but because Thou waitest patiently for me
and art bountiful toward me
that I may refrain from disobedience displeasing to Thee
and abstain from evil deeds that disgrace me,
and because Thou lovest to pardon me more than to punish!

27 But I, my God, am
more numerous in sins,
uglier in footsteps,
more repulsive in acts,
more reckless in rushing into falsehood,
weaker in awakening to Thy obedience,
and less attentive and heedful toward Thy threats,
than that I could number for Thee my faults
or have the power to recount my sins.

28 I only scold my own soul,
craving Thy gentleness,
through which the affairs of sinners are set right,
and hoping for Thy mercy,
through which the necks of the offenders are freed.

29 O God,
this is my neck,
enslaved by sins,
bless Muḥammad and his Household
and release it through Thy pardon!
This is my back,
weighed down by offences,
bless Muḥammad and his Household
and lighten it through Thy kindness!

30 My God,
were I to weep to Thee until my eyelids drop off,
wail until my voice wears out,
stand before Thee until my feet swell up,
bow to Thee until my backbone is thrown out of joint,
prostrate to Thee until my eyeballs fall out,
eat the dirt of the earth for my whole life,
drink the water of ashes till the end of my days,
mention Thee through all of that until my tongue fails,
and not lift my glance to the sky's horizons in shame
before Thee,
yet would I not merit through all of that
the erasing of a single one of my evil deeds!

31 Though Thou forgivest me when I merit Thy forgiveness
and pardonest me when I deserve Thy pardon,
yet I have no title to that through what I deserve,
nor am I worthy of it through merit,
since my repayment from Thee
from the first that I disobeyed Thee
is the Fire!
So if Thou punishest me,
Thou dost me no wrong.

32 My God, since Thou hast
shielded me with Thy covering
and not exposed me,
waited patiently for me through Thy generosity,
and not hurried me to punishment,
and shown me clemency through Thy bounty,
and not changed Thy favour upon me
or muddied Thy kindly acts toward me,

have mercy on my drawn out pleading,
my intense misery,
and my evil situation!

33 O God,
bless Muḥammad and his Household,
protect me from acts of disobedience,
employ me in obedience,
provide me with excellent turning back [to Thee],
purify me through repentance,
strengthen me through preservation from sin,
set me right through well being,
let me taste the sweetness of forgiveness,
make me the freedman of Thy pardon
and the slave released by Thy mercy,
and write for me a security
from Thy displeasure!
Give me the good news of that
in the immediate, not the deferred
- a good news I recognize -
and make known to me therein a sign
which I may clearly see!

34 That will not constrain Thee in Thy plenty,
distress Thee in Thy power,
ascend beyond Thy lack of haste,
or tire Thee in Thy great gifts,
which are pointed to by Thy signs.
Verily Thou dost what Thou wilt,
Thou decreest what Thou desirest.
Thou art powerful over everything.[95]

17

His Supplication when he Mentioned Satan and Sought Refuge from him and from his Enmity and Trickery

1 O God,
we seek refuge in Thee
from the instigations of the accursed Satan,
his trickery, and his traps,
from trust in his false hopes, his promises,
his delusions, and his snares,

2 and lest he should make himself crave
to lead us away from Thy obedience
and to degrade us through our disobeying Thee,
and lest what he has shown us as beautiful be beautiful for us
and what he has shown us as detestable weigh
down upon us.

3 O God,
drive him away from us through Thy worship,
throw him down through our perseverance in Thy love,
and place between him and us a covering
that he cannot tear away
and a solid barrier
that he cannot cut through!

4 O God,
bless Muḥammad and his Household,
distract Satan from us with some of Thy enemies,
preserve us from him through Thy good guarding,
spare us his treachery,
turn his back toward us,
and cut off from us his trace!

5 O God,
bless Muḥammad and his Household,
give us to enjoy guidance
the like of his misguidance,
increase us in piety
against his seduction,

and make us walk in reverential fear
contrary to his path of ruin!

6 O God,
assign him no place of entrance into our hearts and
do not allow him to make his home in that which is
with us!

7 O God,
cause us to recognize the falsehood with which he tempts us,
and once Thou hast caused us to recognize it,
protect us from it!
Make us see what will allow us to outwit him,
inspire us with all that we can make ready for him,
awaken us from the heedless slumber of relying upon him,
and help us well, through Thy giving success, against him!

8 O God,
saturate our hearts with the rejection of his works
and be gentle to us by destroying his stratagems!

9 O God,
bless Muḥammad and his Household,
turn his authority away from us,
cut off his hope from us,
and keep him from craving for us!

10 O God,
bless Muḥammad and his Household,
and place our fathers, our mothers,
our children, our wives,
our siblings, our relatives,
and the faithful among our neighbours,
male and female,
in a sanctuary impregnable to him,
a guarding fortress,
a defending cave!
Clothe them in shields protective against him
and give them arms that will cut him down!

11 O God,

include in that everyone who
witnesses to Thee as Lord,
devotes himself sincerely to Thy Unity,
shows enmity toward him
through the reality of servant hood,
and seeks help from Thee against him
through knowledge of the divine sciences!

12 O God,
undo what he ties,
unstitch what he sews up,
dislocate what he devises,
frustrate him when he makes up his mind,
and destroy what he establishes!

13 O God,
rout his troops,
nullify his trickery,
make his cave collapse,
and rub his nose in the ground!

14 O God,
place us in the ranks of his enemies
and remove us from the number of his friends,
that we obey him not when he entices us
and answer him not when he calls to us!
We command everyone who obeys our command
to be his enemy
and we admonish everyone who follows our prohibition
not to follow him!

15 O God,
bless Muḥammad
the Seal of the prophets and lord of the emissaries,
and the folk of his house,
the good, the pure!
Give refuge to us, our families, our brothers,
and all the faithful, male and female,
from that from which we seek refuge,
and grant us sanctuary from that through fear of which
we seek sanctuary in Thee!

16 Hear our supplication to Thee,
bestow upon us that of which we have been heedless,
and safeguard for us what we have forgotten!
Through all this bring us into the ranks of the righteous
and the degrees of the faithful!
Amen, Lord of the worlds!

18

His Supplication when Perils were Repelled or Requests quickly granted

1 O God,
to Thee belongs praise for Thy excellent accomplishment
and for Thy trial which Thou hast turned away from me!
But make not my share of Thy mercy
the well-being which Thou hast quickly granted to me,
lest I become wretched through what I have loved
and someone else gain felicity through what I have disliked![96]

2 If this well-being in which 1 pass the day or night should precede
a trial that does not cease
and a burden that does not pass away,
then set before me what Thou hadst set behind
and set behind me what Thou hadst set before!

3 For that which ends in annihilation is not great
and that which ends in subsistence is not little.
And bless Muḥammad and his Household!

19

His Supplication in Asking for Water during a Drought

1 O God,
water us with rain,
unfold upon us Thy mercy
through Thy copious rain
from the driven clouds,
so that Thy goodly earth may grow
on all horizons!

2 Show kindness to Thy servants
through the ripening of the fruit,
revive Thy land
through the blossoming of the flowers,
and let Thy angels - the noble scribes - be witness
to a beneficial watering from Thee,
lasting in its abundance,
plenty in its flow,
heavy, quick, soon,

3 through which Thou revivest what has vanished,
bringest forth what is coming,
and providest plentiful foods,
through heaped up, wholesome, productive clouds,
in reverberating layers,
the rain's downpour
not without cease,
the lightning's flashes
not without fruit!

4 O God,
give us water
through rain,
helping, productive, fertilizing,
widespread, plentiful, abundant,
bringing back the risen,
restoring the broken!

5 O God,
give us water with a watering through which Thou wilt

make the stone hills pour,
fill the cisterns,
flood the rivers,
make the trees grow,
bring down prices in all the lands,
invigorate the beasts and the creatures,
perfect for us the agreeable things of provision,
make grow for us the fields,
let flow for us the teats,
and add for us strength to our strength!

6 O God,
make not the cloud's shadow over us a burning wind,
allow not its coldness to be cutting,
let not its pouring down upon us be a stoning,
and make not its waters for us bitter!

7 O God,
bless Muḥammad and his Household
and provide us with the blessings of the heavens and the earth!
Thou art powerful over everything![97]

20

His Supplication on Noble Moral Traits and Acts Pleasing to God

1 O God,
bless Muḥammad and his Household,
cause my faith to reach the most perfect faith,
make my certainty the most excellent certainty,
and take my intention to the best of intentions
and my works to the best of works!

2 O God,
complete my intention through Thy gentleness,
rectify my certainty through what is with Thee,
and set right what is corrupt in me through Thy power!

3 O God,
bless Muḥammad and his Household,
spare me the concerns
which distract me,
employ me
in that about which Thou wilt ask me tomorrow,
and let me pass my days
in that for which Thou hast created me!
Free me from need,
expand Thy provision toward me,
and tempt me not with ingratitude!
Exalt me
and afflict me not with pride!
Make me worship Thee
and corrupt not my worship with self-admiration!
Let good flow out from my hands upon the people
and efface it not by my making them feel obliged![98]
Give me the highest moral traits
and preserve me from vainglory!

4 O God,
bless Muḥammad and his Household,
raise me not a single degree before the people
without lowering me its like in myself
and bring about no outward exaltation for me
without an inward abasement in myself to the same measure!

5 O God,
bless Muḥammad and Muḥammad's Household,
give me to enjoy
a sound guidance
which I seek not to replace,
a path of truth
from which I swerve not,
and an intention of right conduct
in which I have no doubts!
Let me live as long as my life is a free gift in obeying Thee,
but if my life should become a pasture for Satan,
seize me to Thyself
before Thy hatred overtakes me
or Thy wrath against be becomes firm!

6 O God, deposit in me
no quality for which I will be faulted,
unless Thou settest it right,
no flaw for which I will be blamed,
unless Thou makest it beautiful,
no deficient noble trait,
unless Thou completest it!

7 O God,
bless Muḥammad and 'Muḥammad's Household
and replace for me
the animosity of the people of hatred
with love,
the envy of the people of insolence
with affection,
the suspicion of the people of righteousness
with trust,
the enmity of those close
with friendship,
the disrespect of womb relatives
with devotion,
the abandonment of relatives
with help,
the attachment of flatterers
with love set right,

the rejection of fellows
with generous friendliness,
and the bitterness of the fear of wrongdoers
with the sweetness of security!

8 O God,
bless Muḥammad and his Household,
appoint for me
a hand against him who wrongs me,
a tongue against him who disputes with me,
and a victory over him who stubbornly resists me!
Give me
guile against him who schemes against me,
power over him who oppresses me,
refutation of him who reviles me,
and safety from him who threatens me!
Grant me success to
obey him who points me straight
and follow him who guides me right!

9 O God,
bless Muḥammad and his Household
and point me straight to
resist him who is dishonest toward me
with good counsel,
repay him who separates from me
with gentle devotion,
reward him who deprives me
with free giving,
recompense him who cuts me off
with joining,
oppose him who slanders me
with excellent mention,
give thanks for good,
and shut my eyes to evil!

10 O God,
bless Muḥammad and his Household,
adorn me with the adornment of the righteous,
and clothe me in the ornaments of the godfearing, through

spreading justice,
restraining rage,
quenching the flame of hate,
bringing together the people of separation,
correcting discord,
spreading about good behaviour,
covering faults,
mildness of temper,
lowering the wing,[99]
beauty of conduct,
gravity of bearing,
agreeableness in comportment,
precedence in reaching excellence,
preferring bounteousness,
refraining from condemnation,
bestowing bounty on the undeserving,
speaking the truth,
though it be painful,
making little of the good in my words and deeds,
though it be much,
and making much of the evil in my words and deeds,
though it be little!
Perfect this for me through
lasting obedience,
holding fast to the community,
and rejecting
the people of innovation
and those who act in accordance with original opinions!

11 O God,
bless Muḥammad and his Household,
appoint for me
Thy widest provision in my old age
and Thy strongest strength when I am exhausted,
try me not with
laziness in worship of Thee,
blindness toward Thy path,
undertaking what opposes love for Thee,
joining with him who has separated himself from Thee,

and separating from him who has joined himself to Thee!

12 O God,
make me
leap to Thee in times of distress,
ask from Thee in needs,
and plead to Thee in misery!
Tempt me not
to seek help from other than Thee
when I am distressed,
to humble myself in asking from someone else
when I am poor,
or to plead with someone less than Thee
when I fear,
for then I would deserve
Thy abandonment,
Thy withholding,
and Thy turning away,
O Most Merciful of the merciful!

13 O God, make
the wishing, the doubt, and the envy
which Satan throws into my heart
a remembrance of Thy mightiness,
a reflection upon Thy power,
and a devising against Thy enemy!
Make everything he causes to pass over my tongue,
- the indecent or ugly words,
the maligning of good repute,
the false witness,
the speaking ill of an absent man of faith
or the reviling of one present,
and all things similar - a speech in praise of Thee,
a pursual of eulogizing Thee,
an excursion in magnifying Thee,
a thanksgiving for Thy favour,
an acknowledgement of Thy beneficence,
and an enumeration of Thy kindnesses!

14 O God,

bless Muḥammad and his Household,
let me not be wronged
while Thou canst repel from me,
let me not do wrong
while Thou art powerful over holding me back,
let me not be misguided
while Thou art able to guide me,
let me not be poor
while with Thee is my plenty,
let me not be insolent
while from Thee comes my wealth!

15 O God,
I come to Thy forgiveness,
I go straight to Thy pardon,
I yearn for Thy forbearance,
and I trust in Thy bounty,
but there is nothing with me
to make me warrant Thy forgiveness,
nothing in my works
to make me merit Thy pardon,
and nothing on my behalf
after I judge my soul
but Thy bounty,
so bless Muḥammad and his Household
and bestow Thy bounty upon me!

16 O God,
make my speech be guidance,
inspire me with reverential fear,
give me success in that which is most pure,
and employ me in what is most pleasing to Thee!

17 O God,
let me tread the most exemplary path
and make me live and die in Thy creed!

18 O God,
bless Muḥammad and his Household,
give me to enjoy moderation,

make me into one of
the people of right behaviour,
the proofs of right conduct,
and the servants of righteousness,
and provide me with
triumph at the place of Return[100]
and safety from the Ambush![101]

19 O God,
take to Thyself from my soul
what will purify it
and leave for my soul that of my soul
that will set it right,
for my soul will perish
unless Thou preservest it!

20 O God,
Thou art my stores when I sorrow,
Thou art my recourse when I am deprived,
from Thee I seek aid when troubled
and with Thee is
a substitute for everything gone by,
a correction for everything corrupted,
and a change from everything Thou disapprovest.
So show kindness to me with
well-being before affliction,
wealth before asking,
right conduct before misguidance;
suffice me against the burden of shame toward the servants,
give me security on the Day of Return,
and grant me excellent right guidance!

21 O God,
bless Muḥammad and his Household,
repel from me through Thy gentleness,
feed me through Thy favour,
set me right through Thy generosity,
heal me through Thy benefaction,
shade me in Thy shelter,
wrap me in Thy good pleasure,

and give me success to reach
the most guided of affairs when affairs confuse me,
the purest of works when works seem similar,
and the most pleasing to Thee of creeds when creeds conflict!

22 O God,
bless Muḥammad and his Household,
crown me with sufficiency,
place in me excellent guardianship,[102]
give me to guide correctly,
tempt me not with plenty,
grant me excellent ease,
make not my life toil and trouble,
and refuse not my supplication in rejection,
for I make none rival to Thee
and I supplicate none with Thee as equal!

23 O God,
bless Muḥammad and his Household,
hold me back from prodigality,
fortify my provision against ruin,
increase my possessions through blessing them,
and set me upon the path of guidance
through piety in what I spend!

24 O God,
bless Muḥammad and his Household,
spare me the burden of earning,
and provide for me without reckoning,
lest I be distracted from Thy worship through seeking
and carry the load of earning's ill results!

25 O God,
bestow upon me what I seek
through Thy power
and grant me sanctuary from what I fear
through Thy might!

26 O God,
bless Muḥammad and his Household,

save my face through ease,
and demean not my dignity through neediness,
lest I seek provision from those whom Thou hast provided
and asks for bestowal from the worst of Thy creatures!
Then I would be tried
by praising him who gave to me
and afflicted
with blaming him who held back from me,
while Thou - not they - art patron of giving and holding back.

27 O God,
bless Muḥammad and his Household
and provide me with
soundness in worship,
detachment in renunciation,
knowledge put into action,
and abstinence in measure!

28 O God,
seal my term with Thy pardon,
verify my expectation in hoping for Thy mercy,
smooth my paths to reach Thy good pleasure,
and make my works good in all my states!

29 O God,
bless Muḥammad and his Household,
incite me to remember Thee
in times of heedlessness,
employ me in Thy obedience
in days of disregard,
open a smooth road for me
to Thy love,
and complete for me thereby the good
of this world and the next!

30 O God,
and bless Muḥammad and his Household

the best Thou hast blessed
any of Thy creatures before him
and wilt bless
any of them after him,
and *give to us in this World good,*
and in the next world good,
and protect me
through Thy mercy
from the chastisement of the Fire![103]

21

His Supplication when Something Made him Sorrow and Offences Made him Worry

1 O God,
O Sufficer of the isolated and weak
and Protector against terrifying affairs!
Offences have isolated me,
so there is none to be my companion.
I am too weak for Thy wrath
and there is none to strengthen me.
I have approached the terror of meeting Thee
and there is none to still my fear.

2 Who can make me secure from Thee
when Thou hast filled me with terror?
Who can come to my aid
when Thou hast isolated me?
Who can strengthen me
when Thou hast weakened me?

3 None can grant sanctuary to a vassal, my God,
but a lord,
none can give security to one dominated
but a dominator,
none can aid him from whom demands are made
but a demander.

4 In Thy hand, my God, is the thread of all that,
in Thee the place of escape and flight,
so bless Muḥammad and his Household,
give sanctuary to me in my flight,
and grant my request!

5 O God,
if Thou shouldst
turn Thy generous face away from me,
withhold from me Thy immense bounty,
forbid me Thy provision,
or cut off from me Thy thread,
I will find no way to anything of my hope

other than Thee
nor be given power over what is with Thee
through another's aid,
for I am Thy servant and in Thy grasp;
my forelock is in Thy hand.[104]

6 I have no command along with Thy command.
'Accomplished is Thy judgement of me,
just Thy decree for me!'[105]
I have not the strength to emerge from Thy authority
nor am I able to step outside Thy power.
I cannot win Thy inclination,
arrive at Thy good pleasure,
or attain what is with Thee
except through obeying Thee
and through the bounty of Thy mercy.

7 O God,
I rise in the morning and enter into evening
as Thy lowly slave.
I own no profit and loss for myself
except through Thee.
I witness to that over myself
and I confess to the frailty of my strength
and the paucity of my stratagems.
So accomplish what Thou hast promised me
and complete for me what Thou hast given me,
for I am Thy slave,
miserable, abased,
frail, distressed, vile,
despised, poor, fearful,
and seeking sanctuary!

8 O God,
bless Muḥammad and his Household
and let me not
forget to remember Thee in what Thou hast done for me,
be heedless of Thy beneficence in Thy trying me,
or despair of Thy response to me,
though it keep me waiting,

whether I be in
prosperity or adversity,
hardship or ease,
well-being or affliction,
misery or comfort,
wealth or distress,
poverty or riches!

9 O God,
bless Muḥammad and his Household,
make me laud Thee, extol Thee, and praise Thee in all my states
so that I rejoice not over what Thou givest me of this world
or sorrow over that of it which Thou withholdest from me!
Impart reverential fear of Thee to my heart,
employ my body in that which Thou acceptest from me,
and divert my soul through obedience to Thee
from all that enters upon me,
so that I love nothing that displeases Thee
and become displeased at nothing that pleases Thee!

10 O God,
bless Muḥammad and his Household,
empty my heart for Thy love,
occupy it with remembering Thee,
animate it with fear of Thee and quaking before Thee,
strengthen it with beseeching Thee,
incline it to Thy obedience,
set it running in the path most beloved to Thee,
and subdue it through desire for what is with Thee
all the days of my life!

11 Let
my provision in this world
be reverential fear of Thee,[106]
my journey
be toward Thy mercy,
and my entrance

be into Thy good pleasure!
Appoint for me a lodging
in Thy Garden,
give me strength to bear
everything that pleases Thee,
make me flee to Thee
and desire what is with Thee,
clothe my heart in estrangement
from the evil among Thy creatures,
and give me intimacy with Thee,
Thy friends,
and those who obey Thee!

12 Assign to no wicked person or unbeliever
a kindness toward me
or a hand that obliges me,
nor to me a need for one of them!
Rather make
the stillness of my heart,
the comfort of my soul,
my independence and my sufficiency
lie in Thee and the best of Thy creatures!

13 O God,
bless Muḥammad and his Household,
make me their comrade,
make me their helper,
and oblige me with yearning for Thee
and doing for Thee what Thou lovest and approvest!
Thou art powerful over everything[107]
and that is easy for Thee.

22

His Supplication in Hardship, Effort, and Difficult Affairs

1 O God,
Thou hast charged me concerning myself
with that which belongs more to Thee than to me.
Thy power over it and over me is greater than my power,
so give me in myself
what will make Thee pleased with me
and take for Thyself
Thy good pleasure in my self's well-being!

2 O God,
I have
no endurance for effort,
no patience in affliction,
no strength to bear poverty.
So forbid me not my provision
and entrust me not to Thy creatures,
but take care of my need alone
and Thyself attend to sufficing me!

3 Look upon me and look after me in all my affairs,
for if Thou entrustest me to myself,
I will be incapable before myself
and fail to undertake that in which my best interest lies.
If Thou entrustest me to Thy creatures,
they will frown upon me,
and if Thou makest me resort to my kinsfolk,
they will refuse to give to me;
if they give,
they will give little and in bad temper,
making me feel long obliged
and blaming me much.

4 So through Thy bounty, O God,
free me from need,
through Thy mightiness,
lift me up,
through Thy boundless plenty,

open my hand,
and with that which is with Thee,
suffice me!

5 O God,
bless Muḥammad and his Household,
rid me of envy,
encircle me against sins,
make me abstain from things unlawful,
give me not the boldness of disobedient acts,
assign me love for that which is with Thee
and satisfaction with that which comes to me from Thee,
bless me in
that which Thou providest me,
that which Thou conferrest upon me,
and that through which Thou favourest me,
and make me in all my states
safeguarded, watched,
covered, defended,
given refuge, and granted sanctuary!

6 O God,
bless Muḥammad and his Household
and let me accomplish everything which
Thou hast enjoined upon me
or made obligatory for me toward Thee,
in one of the ways of Thy obedience,
or toward one of Thy creatures,
though my body be too frail for that,
my strength too feeble,
my power not able to reach it,
and my possessions and what my hand owns
not encompass it,
and whether I have remembered it or forgotten it.

7 It, my Lord, is among that which Thou hast counted
against me
while I have been heedless of it in myself.
Let me perform it
through Thy plentiful giving

and the abundance which is with Thee
- for Thou art Boundless, Generous - so that nothing of it may remain against me,
lest Thou wouldst wish
to settle accounts for it from my good deeds
or to compound my evil deeds
on the day I meet Thee, my Lord!

8 O God,
bless Muḥammad and his Household
and provide me with desire to serve Thee
for the sake of my state in the hereafter,
such that I know the truthfulness of that [desire] in my heart,
be dominated by renunciation while in this world,
do good deeds with yearning,
and remain secure from evil deeds in fright and fear!
And give me *a light whereby I may walk among the people*,[108]
be guided in the shadows,
and seek illumination in doubt and uncertainty!

9 O God,
bless Muḥammad and his Household
and provide me with fear of the threatened gloom
and yearning for the promised reward,
such that I may find
the pleasure of that for which I supplicate Thee
and the sorrow of that from which I seek sanctuary in Thee!

10 O God,
Thou knowest what will set my affairs right
in this world and the next,
so be ever gracious toward my needs!

11 O God,
bless Muḥammad and Muḥammad's Household
and provide me with what is Thy right
when I fall short in thanking Thee
for that through which Thou hast favoured me
in ease and difficulty,
health and sickness,

such that I may come to know in myself
repose in satisfaction
and serenity of soul
in that which Thou hast made incumbent upon me
in whatever states may occur:
fear and security,
satisfaction and displeasure,
loss and gain!

12 O God,
bless Muḥammad and his Household
and provide me with a breast safe from envy,
such that I envy none of Thy creatures
and in anything of Thy bounty
and such that I see none of Thy favours
toward any of Thy creatures
in religion or this world,
well-being or reverential fear,
plenty or ease,
without hoping for myself better than it
through and from Thee alone,
who hast no associate!

13 O God,
bless Muḥammad and his Household
and provide me in this world and the next
with caution against offences
and wariness against slips
in the state of satisfaction and wrath,
such that I may
remain indifferent toward that which enters upon me
from the two states,[109]
work toward Thy obedience,
and prefer it and Thy good pleasure over all else
in both friends and enemies.
Then my enemy may stay secure
from my wrongdoing and injustice
and my friend may despair
of my inclination
and the bent of my affection.

14 Make me one of those who supplicate Thee with sincerity in ease
with the supplication of those
who supplicate Thee with sincerity in distress!
Verily Thou art Praiseworthy, Glorious.

23

His Supplication when he Asked God for Well-Being and Thanked Him for it

1 O God,
bless Muḥammad and his Household,
clothe me in Thy well-being,
wrap me in Thy well-being,
fortify me through Thy well-being,
honour me with Thy well-being,
free me from need through Thy well-being,
donate to me Thy well-being,
bestow upon me Thy well-being,
spread out for me Thy well-being,
set Thy well-being right for me,
and separate me not from Thy well-being
in this world and the next!

2 O God,
bless Muḥammad and his Household
and make me well with
a well-being sufficient, healing, sublime, growing,
a well-being that will give birth to well-being in my body,
a well-being in this world and the next!

3 Oblige me through
health, security, and safety in my religion and body,
insight in my heart,
penetration in my affairs,
dread of Thee,
fear of Thee,
strength for the obedience
which Thou hast commanded for me,
and avoidance of the disobedience
which Thou hast prohibited for me!

4 O God,
oblige me through
the *hajj,*

the *umra,*[110]
and visiting the graves of Thy Messenger
(Thy blessings, mercy, and benedictions
upon him
and upon his Household)
and the Household of Thy Messenger
(upon them be peace)
for as long as Thou cause me to live,
in this year of mine and in every year,
and make that accepted, thanked, and mentioned
before Thee
and stored away with Thee!

5 Make my tongue utter Thy praise, Thy thanksgiving,
Thy remembrance, and Thy excellent laudation,
and expand my heart
toward the right goals of Thy religion!

6 Give me and my progeny refuge from
the accursed Satan,
the evil of venomous vermin, threatening pests,
swarming crowds, and evil eyes,
the evil of *every rebel satan,*[111]
the evil of every refractory sovereign,
the evil of everyone living in ease and served,
the evil of everyone weak or strong,
the evil of everyone born high or low,
the evil of everyone small or great,
the evil of everyone near or far,
the evil of everyone, jinn or man,
who declares war on Thy Messenger and
his Household,
and the evil of every *crawling creature*
that Thou hast *taken by the forelock!*
Surely Thou art *on a straight path.*[112]

7 O God,
bless Muḥammad and his Household
and if someone desires ill for me
turn him away from me,

drive away from me his deception,
avert from me his evil,
send his trickery back to his own throat,

8 and place before him a barricade, so that Thou mayest
blind his eyes toward me,
deafen his ears toward my mention,
lock his heart toward recalling me,
silence his tongue against me,
restrain his head,
abase his exaltation,
break his arrogance,
abase his neck,
disjoint his pride,
and make me secure from all his injury,
his evil, his slander,
his backbiting, his faultfinding,
his envy, his enmity,
his snares, his traps,
his foot soldiers, and his cavalry!
Surely Thou art Mighty, Powerful!

24

His Supplication for his Parents (upon the two of them be peace)

1 O God,
bless Muḥammad Thy slave and Thy messenger,
and his Household, the pure,
and single them out for the best of Thy blessings, Thy mercy,
Thy benedictions, and Thy peace!

2 And single out my parents, O God,
for honour with Thee and blessings from Thee,
O Most Merciful of the merciful!

3 O God,
bless Muḥammad and his Household,
teach me through inspiration
knowledge of everything incumbent upon me toward
them,
and gather within me
knowledge of all that completely!
Then make me act in accordance
with what Thou hast inspired me
and give me the success to put into practice
the knowledge Thou hast shown to me,
lest I fail to act
according to something Thou hast taught me
or my limbs feel too heavy to perform
that with which Thou hast inspired me!

4 O God,
bless Muḥammad and his Household,
as Thou hast ennobled us through him,
and bless Muḥammad and his Household,
as Thou hast made incumbent upon us
rights toward the creatures because of him![113]

5 O God,
fill me with awe of my parents,
the awe one has toward a tyrannical sovereign,
and let me be devoted to them,
with the devotion of a compassionate mother!

Make my obedience and devotion to them
more gladdening to my eyes
than sleep to the drowsy
and more refreshing to my breast
than drink to the thirsty,
so that I may prefer their inclination
to my inclination,
set their satisfaction
before my satisfaction,
make much of their devotion to me
though it be little,
and make little of my devotion to them
though it be great.

6 O God,
lower before them my voice,
make agreeable to them my words,
make mild before them my temper,
make tender toward them my heart,
and turn me into their kind companion,
their loving friend!

7 O God,
thank them for my upbringing,
reward them for honouring me,
and guard them as they guarded me in my infancy!

8 O God,
and whatever harm has touched them from me,
detested thing has reached them from me,
or right of theirs which has been neglected by me,
allow it to alleviate their sins,
raise them in their degrees,
and add to their good deeds!
O He who changes evil deeds into manifold good deeds![114]

9 O God,
whatever word through which they have transgressed
against me,
act through which they have been immoderate with me,
right of mine which they have left neglected,

or obligation toward me in which they have fallen short,
I grant it to them
and bestow it upon them,
and I beseech Thee
to remove from them its ill consequence,
for I do not accuse them concerning myself,
find them slow in their devotion toward me,
or dislike the way they have attended to my affairs,
my Lord!

10 They have rights against me which are more incumbent,
precedence in beneficence toward me that is greater,
and kindness toward me that is mightier
than that I should settle accounts with justice
or repay them with equivalents.
Where then, my God, would be their long occupation
with bringing me up?
Where the hardship of their toil
in taking care of me?
Where the stinting of themselves
to provide me with plenty?

11 What an idea!
I can never discharge their right against me,
fulfil my obligations toward them,
or accomplish the duty of serving them.
So bless Muḥammad and his Household
and help me, O Best of those whose help we seek!
Give me success, O Most Guiding of those whom we beseech!
Place me not among the people of disrespect to fathers and mothers
on the day *when every soul will be repaid*
for what it has earned,
they shall not be wronged.[115]

12 O God,
bless Muḥammad his Household, and his progeny
and single out my parents for the best
which Thou hast singled out

for the fathers and mothers of Thy faithful servants,
O Most Merciful of the merciful!

13 O God,
let me not forget to remember them after my ritual prayers,
at every time throughout my night,
and in each of the hours of my day!

14 O God,
bless Muḥammad and his Household,
forgive me through my supplication for my parents,
forgive them through their devotion toward me
with unfailing forgiveness,
be well pleased with them through my intercession for them
with resolute good pleasure,
and make them reach through Thy generosity
the abodes of safety!

15 O God,
if Thy forgiveness reaches them first,
make them my intercessors,
and if Thy forgiveness reaches me first,
make me their intercessors,
so that we may gather together through Thy gentleness
in the house of Thy generosity
and the place of Thy forgiveness and mercy!
Verily Thou art Possessor of abounding bounty
and ancient kindness,
and *Thou art the Most Merciful of the merciful!*[116]

25

His Supplication for his Children

1 O God,
be kind to me through
the survival of my children,
setting them right for me,
and allowing me to enjoy them!

2 My God,
make long their lives for me,
increase their terms,
bring up the smallest for me,
strengthen the weakest for me,
rectify for me
their bodies,
their religious dedication,
and their moral traits,
make them well in
their souls,
their limbs,
and everything that concerns me of their affair,
and pour out for me and upon my hand
their provisions!

3 Make them
pious, fearing, insightful, hearing, and obedient
toward Thee,
loving and well-disposed
toward Thy friends,
and stubbornly resistant and full of hate
toward all Thy enemies!
Amen!

4 O God,
through them
strengthen my arm,
straighten my burdened back,
multiply my number,
adorn my presence,
keep alive my mention,

suffice me when I am away,
help me in my needs,
and make them
loving toward me,
affectionate, approaching,
upright, obedient,
never disobedient, disrespectful,
opposed, or offenders!

5 Help me in their upbringing,
their education,
and my devotion toward them,
give me among them from Thyself male children,
make that a good for me,
and make them a help for me
in that which I ask from Thee!

6 Give me and my progeny refuge from the accursed Satan,
for Thou hast created us, commanded us,
and prohibited us,
and made us
desire the reward of what Thou hast commanded,
and fear its punishment!
Thou assigned to us an enemy
who schemes against us,
gave him an authority over us
in a way that Thou didst not give us authority over him,
allowed him to dwell in our breasts
and let him run in our blood vessels;
he is not heedless,
though we be heedless,
he does not forget,
though we forget;
he makes us feel secure from Thy punishment
and fills us with fear toward other than Thee.

7 If we are about to commit an indecency,
he gives us courage to do so,

and if we are about to perform a righteous work,
he holds us back from it.
He opposes us through passions,[117]
and sets up for us doubts.
If he promises us, he lies,
and if he raises our hopes, he fails to fulfil them.
If Thou dost not turn his trickery away from us,
he will misguide us,
and if Thou dost not protect us from his corruption,
he will cause us to slip.

8 O God,
so defeat his authority over us through Thy authority,
such that Thou holdest him back from us
through the frequency of our supplication to Thee
and we leave his trickery
and rise up among those preserved by Thee
from sin!

9 O God,
grant me my every request,
accomplish for me my needs,
withhold not from me Thy response
when Thou hast made Thyself accountable for it to me,[118]
veil not my supplication from Thyself,
when Thou hast commanded me to make it,[119]
and be kind to me through everything that will set me right
in this world and the next,
in everything that I remember or forget,
display or conceal,
make public or keep secret!

10 In all of this, place me through my asking Thee among
those who set things right,
those who are answered favourably
when they request from Thee
and from whom is not withheld
when they put their trust in Thee,

11 those accustomed to seek refuge in Thee,
those who profit through commerce with Thee,

those granted sanctuary
through Thy might,
those given lawful provision in plenty from Thy
boundless bounty
through Thy munificence and generosity,
those who reach exaltation after abasement
through Thee,
those granted sanctuary from wrong
through Thy justice,
those released from affliction
through Thy mercy,
those delivered from need after poverty
through Thy riches,
those preserved from sins, slips, and offences
through reverential fear toward Thee,
those successful in goodness, right conduct, and propriety
through obeying Thee,
those walled off from sins
through Thy power,
the refrainers from every act of disobedience toward Thee,
the dwellers in Thy neighbourhood!

12 O God,
give me all of that through Thy bestowal of success and
Thy mercy,
grant us refuge from the chastisement of the burning,
and give to
all the Muslims, male and female,
and all the faithful, male and female,
the like of what I have asked for myself and my children,
in the immediate of this world
and the deferred of the next!
Verily Thou art the Near, the Responder,
the All-hearing, the All-knowing,
the Pardoner, the Forgiving,
the Clement, the Merciful!

13 And *give to us in this world good,*
and in the next world good,
and protect us from the chastisement of the Fire![120]

26

His Supplication for his Neighbours and Friends w hen he Mentioned them.

1 O God,
bless Muḥammad and his Household
and attend to me with Thy best attending
in my neighbours and friends
who recognize our right[121]
and war against our enemies!

2 Give [my neighbours and friends] success in
performing Thy prescriptions
and taking on the beauties of Thy courtesy through
acting gently with their weak,
remedying their lacks,
visiting their sick,
guiding their seeker of right guidance,
giving good counsel to their seeker of advice,
attending to the one among them who returns
from travel,
hiding their secrets,
covering over their shameful things,
helping their wronged,
sharing kindly with them in goods,
turning toward them with wealth and bestowal of
bounty,
and giving what is due to them before they ask!

3 Let me, O God,
repay their evildoer
with good-doing,
turn away from their wrongdoer
with forbearance.
have a good opinion
of every one of them,
attend to all of them
with devotion,
lower my eyes before them
in continence,

make mild my side toward them
    in humility,
be tender toward the afflicted among them
    in mercy,
make them happy in absence
    through affection,
love that they continue to receive favour
    through good will,
grant them
    what I grant my next of kin,
and observe for them
    what I observe for my special friends!

4 O God,
bless Muḥammad and his Household,
provide me the like of that from them,
appoint for me the fullest share of what is with them,
increase them
    in insight toward my right
    and knowledge of my excellence
so that they will be fortunate through me
    and I fortunate through them!
Amen, Lord of the worlds!

27

His Supplication for the People of the Frontiers

1 O God,
bless Muḥammad and his Household,
fortify the frontiers of the Muslims through Thy might,
support their defenders through Thy strength,
and lavish upon them gifts through Thy wealth!

2 O God,
bless Muḥammad and his Household,
increase their number,
hone their weapons,
guard their territory,
defend their midst,
unite their throng,
arrange their affair,
send them supplies in a steady string,
undertake Thyself to suffice them with provisions,
support them with victory,
help them with patience,
and give them subtlety in guile![122]

3 O God,
bless Muḥammad and his Household,
give them the knowledge of that of which they are ignorant,
teach them what they do not know,
and show them what they do not see!

4 O God,
bless Muḥammad and his Household,
make them forget when they meet the enemy
to remember this cheating and delusive world of theirs,
erase from their hearts the thought of enchanting possessions,
place the Garden before their eyes,
and display to their sight that part of it
which Thou hast prepared for them
- the homes of everlastingness and mansions of honour,
the beautiful houris,
the rivers gushing forth with all sorts of drinks,

the trees hanging, low with all kinds of fruits -
lest any of them think of turning his back
or suggest to himself to flee his opponent!

5 O God,
defeat their enemy through that,
trim their nails from them,
separate them from their weapons,
pull out the firm ties from their hearts,
keep them far away from their stores,
bewilder them in their roads,
turn them astray from their direction,
cut off reinforcements from them,
chop them down in numbers,
fill their hearts with terror,
hold back their hands from stretching forth,
tie back their tongues from speaking,
scatter by them the ones behind them[123]
make them a lesson for those beyond them,
and through their degradation
cut off the hopes of those who come after them!

6 O God,
make the wombs of their women barren,
dry up the loins of their men,
cut off the breeding of their mounts and their cattle,
and permit not their sky to rain
or their earth to grow!

7 O God, through that
strengthen the prowess[124] of the People of Islam,
fortify their cities,
increase their properties,
give them ease
from their fighting to worship Thee
and from their warfare to be alone with Thee,
so that none will be worshipped
in the regions of the earth but Thee
and no forehead of theirs may be rubbed in dust
for less than Thee!

8 O God,
send out the Muslims of every region on raids against
the idolaters who face them!
Reinforce them with angels in ranks from Thee,
till the idolaters are routed by them to the end of the land,
slain in Thy earth or taken captive,
or till they admit that Thou art God,
other than whom there is no god,
Thou alone, who hast no associate!

9 O God,
include in this Thy enemies in the regions of the lands,
the Indians, the Byzantines, the Turks,
the Khazars, the Abyssinians, the Nubians,
the Zanjis, the Slavs, the Daylamites,
and the rest of the idol-worshipping nations,
those whose names and attributes are concealed,
but whom Thou countest in Thy cognizance
and overseest through Thy power!

10 O God,
distract the idolaters from reaching for the borders
of the Muslims
through the idolaters,
bar them from cutting them down
through being cut down,
and hold them back from massing together against them
through dissension!

11 O God,
empty their hearts of security
and their bodies of strength,
distract their hearts from thinking of stratagems,
make their limbs too feeble for clashing with men,
make them too cowardly for contending with champions,
send against them a troop of Thy angels
with some of Thy severity
as Thou didst on the Day of Badr,[125]
so that through it Thou mayest
cut off their roots,
harvest their thorns,
and disperse their number!

12 O God,
mix their waters with pestilence
and their foods with maladies,
hurl down their cities,
harass them with peltings,
hinder them through drought,
place their supplies in the most ill-omened part of Thy earth
and the farthest from them,
bar them from its fortresses,
and strike them with constant hunger and painful illness!

13 O God,
if a warrior from the people of Thy creed
wars against them
or a struggler from the followers of Thy prescriptions
struggles against them
so that Thy religion may be the highest,
Thy party the strongest,
and Thy share the fullest,
cast ease to him,
arrange his affair,
attend to him by granting success,
select for him his companions,
strengthen his back,
lavish upon him livelihood,
give him enjoyment of joyous vitality,
cool for him the heat of yearning,
give him sanctuary from the gloom of loneliness,
make him forget the remembrance of wife and child,

14 pass along to him an excellent intention,
attend to him with well-being,
make safety his companion,
release him from cowardice,
inspire him with boldness,
provide him with strength,
support him with help,
teach him right conduct and the norms of the *Sunna*,
point him straight in judgement,
remove from him hypocrisy,
purify him from seeking fame,
and make his thinking and remembrance,

his departing and his staying,
be in Thee and for Thee!

15 When he stands in ranks before Thy enemy and his enemy,
make them few in his eye,
diminish their importance in his heart,
give him a turn to prevail over them,
not them a turn to prevail over him!
But if Thou sealest him with felicity
and decreest for him martyrdom,
then let it be after
he has exterminated Thy enemies by slaying,
captivity has afflicted them,
the borders of the Muslims are secure,
and Thy enemy has turned his back in flight!

16 O God,
and if a Muslim should
take the place of a warrior or a soldier in his home,
attend to those left behind in his absence,
help him with a portion of his property,
assist him with equipment,
hone him for the struggle,
send along with him a supplication for his purpose,
or guard his honour in his absence,
reward him with the like of his reward
measure for measure,
like for like,
and recompense him for his act with an immediate compensation
through which he will hasten to
the profit of what he has sent forth
and the joy of what he has given,
till the present moment takes him to
the bounty Thou hast granted to him
and the generosity Thou hast prepared for him!

17 O God,
and if the affair of Islam
should worry a Muslim
and the alliance of the idolaters' against Islam
should grieve him,

so that he has the intention to go to war
and is about to enter the struggle,
but frailty keeps him seated,
neediness keeps him waiting,
a mishap delays him,
or an obstruction prevents him from his wish,
write his name
among the worshipers,
make incumbent for him
the reward of the strugglers,
and place him among the ranks
of the martyrs and the righteous!

18 O God,
bless Muḥammad , Thy slave and Thy messenger,
and the Household of Muḥammad
with a blessing high above all other blessings,
towering beyond all other salutations,
a blessing whose end is never reached
and whose number is never cut off,
like the most perfect of Thy blessings that has passed
to any one of Thy friends!
Thou art All-kind, Praiseworthy,
the Originator who takes back again,
Accomplisher of what Thou desirest.

28

His Supplication in Fleeing to God

1 O God,
I showed sincerity by cutting myself off from everything but Thee.

2 I approached Thee with my whole self.

3 I averted my face from everyone who needs Thy support.

4 I ceased to ask from any who cannot do without Thy bounty.

5 I saw that the needy who seeks from the needy
is foolish in his opinion,
and misguided in his intellect.

6 How many people have I seen, my God,
who sought exaltation through other than Thee
and were abased,
who wanted wealth from someone else
and became poor,
who tried to rise high
and fell down low!

7 Observing the likes of them
corrects a prudent man;
his taking heed
gives him success;
his choosing the best
guides him to the path of right.

8 So Thou, my Master,
art the object of my asking
to the exclusion of all those who are asked
and the patron of my need
to the exclusion of all those from whom requests are made.

9 Thou art singled out for my call before all who are called;
none is associated with Thee in my hope,

none comes along with Thee in my supplication,
nor does any join with Thee within it,
for to Thee is my appeal.

10 To Thee, my God, belongs
the Unity of number,
the property of eternal power,
the excellence of force and strength,
the degree of sublimity and elevation.

11 Everyone other than Thee is
the object of compassion in his lifetime,
overcome in his affair,
overwhelmed in his situation,
diverse in states,
constantly changing in attributes.

12 So Thou art high exalted
above likenesses and opposites,
proudly magnified
beyond similitudes and rivals!
Glory be to Thee!
There is no God but Thou.

29

His Supplication when his Provision was Stinted

1 O God,
Thou hast tried us with
distrust in our provisions
and the expectation of long lives,
until we begged for provisions
from those who are provided
and craved in our expectations
the life-spans of the long-lived!

2 So bless Muḥammad and his Household,
give us a true certainty
that will suffice us the burden of seeking,
and inspire us with a sincere trust
that will release us from the hardship of exertion!

3 Let Thy clear promise in Thy Revelation
which Thou hast followed in Thy Book with Thy oath
cut off our worry
about the provision for which
Thou hast made Thyself responsible
and sever our occupation
with everything
whose sufficiency Thou hast guaranteed!

4 For Thou hast said
- and Thy word is the most truthful truth -
and Thou hast sworn
- and Thy oath is the most kept and fulfilled -
In the heaven are your provision and everything you are promised!

5 And then Thou hast said,
So by the Lord of heaven and earth,
it is as surely true as that you have speech![126]

30

His Supplication for Help in Repaying Debts

1 O God,
bless Muḥammad and his Household
and release me from a debt
which makes me lose face,
confuses my mind,
disrupts my thinking,
and prolongs my occupation with attending to it!

2 I seek refuge in Thee, my Lord,
from worry and thought about debt,
from the distraction and sleeplessness of debt;
so bless Muḥammad and his Household
and give me refuge from it!
I seek sanctuary in Thee, my Lord, from
debt's abasement in life
and its ill effects after death,
so bless Muḥammad and his Household
and give me sanctuary from it through
a bountiful plenty
or a continually arriving sufficiency!

3 O God,
bless Muḥammad and his Household
prevent me from extravagance and excess,
put me on the course of generous spending and moderation,
teach me excellent distribution,
hold me back through Thy gentleness from squandering,
allow me to attain my provisions through lawful means,
direct my spending toward the gateways of devotion,
and take away from me any possession
which will bring forth pride in me,
lead to insolence,
or drag me in its heels to rebellion!

4 O God,
make me love the companionship of the poor
and help me be their companion with excellent patience!

5 Whenever Thou takest away from me
the goods of this perishing world,
store them for me in Thy abiding treasuries!

6 Make this world's broken pieces
which Thou hast conferred upon me
and its goods
which Thou hast quickly granted to me
a way to reach Thy neighbourhood,
a link to Thy nearness,
and a means to Thy Garden!
Verily Thou art Possessor of bounty abounding,
and Thou art the Munificent, the Generous.

31

His Supplication in Mentioning and Asking for Repentance

1 O God,
O He whom the depiction of the describers
fails to describe!

2 O He beyond whom passes not
the hope of the hopers!

3 O He with whom is not lost
the wage of the good-doers!

4 O He who is the ultimate object
of the fear of the worshipers!

5 O He who is the utmost limit
of the dread of the godfearing!

6 This is the station of him
whom sins have passed from hand to hand.
Offences' reins have led him on,
and Satan has gained mastery over him.
He fell short of what Thou hast commanded
through neglect
and he pursued what Thou hast prohibited
in delusion,

7 like one ignorant of Thy power over him
or one who denies the bounty of Thy beneficence
toward him,
until, when the eye of guidance was opened for him
and the clouds of blindness were dispelled,
he reckoned that through which he had wronged himself
and reflected upon that in which he had opposed
his Lord.
He saw his vast disobedience as vast
and his great opposition as great.

8 So turned to Thee,
hoping in Thee
and ashamed before Thee,

and he directed his beseeching toward Thee,
having trust in Thee.
He repaired to Thee in his longing
with certitude
and he went straight to Thee in fear
with sincerity.
His longing was devoid of every object of longing but Thee,
and his fright departed from every object of fear
but Thee.

9 So he stood before Thee pleading,
his eyes turned toward the ground in humbleness,
his head bowed before Thy might in lowliness;
he revealed to Thee in meekness
those secrets of his which Thou knowest better than he;
he numbered for Thee in humility
those sins of his which Thou countest better than he;
he sought help from Thee
before the dreadful into which he has fallen
in Thy knowledge
and the ugly which has disgraced him
in Thy judgement:
the sins
whose pleasures have turned their backs
and gone
and whose evil consequences have stayed
and stuck fast.

10 He will not deny Thy justice, my God,
if Thou punishest him,
nor will he consider Thy pardon great
if Thou pardonest him and hast mercy upon him,
for Thou art the Generous Lord
for whom the forgiveness of great sins
is nothing great!

11 O God,
so here I am:
I have come to Thee
obeying Thy command

(for Thou hast commanded supplication)
and asking the fulfilment of Thy promise,
(for Thou hast promised to respond)
Thou hast said,
Supplicate Me and I will respond to you.[127]

12 O God,
so bless Muḥammad and his Household,
meet me with Thy forgiveness
just as I have met Thee with my confession,
lift me up from the fatal infirmities of sins
just as I have let myself down before Thee,
and cover me with Thy covering
just as Thou hast shown no haste to take vengeance on me!

13 O God,
make firm my intention to obey Thee,
strengthen my insight in worshipping Thee,
give me the success of works
which will wash away the defilement of offences,
and take me when Thou takest me
in the creed of Thy prophet Muḥammad
(upon him be peace).

14 O God,
I repent to Thee in this my station from
my sins,
great and small,
my evil deeds,
inward and outward,
my lapses,
past and recent,
with the repentance of one who does not
tell himself that he might disobey
or secretly think that he might return to an offence.

15 Thou hast said, my God,
in the firm text of Thy Book,
that Thou acceptest repentance from Thy servants,[128]
pardonest evil deeds,[129]

and lovest the repenters,[130]
so accept my repentance
as Thou hast promised,
pardon my evil deeds as thou hast guaranteed,
and make obligatory toward me
Thy love as Thou hast stipulated!

16 To Thee, my Lord, belongs
my stipulation
that I will not return
to what is disliked by Thee,
my guarantee
that I will not go back
to what Thou blamest,
and my covenant
that I will stay away
from acts of disobedience to Thee.

17 O God,
Thou knowest better what I have done,
so forgive me what Thou knowest
and turn me through Thy power to what Thou lovest!

18 O God,
counted against me are
claims that stay in my memory
and claims that I have forgotten,
while all of them remain in
Thy eye that does not sleep
and Thy knowledge that does not forget!
So compensate their owners,
lighten their load upon me,
lift up their weight from me,
and preserve me from approaching their like!

19 O God,
but I can not be faithful to my repentance
without Thy preservation,
nor can I refrain from offences
without Thy strength.
So strengthen me with a sufficient strength

and attend to me with a defending preservation!

20 O God,
if any servant repents to Thee,
while in Thy knowledge of the Unseen he
will break his repentance
and return to his sin and offence,
I seek refuge in Thee lest I be like that!
So make this my repentance
a repentance
after which I will need no repentance
and a repentance
which will obligate the erasing of what has gone by
and safety in what remains!

21 O God,
I ask pardon from Thee for my ignorance,
and I ask Thee to disregard my evil acts!
So join me to the shelter of Thy mercy
through graciousness
and cover me with the covering of Thy well-being
through bounteousness!

22 O God,
I repent to Thee from everything opposed to Thy will
or far from Thy love
- the thoughts of my heart,
the glances of my eye,
the tales of my tongue -
with a repentance through which each bodily part will by itself
stay safe from ill consequences with Thee
and remain secure from Thy painful penalties
feared by transgressors!

23 O God,
so have mercy on
my being alone before Thee,
the pounding of my heart in dread of Thee,
the trembling of my limbs in awe of Thee!
My sins, my God, have stood me in the station
of degradation in Thy courtyard.

If I remain silent,
none will speak for me;
if I seek an intercessor,
I am not worthy for intercession.

24 O God,
bless Muḥammad and his Household,
make Thy generosity intercede for my offences,
follow up my evil deeds with Thy pardon,
repay me not with the punishment that is my proper repayment,
spread over me Thy graciousness,
wrap me in Thy covering,
and do with me what is done
by a mighty man,
when a lowly slave pleads to him
and he shows him mercy,
or a rich man,
when a poor slave submits himself
and he raises him to wealth!

25 O God,
I have no protector against Thee,
so let Thy might be my protector!
I have no intercessor with Thee,
so let Thy bounty be my intercessor!
My offences have set me quaking,
so let Thy pardon give me security!

26 Not all that I have said rises up from
my ignorance of my evil footsteps
or forgetfulness of my blameworthy acts in the past,
but in order that Thy heaven and those within it
and Thy earth and those upon it
may hear the remorse which I have professed to Thee
and the repentance through which I have sought asylum with Thee.

27 Then perhaps one of them, through Thy mercy,
may show mercy upon my evil situation
or be seized by tenderness for my evil state.

There may come from him for my sake
a supplication to which Thou givest ear
more than to my supplication
or an intercession surer with Thee
than my intercession
through which I may be delivered from Thy wrath
and attain to Thy good pleasure!

28 O God,
if remorse is a repentance toward Thee,[131]
then I am the most remorseful of the remorseful!
If refraining from disobedience is a turning back to Thee,
then I am the first of those who turn back!
If praying for forgiveness alleviates sins,
surely I am one of those who pray for Thy
forgiveness!

29 O God,
as Thou hast commanded repentance
and guaranteed acceptance,
as Thou hast urged supplication,
and promised to respond,
so also bless Muḥammad and his Household,
accept my repentance,
and return me not to the returning place
of disappointment in Thy mercy!
Surely Thou art Ever-turning toward the sinners,
All-compassionate[132] toward the offenders who turn back!

30 O God,
bless Muḥammad and his Household
just as Thou hast guided us by him!
Bless Muḥammad and his Household
just as Thou hast rescued us through him![133]
Bless Muḥammad and his Household,
with a blessing that will intercede for us
on the Day of Resurrection,
the day of neediness toward Thee!
Thou art powerful over everything,[134]
and that is easy for Thee!

32

His Supplication for himself in Confessing Sins after Finishing the Night Prayer

1 O God,
O Possessor of
kingdom perpetual in everlastingness,

2 authority invincible without armies or helpers,

3 might abiding through aeons past,
years gone by,
times and days elapsed!

4 Thy authority is mighty
with a might that knows no bound by being first
nor utmost end by being last!

5 Thy kingdom towers high with a towering
before which all things fall down without reaching
its term;

6 the least of it which Thou hast kept to Thyself is not reached
by the furthest description of the describers!

7 Attributes go astray in Thee,
descriptions fall apart below Thee,
the subtlest of imaginations are bewildered
by Thy magnificence!

8 So art Thou:
God, the First in Thy firstness,
and so art Thou everlastingly.
Thou dost not pass away.

9 But I am the slave,
feeble in works,
immense in hopes.
The tying links are outside my hand,
except what is tied by Thy mercy;
the bonds of hopes have been cut away from me,
except the pardon to which I hold fast.

10 Little on my part is
the obedience toward Thee upon which I count,
and great against me
the disobedience toward Thee to which I have reverted.
But pardoning Thy slave will not constrain Thee,
even if he be bad,
so pardon me!

11 O God,
Thy knowledge watches over hidden works,
every covered thing is exposed before Thy awareness,
the intricacies of things are not concealed from Thee,
and unseen mysteries slip not away from Thee.

12 But over me Thy enemy has gained mastery:
He asked a delay from Thee to lead me astray,
and Thou gavest him the delay!
He asked a respite from Thee until the Day of Doom to misguide me,
and Thou gavest him the respite![135]

13 So he threw me down,
though I had fled to Thee from
small, ruinous sins
and great, deadly works,
until, when I had yielded to disobeying Thee
and merited Thy anger through my bad efforts,
he turned the bridle of his treachery away from me,
met me with the word of his ingratitude,
undertook to be quit of me,[136]
turned his back to flee from me,
threw me to the desert of Thy wrath alone,
and sent me as an outcast
into the courtyard of Thy vengeance.

14 There is no intercessor to intercede for me with Thee,
no protector to make me feel secure against Thee,
no fortress to veil me from Thee,
no shelter in which to seek asylum apart from Thee!

15 This is the station of him who takes refuge with Thee,
the place of the confessor to Thee:

Let not Thy bounty be too narrow for me,
let not Thy pardon fall short of me!
Let me not be the most disappointed
of Thy repentant servants,
nor the most despairing
of those who come to Thee with expectations!
Forgive me,
surely Thou art the best of the forgivers!

16 O God,
Thou commanded me,
and I refrained,
Thou prohibited me,
and I committed.
evil thoughts tempted me to offend,
and I was negligent.

17 I cannot call upon daytime to witness my fasting,
nor can I seek sanctuary in night because of my vigil;
no *Sunna* praises me for keeping it alive,
only Thy obligations,
he who neglects which has perished.

18 I cannot seek access to Thee
through the excellence of a supererogatory work,
given the many duties of Thy obligations
of which I have been heedless
and the stations of Thy bounds which I have transgressed,
thereby violating sacred things and committing great sins,
though Thou hast given me safety from their disgraces as a covering.

19 This is the station of him who is
ashamed of himself before Thee,
angry with himself,
and satisfied with Thee.
He meets Thee
with a humble soul,
a neck bent down,
a back heavy with offences,
hesitating between longing for Thee and fear of Thee.

20 Thou art the most worthy of those in whom he might hope,
the most deserving for him to dread and fear.
So give me, my Lord, what I hope for,
make me secure against what frightens me,
and act kindly toward me with the kindly act of mercy!
Surely Thou art the most generous
of those from whom are asked!

21 O God,
since Thou hast covered me with Thy pardon
and shielded me with Thy bounty
in the abode of annihilation and the presence of equals,
grant me sanctuary from the disgraces of the Abode of
Subsistence
at the standing places of the Witnesses
(the angels brought nigh,
the messengers honoured,
the martyrs, the righteous)
before the neighbour
from whom I have hidden my evil deeds
and the womb relative
before whom I feel ashamed in my secret thoughts!

22 I trust them not, my Lord,
to cover me over,
but I trust Thee, my Lord,
to forgive me!
Thou art the most worthy of those in whom confidence is had,
the most giving of those who are besought,
and the most clement of those from whom mercy
is asked.
So have mercy upon me!

23 O God,
Thou caused me to descend as mean water
from loins of narrow bones and tight passages
into a constricted womb
which Thou hadst covered with veils;[137]
Thou turned me about from state to state
until Thou tookest me to the completion of the form
and fixed within me the bodily parts,
as Thou hast described in Thy Book:

a drop,
then a clot,
then a tissue,
then bones,
then Thou garmented the bones with flesh,
then Thou produced me as another creature
as Thou willed.[138]

24 Then, when I needed Thy provision,
and could not do without the aid of Thy bounty,
Thou appointed for me a nourishment
from the bounty of the food and drink
which Thou bestowed upon Thy handmaid
in whose belly Thou gavest me to rest
and in the lodging of whose womb
Thou deposited me.

25 Hadst Thou entrusted me in those states, my Lord,
to my own force
or driven me to have recourse to
my own strength,
force would have been removed from me
and strength taken far away.

26 So Thou hast fed me through Thy bounty
with the food of the Good, the Gentle;
Thou hast done that for me in graciousness toward me
up to this my present point.
I do not lack Thy goodness,
nor does Thy benefaction keep me waiting.
Yet with all that,
my trust has not become firm enough
that I might free myself
for that which is more favoured by Thee.

27 Satan has taken possession of my reins
through my distrust and frail certainty.
I complain of his evil neighbourhood with me
and my soul's obedience toward him!
I ask Thee to preserve me against his domination,
and I plead with Thee to turn his trickery away from me!

28 I ask Thee
to make the path to my provision easy,
since to Thee belongs praise for
Thy beginning with immense favours
and Thy inspiring gratitude
for beneficence and bestowing favour!
Bless Muḥammad and his Household,
and make the way to my provision easy for me!
[I ask Thee] to make me content
with Thy ordainment for me,
to make me satisfied with my lot
in that which Thou hast apportioned for me
and to place what has gone of my body and my life-span
into the path of Thy obedience![139]
Surely Thou art the Best of providers!

29 O God, I seek refuge in Thee
from the Fire
through which Thou art harsh
toward him who disobeys Thee
and by which Thou hast threatened
him who turns away from Thy good pleasure;
from the Fire
whose light is darkness,
whose ease is pain,
and whose far is near;
from the Fire
parts of which devour parts
and parts of which leap upon parts;

30 from the Fire which
leaves bones decayed
and lets its people drink boiling water;
from the Fire which
'does not spare him who pleads to it,'[140]
has no mercy on him who seeks sympathy from it,
and has no power to relieve him
who humbles himself before it
and yields himself to it;
it meets its inhabitants with the hottest that it possesses:
painful punishment and intense noxiousness.

31 I seek refuge in Thee from
its gaping-jawed scorpions,
its scraping-toothed serpents,
and its drinks, which
tear apart the intestines and hearts of its inhabitants
and root out their marrows.
I ask guidance from Thee
to that which will keep far from it
and make it retreat!

32 O God,
bless Muḥammad and his Household,
grant me sanctuary from it through the bounty of Thy mercy,
release me from my stumbles through Thy good releasing,
and abandon me not,
O Best of the sanctuary-granters!

33 O God,
Thou protectest from the disliked,
givest the good,
dost what Thou wilt,
and *Thou art powerful over everything.*[141]

34 O God,
bless Muḥammad and his Household
when the pious are mentioned
and bless Muḥammad and his Household
as long as night and day come and go
with a blessing
whose replenishment is never cut off
and whose number cannot be counted,
a blessing
that will fill up the air
and crowd the earth and the heaven!

35 God bless him
until he is well pleased
and God bless him and his Household
after good pleasure
with a blessing that has neither bound
nor utmost limit!
O Most Merciful of the merciful!

33

His Supplication in Asking for the Best

1 O God,
I ask from Thee the best in Thy knowledge,
so bless Muḥammad and his Household
and decree for me the best!

2 Inspire us with knowledge to chose the best
and make that a means to
being pleased with what Thou hast decreed for us
and submitting to what Thou hast decided!
Banish from us the doubt of misgiving
and confirm us with the certainty of the sincere!

3 Visit us not with incapacity
to know what Thou hast chosen, lest we
despise Thy measuring out,
dislike the place of Thy good pleasure,
and incline toward that which is
further from good outcome
and nearer to the opposite of well-being!

4 Make us love what we dislike in Thy decree
and make easy for us what we find difficult in Thy decision!

5 Inspire us to yield
to that which Thou bringest upon us by Thy will,
lest we
love the delay of what Thou hast hastened
and the hastening of what Thou hast delayed,
dislike what Thou lovest,
and choose what Thou dislikest!

6 Seal us with that which is most praised in outcome
and most generous in issue!
Surely Thou givest generous gain,
bestowest the immense,
dost what Thou wilt, *and Thou art powerful over everything.*[142]

34

His Supplication when he was Afflicted or saw Someone Afflicted with the Disgrace of Sin

1 O God,
to Thee belongs praise for
Thy covering over after Thy knowledge
and Thy pardon after Thy awareness!
Each of us has committed faults,
but Thou hast not made him notorious,
done indecencies,
but Thou hast not disgraced him,
and covered over evil deeds,
but Thou hast not pointed to him.

2 How many are Thy prohibited acts
which we have performed,
Thy commandments of which Thou hast told us
which we have transgressed,
the evil deeds
which we have earned,
the offences
which we have committed!
Thou seest them
to the exclusion of all observers;
Thou hast the power to make them public
above all the powerful!
By giving us safety
Thou hast veiled their eyes
and stoppled their ears.

3 So make
the shameful things Thou hast covered over
and the inward reality Thou hast concealed
our admonisher,
a restrainer upon bad character traits and committing offences,
and a striving toward the repentance that erases [sins]
and the praiseworthy path!

4 Bring the time of striving near
and visit us not with heedlessness of Thee!

Surely we are Thy beseechers,
the repenters of sins.

5 And bless Thy chosen, O God, from Thy creation,
Muḥammad and his descendants,
the friends selected from among Thy creatures, the pure,
and make us listeners to them and obeyers,
as Thou hast commanded![143]

35

His Supplication in Satisfaction when he Looked upon the Companions of this World

1 Praise belongs to God
in satisfaction with God's decision!
I bear witness that
God has apportioned the livelihoods of His servants
with justice
and undertaken bounty for all His creatures.

2 O God,
bless Muḥammad and his Household,
tempt me not with what Thou hast given to Thy creatures
and tempt them not with what Thou hast withheld from me.
Lest I envy Thy creatures
and despise Thy decision!

3 O God,
bless Muḥammad and his Household,
delight my soul through Thy decree,
expand my breast through the instances of Thy decision,
give to me a trust through which I may admit
that Thy decree runs only to the best,
and let my gratitude to Thee
for what Thou hast taken away from me
be more abundant than my gratitude to Thee
for what Thou hast conferred upon me!

4 Preserve me from imagining any meanness
in someone who is destitute
or imagining any superiority
in someone who possesses wealth,
for the noble is he
whom obedience to Thee has ennobled
and the exalted is he
whom worship of Thee has exalted!

5 So bless Muḥammad and his Household,
give us to enjoy a wealth
which does not run out,

confirm us with an exaltation
which will never be lost,
and let us roam freely
in the kingdom of everlastingness!
Surely Thou art the One, *the Unique, the Eternal Refuge;*
Thou hast not begotten,
nor hast Thou been begotten,
and equal to Thee is not any one![144]

36

His Supplication when he Looked upon Clouds and Lightening and Heard the Sound of Thunder

1 O God,
these are two of Thy signs
and these are two of Thy helpers.
They rush to obey Thee
with beneficial mercy
or injurious vengeance,
so rain not down upon us from them
the evil rain[145]
and clothe us not through them
in the garment of affliction!

2 O God,
bless Muḥammad and his Household,
send down upon us the benefit of these clouds
and their blessing,
turn away from us their harm and their injury,
strike us not through them with blight,
and loose not upon our livelihoods any bane!

3 O God,
if Thou hast incited them as vengeance
and loosed them in anger,
we seek sanctuary with Thee from Thy wrath
and implore Thee in asking Thy pardon!
So incline with wrath
toward the idolaters
and set the millstone of Thy vengeance
turning upon the heretics![146]

4 O God,
take away the barrenness of our lands
with Thy watering,
dislodge the malice from our breasts
with Thy providing,
distract us not from Thee

through other than Thee,
and cut none of us off
from the stuff of Thy goodness,
for the rich is he to whom Thou hast given riches,
and the safe he whom Thou hast protected!

5 No one has any defence against Thee,
nor any means to bar Thy penalty.
Thou decidest what Thou wilt
for whom Thou wilt
and Thou decreest what Thou desirest
for any whom Thou desirest!

6 So to Thee belongs praise
for protecting us from affliction
and to Thee belongs thanks
for conferring upon us blessings,
a praise which will leave behind the praise of the praisers,
a praise which will fill the earth and the heaven!

7 Surely Thou art the All-kind through immense kindnesses,
the Giver of abounding favours,
the Accepter of small praise,
the Grateful for little gratitude,
the Beneficent, the Benevolent,
Possessor of graciousness!
There is no god but Thou;
unto Thee is the homecoming.[147]

37

His Supplication when Confessing his Shortcomings in Giving Thanks

1 O God,
no one reaches a limit in thanking Thee
without acquiring that of Thy beneficence
which enjoins upon him thanksgiving,

2 nor does anyone reach a degree in obeying Thee,
even if he strives,
without falling short of what Thou deservest
because of Thy bounty.

3 The most thankful of Thy servants
has not the capacity to thank Thee,
and the most worshipful of them
falls short of obeying Thee.

4 To none of them is due
Thy forgiveness through what he himself deserves
or Thy good pleasure for his own merit.

5 When Thou forgivest someone,
it is through Thy graciousness,
and when Thou art pleased with someone,
it is through Thy bounty.

6 Thou showest gratitude
for the paltry for which Thou showest gratitude[148]
and Thou rewardest
the small act in which Thou art obeyed,
so that it seems as if Thy servants' thanksgiving
for which Thou hast made incumbent their reward
and made great their repayment
is an affair
from which they could have held back
without Thee,
and hence Thou wilt recompense them,
and whose cause is not in Thy hand,
and hence Thou wilt repay them.

7 Nay, my God, Thou hadst power over their affair
before they had power to worship Thee,
and Thou hadst prepared their reward
before they began to obey Thee;
and that because Thy wont is bestowal of bounty,
Thy custom beneficence,
Thy way pardon.

8 So all creatures confess
that Thou wrongest not him whom Thou punishest
and bear witness
that Thou bestowest bounty upon him whom
Thou pardonest.
Each admits
that he has fallen short of what Thou meritest.

9 Had Satan not misled them from Thy obedience,
no disobeyer would have disobeyed Thee,
and had he not shown falsehood to them in the likeness
of truth
no strayer would have gone astray from Thy path.

10 So glory be to Thee!
How manifest is Thy generosity
in dealing with him who obeys or disobeys Thee!
Thou showest gratitude to the obedient
for that which Thou undertakest for him,
and Thou grantest a respite to the disobedient
in that within which Thou art able to hurry him.

11 Thou givest to each of them
that which is not his due,
and Thou bestowest bounty upon each
in that wherein his works fall short.

12 Wert Thou to counterbalance for the obedient servant
that which Thou Thyself hadst undertaken,
he would be on the point of losing Thy reward
and seeing the end of Thy favour,
but through Thy generosity Thou hast repaid him
for a short, perishing term
with a long, everlasting term,
and for a near, vanishing limit

with an extended, abiding limit.

13 Then Thou dost not visit him with a settling of accounts
for Thy provision
through which he gained strength to obey Thee,
nor dost Thou force him to make reckonings
for the organs he employed
to find the means to Thy forgiveness.
Wert Thou to do that to him,
it would take away
everything for which he had laboured
and all wherein he had exerted himself
as repayment for the smallest of Thy benefits
and kindnesses,
and he would remain hostage before Thee
for Thy other favours.
So how can he deserve something of Thy reward?
Indeed, how?

14 This, my God, is the state of him who obeys Thee
and the path of him who worships Thee.
But as for him who disobeys Thy command
and goes against Thy prohibition,
Thou dost not hurry him to Thy vengeance,
so that he may seek to replace
his state in disobeying Thee
with the state of turning back to obey Thee,
though he deserved from the time he set out to disobey Thee
every punishment which Thou hast prepared
for all Thy creatures.

15 Through each chastisement
which Thou hast kept back from him
and each penalty of Thy vengeance and Thy punishment
which Thou hast delayed from him,
Thou hast refrained from Thy right
and shown good pleasure
in place of what Thou hast made obligatory.

16 So who is more generous, my God, than Thou?
And who is more wretched than he who perishes
in spite of Thee?
Indeed, who?

Thou art too blessed to be described
by any but beneficence
and too generous for any but justice
to be feared from Thee!
There is no dread that Thou wilt be unjust
toward him who disobeys Thee,
nor any fear of Thy neglecting to reward
him who satisfies Thee.[149]
So bless Muhammad and his Household,
give me my hope,
and increase me in that of Thy guidance
through which I may be successful in my works!
Surely Thou art All-kind, Generous.

38

His Supplication in Asking Pardon for Misdeeds to God's Servants and for Falling Short in their Rights and that his Neck be Set Free from the Fire

1 O God,
I ask pardon from Thee for
the person wronged in my presence
whom I did not help,
the favour conferred upon me
for which I returned no thanks,
the evildoer who asked pardon from me
and whom I did not pardon,
the needy person who asked from me
and whom I preferred not over myself,
the right of a believer who possesses a right incumbent upon me
which I did not fulfil,
the fault of a believer which became evident to me
and which I did not conceal,
and every sin which presented itself to me
and which I failed to avoid.

2 I ask pardon, my God,
for all of these and their likes,
with an asking of pardon in remorse
which may act as an admonisher
against similar things ahead of me.

3 So bless Muḥammad and his Household
and make
my remorse for the slips
into which I have fallen
and my determination to refrain from the evil deeds
which present themselves to me
a repentance which will make Thy love for me obligatory,
O lover of those who repent![150]

39

His Supplication in Seeking Pardon and Mercy

1 O God,
bless Muḥammad and his Household,
break my passion for every unlawful thing,
take away my craving for any sin,
and bar me from harming any believer, male or female,
and any Muslim, male or female!

2 O God,
if any of Thy servants should harm me in what Thou hast forbidden
or violate me in what Thou hast interdicted,
and if he should pass into death with my complaint
or I come to have a complaint against him while he is alive,
forgive him what he did to me
and pardon him that through which he turned his back on me!
Inquire not from him about what he committed toward me
and expose him not through what he earned by me!
Make my open-handedness in pardoning such servants
and my contribution in charity toward them
the purest charity of the charitable
and the highest gift of those seeking nearness to Thee!

3 Recompense me for my pardoning them with Thy pardon
and for my supplicating for them with Thy mercy
so that each one of us may gain felicity through Thy bounty
and each may attain deliverance through Thy kindness!

4 O God,
if there is a servant from among Thy servants whom
an ill visits on my account,
a harm touches from my direction,
or a wrong overtakes through me or because of me,
and should I fail to take care of his right
or go before him [in death] with his complaint,
bless Muḥammad and his Household,
satisfy him toward me through Thy wealth,

and give him his full right from Thyself!

5 Then protect me from what Thy decision mandates
and save me from what Thy justice decides,
for my strength cannot bear Thy vengeance
and my obedience cannot stand up to Thy displeasure!
If Thou recompensest me with the right,
Thou wilt destroy me,
and if Thou dost not shield me in Thy mercy,
Thou wilt lay me waste.

6 O God,
I ask Thee to grant, my God,
that whose giving will not decrease Thee,
and I ask Thee to carry
that whose carrying will not weigh Thee down:

7 My God, I ask Thee to give my soul,
which Thou didst not create
to keep Thyself from evil
nor to find the way to profit.
No, Thou brought it forth
to demonstrate Thy power over its like
and to provide an argument against its similar.

8 I ask Thee to carry those of my sins
whose carrying weighs me down
and I seek help from Thee in
that whose heaviness oppresses me.

9 So bless Muḥammad and his Household,
give to me my soul in spite of its wrongdoing,[151]
and appoint Thy mercy to carry my burden!
How many evildoers Thy mercy has overtaken!
How many wrongdoers Thy pardon has embraced!

10 So bless Muḥammad and his Household
and make me the model of him whom Thou hast
aroused through Thy forbearance
from the deadly infirmities of the Senders
and saved through Thy giving success
from the tangled plights of the sinners,

so that I may rise up
freed by Thy pardon from the bonds of Thy displeasure
and released by Thy benefaction from the ties of
Thy justice!

11 Surely if Thou dost that, my God,
Thou wilt do it to one who does not
deny deserving Thy punishment
or acquit himself from merit for Thy vengeance.

12 Do that, my God, for one
whose fear of Thee is greater
than his craving from Thee,
whose hopelessness of deliverance
is firmer than his hope for salvation!
Not that his hopelessness is despair,
nor that his expectation is deluded.
No, rather his good deeds are few
among his evil deeds
and his arguments are frail
in face of everything due from his acts.

13 But Thou, my God, art worthy that
the righteous not be deluded concerning Thee
and the sinners not lose hope in Thee,
for Thou art the All-mighty Lord who
holds back His bounty from none
and takes His full right from no one.

14 High exalted is Thy mention
above those mentioned!
Holy are Thy names
beyond those described!
Spread is Thy favour
among all creatures!
Thine is the praise for that,
O Lord of the worlds!

40

His Supplication when Someone's Death was Announced to him or when he Remembered Death

1 O God,
Bless Muḥammad and his Household,
spare us drawn out expectations
and cut them short in us through sincerity of works,
that we may not hope expectantly for
completing an hour after an hour,
closing a day after a day,
joining a breath to a breath,
or overtaking a step with a step!

2 Keep us safe from the delusions of expectations,
make us secure from their evils,
set up death before us in display.
and let not our remembering of it come and go!

3 Appoint for us from among the righteous works a work
through which we will feel the homecoming to Thee as slow
and crave a quick joining with Thee,
so that death may be
our intimate abode with which we are intimate,
our familiar place toward which we yearn,
and our next of kin whose coming we love!

4 When Thou bringest it to us
and send it down upon us,
make us happy with it as a visitor,
comfort us with its arrival,
make us not wretched through entertaining it,
degrade us not through its visit,
and appoint it one of the gates to Thy forgiveness
and the keys to Thy mercy!

5 Make us die
guided, not astray,
obedient, not averse,
repentant, not disobedient or persisting,
O He who guarantees the repayment of the good-doers
and seeks to set right the work of the corrupt!

41

His Supplication in Asking for Covering and Protection

1 O God,
bless Muḥammad and his Household,
spread for me the bed of Thy honour,
bring me to the wateringholes of Thy mercy,
set me down in the midst of Thy Garden,
stamp me not with rejection by Thee,
deprive me not through disappointment by Thee,

2 settle not accounts with me for what I have committed,
make no reckoning with me for what I have earned,
display not what I have hidden,
expose not what I have covered over,
weigh not my works on the scales of fairness,
and make not my tidings known to the eyes of the crowd!

3 Conceal from them
everything whose unfolding would shame me
and roll up before them
all which would join me to disgrace with Thee!

4 Ennoble my degree through Thy good pleasure,
perfect my honour through Thy forgiveness,
rank me among the companions of the right hand,
direct me to the roads of the secure,
place me in the throng of the triumphant,
and through me let the sessions of the righteous thrive![152]
Amen, Lord of the worlds!

42

His Supplication upon Completing a Reading of the Qur'ān

1 O God,
Thou hast helped me complete Thy Book,
which Thou sent down as a light[153] and appointed as
a guardian over every book Thou hast sent down,[154]
preferring it over every narrative
which Thou hast recounted,[155]

2 a separator, through which Thou hast separated
Thy lawful from Thy unlawful,[156]
a Qur'an, through which Thou hast made plain
the approaches to Thy ordinances,[157]
a book, which Thou hast distinguished very distinctly
for Thy servants,[158]
a revelation, which Thou hast sent down,
a sending down,
upon Thy prophet Muḥammad[159]
(Thy blessings be upon him and his Household).

3 Thou appointed it
a light through following which
we may be guided from the shadows
of error and ignorance,[160]
a healing for him
who turns ear toward hearing it
with the understanding of attestation,[161]
a just balance
whose tongue does not incline away from truth,[162]
a light of guidance
whose proof is not extinguished before
the witnesses,[163]
and a guidepost of deliverance, so that
he who repairs straightway to its prescription
will not go astray
and he who clings to its preservation's handhold
will not be touched by the hands of disasters.

4 O God,
since Thou hast given us help to recite it

and made smooth the roughness of our tongues
through the beauty of its expression,
place us among those who
observe it as it should be observed,
serve Thee by adhering in submission
to the firm text of its verses,
and seek refuge in admitting both its ambiguous parts
and the elucidations of its clear signs!

5 O God,
Thou sent it down upon Thy prophet Muḥammad
(God bless him and his household) in summary form,
Thou inspired him with the science of its wonders
to complement it,
Thou made us the heirs of its knowledge
as interpreters,[164]
Thou made us to surpass
him who is ignorant of its knowledge,
and Thou gave us strength over it
to raise us above those not able to carry it.

6 O God,
just as Thou hast appointed our hearts
as its carriers
and made known to us through Thy mercy
its nobility and excellence,
so also bless Muḥammad its preacher,
and his Household, its guardians,
and place us among those who confess that it has come
from Thee,
lest doubt about attesting to it assail us,
or deviation from its straightforward path shake us!

7 O God,
bless Muḥammad and his Household
and make us one of those who
hold fast to its cord,
seek haven from its ambiguities in its
fortified stronghold,
rest in the shadow of its wing,
find guidance in the brightness of its morning,
follow the shining of its disclosure,

acquire light from its lamp,
and beg not guidance from any other!

8 O God,
just as through it
Thou hast set up Muḥammad as a guidepost to point to Thee
and through his Household
Thou hast made clear Thy good pleasure's roads to Thee,
so also bless Muḥammad and his Household
and make the Qur'an
our mediation to the noblest stations
of Thy honour,
a ladder by which we may climb
to the place of safety,
a cause for our being repaid
with deliverance at the Plain of Resurrection,
and a means whereby we may reach
the bliss of the House of Permanence!

9 O God,
bless Muḥammad and his Household,
lessen for us through the Qur'an the weight of heavy sins,
give to us the excellent qualities of the pious,
and make us follow the tracks of those who stood before Thee
in the watches of the night and the ends of the day,[165]
such that Thou purifiest us from every defilẹment
through its purification
and makest us to follow the tracks of those
who have taken illumination from its light
and whom expectation has not distracted from works,
cutting them off through its delusions' deceptions!

10 O God,
bless Muḥammad and his Household
and appoint the Qur'an
for us an intimate
in the shadows of nights
and a guardian
against the instigations of Satan
and confusing thoughts,
for our feet an obstruction

from passing to acts of disobedience,
for our tongues a silencer without blight
preventing a plunge into falsehood,
for our limbs a restrainer
from committing sins,
and for the scrutiny of heedfulness
rolled up in heedlessness
an unroller,
such that Thou attachest to our hearts
the understanding of the Qur'ān's wonders
and its restraining similitudes
which immovable mountains in all their solidity
were too weak to carry![166]

11 O God,
bless Muḥammad and his Household
and through the Qur'an
make permanent the rightness
of our outward selves,
veil the ideas of confusing thoughts
from the soundness of our innermost minds,
wash away the dirt of our hearts
and the ties of our heavy sins,
gather our scattered affairs,
quench the thirst of our burning heat
in the standing place of the presentation to Thee,
and clothe us in the robes of security
on the Day of the Greatest Terror at our uprising![167]

12 O God,
bless Muḥammad and his Household
and through the Qur'ān
redress our lack - our destitution in poverty -
drive toward us the comforts of life
and an abundance of plentiful provisions,
turn aside blameworthy character traits
and base moral qualities,
and preserve us from the pit of unbelief
and the motives for hypocrisy,
such that the Qur'an may be
for us at the resurrection a leader

to Thy good pleasure and Thy gardens,
for us in this world a protector
against Thy displeasure and transgressing Thy bounds,
and for what is with Thee a witness
by its declaring lawful the lawful
and its declaring unlawful the unlawful!

13 O God,
bless Muḥammad and his Household
and through the Qur'an make easy for our souls at death
the distress of the driving,[168]
the effort of the moaning,
and the succession of the rattling,
when souls *reach the throats*
and it is said, 'Where is the enchanter?';[169]
when the angel of death discloses himself
to seize them from behind the veils of unseen things,
letting loose at them from the bow of destinies
the arrows of the terror of lonesome separation,
and mixing for them from sudden death
a cup poisoned to the taste;
and when departure and release for the hereafter come close to us,
works become collars around the necks,[170]
and the graves become the haven
until the appointed time of the Day of Encounter!

14 O God,
bless Muḥammad and his Household,
make blessed for us the arrival at the house of decay
and the drawn out residence between the layers of the earth,
appoint the graves, after separation from this world,
the best of our waystations,
make roomy for us through Thy mercy the narrowness of our tombs,
and disgrace us not among those present at the Resurrection
through our ruinous sins!

15 Through the Qur'an
have mercy upon the lowliness of our station
at the standing place of presentation to Thee,

make firm the slips of our feet
during the shaking of the bridge across hell
on the day of passage over it,
illuminate the darkness of our graves
before the Uprising,
and deliver us from every distress on the Day of Resurrection
and from the hardships of terrors on the Day of Disaster!

16 Whiten our faces
on the day when the faces of wrongdoers are blackened[171]
during the Day of Regret and Remorse,
appoint love for us in the breasts of the faithful,
and make not life for us troublesome!

17 O God,
bless Muḥammad ,Thy servant and Thy messenger,
just as He delivered Thy message,
executed Thy command,
and counselled Thy servants!

18 O God,
on the Day of Resurrection make our Prophet
(Thy blessings be upon him and his Household)
the nearest of the prophets to Thee in seat,
the ablest of them before Thee with intercession,
the greatest of them with Thee in measure,
and the most eminent of them with Thee in rank!

19 O God,
bless Muḥammad and the Household of Muḥammad ,
ennoble his edifice,
magnify his proof,
make weighty his balance,
accept his intercession,
bring near his mediation,[172]
whiten his face,
complete his light,
and raise his degree!

20 Make us live according to his *Sunna,*
make us die in his creed,
take us on his road,

make us travel his path,
place us among the people who obey him,
muster us in his band,
lead us to up his pool,[173]
and give us to drink of his cup!

21 And bless Muḥammad and his Household,
with a blessing
through which Thou wilt take him to the most excellent
of Thy good, Thy bounty, and Thy generosity
for which he hopes!
Thou art Possessor of boundless mercy
and generous bounty.

22 O God,
repay him for
Thy messages which he delivered,
Thy signs which he passed on,
the good counsel he gave to Thy servants,
and the struggle he undertook in Thy way,
with the best Thou hast repaid any of Thy angels brought nigh
and Thy prophets sent out and chosen!
And upon him and his Household,
the good, the pure,
be peace, God's mercy, and His blessings!

43

His Supplication when he Looked at the New Crescent Moon

1 O obedient creature,
speedy and untiring,
frequenter of the mansions of determination,[174]
moving about in the sphere of governance!

2 I have faith in Him who
lights up darknesses through thee,
illuminates jet-black shadows by thee,
appointed thee one of the signs of His kingdom
and one of the marks of His authority,
and humbled thee through increase and decrease,
rising and setting,
illumination and eclipse.
In all of this thou art obedient to Him,
prompt toward His will.

3 Glory be to Him!
How wonderful is what He has arranged in thy situation!
How subtle what He has made for thy task!
He has made thee the key
to a new month
for a new situation.

4 So I ask God, my Lord and thy Lord,
my Creator and thy Creator,
my Determiner and thy Determiner,
my Form-giver and thy Form-giver,
that He bless Muḥammad and his Household
and appoint thee
a crescent of blessings not effaced by days
and of purity not defiled by sins;

5 a crescent of security from blights
and of safety from evil deeds;
a crescent of auspiciousness containing no misfortune,
of prosperity accompanied by no adversity,
of ease not mixed with difficulty,
of good unstained by evil;

a crescent of security and faith,
favour and good-doing,
safety and submission!

6 O God,
bless Muḥammad and his Household,
place us among
the most satisfied of those
over whom the crescent has risen,
the purest of those
who have looked upon it,
the most fortunate of those
who have worshipped Thee under it;
give us the success during [the new month] to repent,
preserve us within it from misdeeds,
guard us therein from pursuing disobedience to Thee,

7 allot to us within it thanksgiving for Thy favour,
clothe us during it in the shields of well-being,
and complete for us Thy kindness
by perfecting therein obedience to Thee!
Surely Thou art All-kind, Praiseworthy.
And bless Muḥammad and his Household, the good, the pure.

44

His Supplication for the Coming of the Month of Ramadan

1 Praise belongs to God who guided us to His praise
and placed us among the people of praise,
that we might be among the thankful for His beneficence
and that He might recompense us for that
with the recompense of the good-doers!

2 And praise belongs to God who
showed favour to us through His religion,
singled us out for His creed,
and directed us onto the roads of His beneficence,
in order that through His kindness we might travel
upon them
to His good pleasure,
a praise which He will accept from us
and through which He will be pleased with us!

3 And praise belongs to God who appointed among those roads His month,
the month of Ramadan,
the month of fasting,
the month of submission,
the month of purity,
the month of putting to test,
the month of standing in prayer,
in which the Qur'an was sent down as guidance to the people,
and as clear signs of the Guidance and the Separator![175]

4 He clarified its excellence over other months
by the many sacred things and well-known excellencies
which He placed therein,
for He made unlawful in it what He declared lawful in others
to magnify it,
He prohibited foods and drinks in it
to honour it,
and He appointed for it a clear time which He
(majestic and mighty is He)
allows not to be set forward
and accepts not to be placed behind.

5 Then He made one of its nights surpass the nights

of a thousand months
and named it the Night of Decree;
in it the angels and the Spirit descend
by the leave of their Lord upon every command,
a peace[176] constant in blessings
until the rising of the dawn
upon whomsoever He will of His servants
according to the decision He has made firm.

6 O God,
bless Muḥammad and his Household,
inspire us
with knowledge of its excellence,
veneration of its inviolability,
and caution against what Thou hast forbidden within it,
and help us to fast in it
by our restraining our limbs
from acts of disobedience toward Thee
and our employing them
in that which pleases Thee,
so that we lend not our ears to idle talk
and hurry not with our eyes to diversion,

7 we stretch not our hands toward the forbidden
and stride not with our feet toward the prohibited,
our bellies hold only what Thou hast made lawful
and our tongues speak only what Thou
hast exemplified,
we undertake nothing but what brings close to
Thy reward
and pursue nothing but what protects from
Thy punishment!
Then rid all of that from the false show of the false showers
and the fame seeking of the fame seekers,
lest we associate therein anything with Thee
or seek therein any object of desire but Thee!

8 O God,
bless Muḥammad and his Household,
in it make us attend
to the appointed moments of the five prayers within
the bounds Thou hast set,

the obligations Thou hast decreed,
the duties Thou hast assigned,
and the times Thou hast specified;

9 and in the prayers make us alight in the station of
the keepers of their stations,
the guardians of their pillars,
their performers in their times,
as Thy servant and Thy messenger set down in
his *Sunna*
(Thy blessings be upon him and his Household)
in their bowings, their prostrations, and all their
excellent acts,
with the most complete and ample ritual purity
and the most evident and intense humility!

10 Give us success in this month to
tighten our bonds of kin with devotion and gifts,
attend to our neighbours with bestowal and giving,
rid our possessions from claims,
purify them through paying the alms,
go back to him who has gone far from us,
treat justly him who has wronged us,
make peace with him who shows enmity toward us
(except him who is regarded as an enemy
in Thee and for Thee,
for he is the enemy whom we will not befriend,
the party whom we will not hold dear),

11 and seek nearness to Thee through blameless works
which will purify us from sins
and preserve us from renewing faults,
so that none of Thy angels will bring for Thee
the kinds of obedience and sorts of
nearness-seeking
unless they be less than what we bring![177]

12 O God,
I ask Thee by the right of this month
and by the right of him who worships Thee within it
from its beginning to the time of its passing,
whether angel Thou hast brought nigh to Thee,

prophet Thou hast sent,
or righteous servant Thou hast singled out,
that Thou bless Muḥammad and his Household,
make us worthy of the generosity Thou hast promised
Thy friends,
make incumbent for us
what Thou hast made incumbent
for those who go to great lengths in obeying Thee,
and place us in the ranks of those
who deserve through Thy mercy the highest elevation!

13 O God,
bless Muḥammad and his Household,
turn us aside from
deviation in professing Thy Unity,
falling short in magnifying Thee,
in Thy religion,
blindness toward Thy path,
heedlessness of Thy inviolability,
and being deceived by Thy enemy, the accursed Satan!

14 O God,
bless Muḥammad and his Household,
and when in every night of this month's nights
Thou hast necks
which Thy pardon will release
and Thy forgiveness disregard,
place our necks among those necks
and place us among the best folk and companions
of this our month!

15 O God,
bless Muḥammad and his Household,
efface our sins along with the effacing of its crescent moon,
and make us pass forth from the ill effects of our acts
with the passing of its days,
until it leaves us behind,
while within it Thou hast purified us of offences
and rid us of evil deeds!

16 O God,
bless Muḥammad and his Household,

and should we go off to one side in this month,
set us aright;
should we swerve,
point us straight;
and should Thy enemy Satan enwrap us,
rescue us from him!

17 O God,
fill this month with our worship of Thee,
adorn its times with our obedience toward Thee,
help us during its daytime with its fast,
and in its night with prayer and pleading toward Thee,
humility toward Thee,
and lowliness before Thee,
so that its daytime may not bear witness
against our heedlessness,
nor its night against our neglect!

18 O God,
make us like this in the other months and days
as long as Thou givest us life,
and place us among Thy righteous servants,
those who shall inherit Paradise,
therein dwelling forever,[178]
those who give what they give,
while their hearts quake,
that they are returning to their Lord,[179]
those who vie in good works,
outracing to them![180]

19 O God,
bless Muḥammad and his Household
in every time, in all moments, and in every state,
to the number that Thou hast blessed whomsoever
Thou hast blessed
and to multiples of all that, through multiples
which none can count but Thee!
Surely Thou art Accomplisher of what Thou desirest

45

His Supplication in Bidding Farewell to the Month of Ramadan

1 O God,
O He who desires no repayment!

2 O He who shows no remorse at bestowal!

3 O He who rewards not His servant tit for tat!

4 Thy kindness is a new beginning,
Thy pardon gratuitous bounty,[181]
Thy punishment justice,
Thy decree a choice for the best!

5 If Thou bestowest,
Thou stainest not Thy bestowal with obligation,
and if Thou withholdest,
Thou withholdest not in transgression.

6 Thou showest gratitude to him who thanks Thee,
while Thou hast inspired him to thank Thee.

7 Thou rewardest him who praises Thee,
while though Thou hast taught him Thy praise.

8 Thou coverest him whom,
if Thou willed,
Thou wouldst expose,
and Thou art generous toward him from whom,
if Thou willed,
Thou wouldst withhold.
Both are worthy of Thy exposure and withholding,
but Thou hast
founded Thy acts upon gratuitous bounty,
channelled Thy power into forbearance,

9 received him who disobeyed Thee with clemency,
and disregarded him who intended wrongdoing against himself.
Thou awaitest their turning back without haste

and refrainest from rushing them toward repentance,
so that the perisher among them may not perish
because of Thee
and the wretched may not be wretched through
Thy favour,
but only after Thy prolonged excusing him
and successive arguments against him,
as an act of generosity through Thy pardon, O Generous,
and an act of kindliness through Thy tenderness,
O Clement!

10 It is Thou who hast opened for Thy servants
a door to Thy pardon,
which Thou hast named 'repentance'.
Thou hast placed upon that door
a pointer from Thy revelation,
lest they stray from it:
Thou hast said (blessed are Thy names),
Repent toward God with unswerving repentance!
It may be that Thy Lord will acquit of your evil deeds
and will admit you into gardens
beneath which rivers flow,

11 *upon the day when God will not degrade the Prophet*
and those who have faith along with him,
their light running before them
and on their right hands,
and they say:
'Our Lord, complete for us our light, and forgive us!
Surely Thou art powerful over everything.'[182]
What is the excuse
of him who remains heedless of entering that house
after the opening of the door
and the setting up of the pointer?

12 It is Thou who hast raised the price against Thyself
to the advantage of Thy servants,
desiring their profit in their trade with Thee,
their triumph through reaching Thee,
and their increase on account of Thee,
for Thou hast said
(blessed is Thy Name and high art Thou exalted),

Whoso brings a good deed
shall have ten the like of it,
and whoso brings an evil deed
shall only be recompensed the like of it.[183]

13 Thou hast said,
The likeness of those who expend their wealth
in the way of God
is as the likeness of a grain of corn
that sprouts seven ears,
in every ear a hundred grains;
so God multiplies unto whom He wills.[184]
Thou hast said,
Who is he that will lend to God a good loan,
and He will multiply it for him manifold?[185]
And Thou hast sent down in the Qur'an
similar verses on the multiplying of good deeds.

14 It is Thou who hast pointed them
through Thy speech from Thy Unseen
and Thy encouragement in which lies their good fortune
toward that which
- hadst Thou covered it from them -
their eyes would not have perceived,
their ears would not have heard,
and their imaginations would not have grasped,
for Thou hast said,
Remember Me
and I will remember you
be thankful to Me,
and be you not thankless towards Me![186]
Thou hast said,
If you are thankful,
surely I will increase you,
but if you are thankless,
My chastisement is surely terrible;[187]

15 And Thou hast said,
Supplicate Me
and I will respond to you,
surely those who wax too proud to worship Me
shall enter Gehenna utterly abject.[188]

Hence Thou hast named supplicating Thee 'worship'
and refraining from it 'waxing proud',
and Thou hast threatened that the refraining from it
would yield entrance into Gehenna in utter abjection.

16 So they remember Thee for Thy kindness,
they thank Thee for Thy bounty,
they supplicate Thee by Thy command,
and they donate for Thee
in order to seek Thy increase;
in all this lies their deliverance from Thy wrath
and their triumph through Thy good pleasure.

17 Were any creature himself to direct another creature
to the like of that to which
Thou Thyself hast directed Thy servants,
he would be described by beneficence,
qualified by kindness,
and praised by every tongue.
So to Thee belongs praise
as long as there is found a way to praise Thee
and as long as there remains for praising
words by which Thou may be praised
and meanings which may be spent in praise!

18 O He who shows Himself praiseworthy to His servants
through beneficence and bounty,
flooding them with kindness and graciousness!
How much Thy favour has been spread about among us,
Thy kindness lavished upon us,
and Thy goodness singled out for us!

19 Thou hast guided us to
Thy religion which Thou hast chosen,
Thy creed with which Thou art pleased,
and Thy path which Thou hast made smooth,
and Thou hast shown us proximity to Thee
and arrival at Thy generosity!

20 O God,
among the choicest of those duties
and the most special of those obligations

Thou hast appointed the month of Ramadan,
which Thou hast singled out from other months,
chosen from among all periods and eras,
and preferred over all times of the year
through the Qur'an and the Light
which Thou sent down within it,
the faith
which Thou multiplied by means of it,
the fasting
which Thou obligated therein,
the standing in prayer
which Thou encouraged at its time,
and the Night of Decree
which Thou magnified therein,
the night which is *better than a thousand months.*[189]

21 Through it Thou hast preferred us
over the other communities
and through its excellence Thou hast chosen us
to the exclusion of the people of the creeds.
We fasted by Thy command in its daylight,
we stood in prayer with Thy help in its night,
presenting ourselves by its fasting and its standing
to the mercy which Thou hast held up before us,
and we found through it the means to Thy reward.
And Thou art full of what is sought from Thee,
munificent with what is asked of Thy bounty,
and near to him who strives for Thy nearness.

22 This month stood among us
in a standing place of praise,
accompanied us
with the companionship of one approved,
and profited us
with the most excellent profit of the world's creatures.
Then it parted from us at the completion of its time,
the end of its term,
and the fulfilment of its number.

23 So we bid farewell to it with the farewell of one

whose parting pains us,
whose leaving fills us with gloom and loneliness,
and to whom we have come to owe
a safeguarded claim,
an observed inviolability,
and a discharged right.
We say:
Peace be upon thee,
O greatest month of God!
O festival of His friends!

24 Peace be upon thee,
O most noble of accompanying times!
O best of months in days and hours!

25 Peace be upon thee,
month in which
expectations come near
and good works are scattered about!

26 Peace be upon thee,
comrade
who is great in worth when found
and who torments through absence when lost,
anticipated friend
whose parting gives pain!

27 Peace be upon thee,
familiar
who brought comfort in coming,
thus making happy,
who left loneliness in going,
thus giving anguish!

28 Peace be upon thee,
neighbour in whom
hearts became tender
and sins became few!

29 Peace be upon thee,
helper
who aided against Satan,
companion

who made easy the paths of good-doing!

30 Peace be upon thee -
How many became freedmen of God within thee!
How happy those who observed the respect due to thee!

31 Peace be upon thee -
How many the sins thou erased!
How many the kinds of faults thou covered over!

32 Peace be upon thee -
How drawn out wert thou for the sinners!
How awesome wert thou in the hearts of the faithful!

33 Peace be upon thee,
month with which no days compete!

34 Peace be upon thee,
month which is peace in all affairs!

35 Peace be upon thee,
thou whose companionship is not disliked,
thou whose friendly mixing is not blamed!

36 Peace be upon thee,
just as thou hast entered upon us with blessings
and cleansed us of the defilement of offences!

37 Peace be upon thee -
Thou art not bid farewell in annoyance
nor is thy fasting left in weariness!

38 Peace be upon thee,
object of seeking before thy time,
object of sorrow before thy passing!

39 Peace be upon thee -
How much evil was turned away from us through thee!
How much good flowed upon us because of thee!

40 Peace be upon thee

and upon the Night of Decree
which is *better than a thousand months!*[190]

41 Peace be upon thee -
How much we craved thee yesterday!
How intensely we shall yearn for thee tomorrow!

42 Peace be upon thee
and upon thy bounty
which has now been made unlawful to us
and upon thy blessings gone by
which have now been stripped away from us!

43 O God,
we are the people of this month.
Through it Thou hast ennobled us
and given us success
because of Thy kindness,
while the wretched are ignorant of its time.
Made unlawful to them is its bounty
because of their wretchedness.

44 Thou art the patron
of the knowledge of it by which Thou hast preferred us,
and its prescribed practices to which Thou hast
guided us.
We have undertaken, through Thy giving success,
its fasting and its standing in prayer,
but with shortcomings,
and we have performed little of much.

45 O God,
so to Thee belongs praise,
in admission of evil doing
and confession of negligence,
and to Thee belongs
remorse firmly knitted in our hearts
and seeking of pardon sincerely uttered by our tongues.
Reward us,
in spite of the neglect that befell us in this month,
with a reward through which
we may reach the bounty desired from it
and win the varieties of its craved stores!

46 Make incumbent upon us Thy pardon
for our falling short of Thy right in this month
and make our lives which lie before us
reach the coming month of Ramadan!
Once Thou hast made us reach it,
help us perform the worship of which Thou art worthy,
cause us to undertake the obedience which Thou deservest,
and grant us righteous works
that we may fulfil Thy right
in these two months of the months of time.[191]

47 O God,
as for the small and large sins
which we have committed in this our month,
the misdeeds into which we have fallen,
and the offences which we have earned
purposefully or in forgetfulness,
wronging ourselves thereby
or violating the respect due to others,
bless Muḥammad and his Household,
cover us over with Thy covering,
pardon us through Thy pardoning,
place us not before the eyes of the gloaters because of that,
stretch not toward us the tongues of the defamers,
and employ us in that which will alleviate and expiate
whatever Thou disapprovest from us within it
through Thy clemency which does not run out,
and Thy bounty which does not diminish!

48 O God,
bless Muḥammad and his Household,
redress our being afflicted by our month,[192]
bless us in this day of our festival and our fast-breaking,
make it one of the best of days that have passed over us,
the greatest in attracting Thy pardon,
and the most effacing toward sins,
and forgive us our sins, both the concealed and the public!

49 O God,
with the passing of this month
make us pass forth from our offences,

with its departure
make us depart from our evil deeds,
and appoint us thereby among its most felicitous people,
the most plentiful of them in portion,
and the fullest of them in share!

50 O God,
when any person observes this month as it should be observed,
safeguards its inviolability as it should be safeguarded,
attends to its bounds as they should be attended to,
fears its misdeeds as they should be feared,
or seeks nearness to Thee with any act of nearness-seeking
which
makes incumbent upon him Thy good pleasure
and bends toward him Thy mercy,
give to us the like [of that][193] from Thy wealth
and bestow it upon us in multiples through Thy bounty,
for Thy bounty does not diminish,
Thy treasuries do not decrease but overflow,
the mines of Thy beneficence are not exhausted,
and Thy bestowal is the bestowal full of delight!

51 O God,
bless Muḥammad and his Household
and write for us the like of the wages
of him who fasted in it
or worshipped Thee within it
until the Day of Resurrection!

52 O God,
we repent to Thee in our day of fast-breaking,
which Thou hast appointed
for the faithful
a festival and a joy
and for the people of Thy creed
a time of assembly and gathering,
from every misdeed we did,
ill work we sent ahead,
or evil thought we secretly conceived,
the repentance of one who does not harbour a return to sin
and who afterwards will not go back to offence,
an unswerving repentance rid of doubt and wavering.

So accept it from us,
be pleased with us,
and fix us within it!

53 O God,
provide us with fear of the threatened punishment
and yearning for the promised reward,
so that we may find
the pleasure of that for which we supplicate Thee
and the sorrow of that from which we seek sanctuary in Thee!

54 And place us with Thee among the repenters,
those upon whom Thou hast made Thy love obligatory
and from whom Thou hast accepted
the return to obeying Thee![194]
O Most Just of the just!

55 O God,
show forbearance toward our fathers and our mothers
and all the people of our religion,
those who have gone and those who will pass by,
until the Day of Resurrection!

56 O God,
bless our prophet Muḥammad and his Household,
as Thou hast blessed Thy angels brought nigh,
bless him and his Household,
as Thou hast blessed Thy prophets sent out,
bless him and his Household,
as Thou hast blessed Thy righteous servants
- and better than that, O Lord of the worlds! -
a blessing whose benediction will reach us,
whose benefit will attain to us,
and through which our supplication may be granted!
Thou art the most generous of those who are beseeched,
the most sufficient of those in whom confidence is had,
the most bestowing of those from whom bounty is asked,
and *Thou art powerful over everything!*[195]

46

His Supplication on the Day of Fast-Breaking and on Friday

When he finished his prayer,
He would stand in place, face the *qibla,* and say:

1 O He who has mercy upon him toward whom the servants show no mercy!

2 O He who accepts him whom the cities will not accept!

3 O He who looks not down upon those who have need of Him!

4 O He who disappoints not those who implore Him!

5 O He who slaps not the brow of the people of boldness toward Him with rejection!

6 O He who collects the little that is given to Him
and shows gratitude for the paltry that is done for Him!

7 O He who shows gratitude for the small and rewards with the great!

8 O He who comes close to him who comes close to Him!

9 O He who invites to Himself him who turns his back on Him!

10 O He who changes not favour[196] and rushes not to vengeance!

11 O He who causes the good deed to bear fruit
so that He may make it grow,
and overlooks the evil deed
so that He may efface it!

12 Hopes turn back with needs fulfilled
short of the extent of Thy generosity,
the cups of requests fill up
with the overflow of Thy munificence,
and attributes fall apart
without reaching Thy description.
For to Thee belongs the highest highness
above everything high,
and the most glorious majesty

beyond every majesty!

13 Everything majestic before Thee is small,
everything eminent beside Thy eminence vile!
Those who reach other than Thee are disappointed,
those who present themselves to other than Thee
have lost,
those who stay with other than Thee have perished,
and those who retreat
- except those who retreat to Thy bounty -
are desolate!

14 Thy door is open to the beseechers,
Thy munificence free to the askers,
Thy help near to the help-seekers!

15 The expectant are not disappointed by Thee,
those who present themselves
despair not of Thy bestowal,
the forgiveness-seekers
become not wretched through Thy vengeance!

16 Thy provision is spread among those who disobey Thee,
Thy clemency presents itself to those hostile toward
Thee,
Thy habit is beneficence toward the evildoers,
and Thy wont is to spare the transgressors,
so much so that Thy lack of haste deludes them from
returning,
and Thy disregard bars them from desisting!

17 Thou actest without haste toward them
so that they will come back to Thy command
and Thou disregardest them
confident in the permanence of Thy kingdom,
so Thou sealest him who is worthy of it with felicity,
and Thou abandonest him who is worthy of it to
wretchedness!

18 All of them come home to Thy decree,
their affairs revert to Thy command;
Thy authority grows not feeble through their drawn out
term,

Thy proof is not refuted by the failure to hurry after them.

19 Thy argument is established, never refuted,
Thy authority fixed, never removed.
Permanent woe belongs
to him who inclines away from Thee,
forsaking disappointment
to him who is disappointed by Thee,
and the most wretched wretchedness
to him who is deluded about Thee!

20 How much he will move about in Thy chastisement!
How long he will frequent Thy punishment!
How far his utmost end from relief!
How he will despair of an easy exit!
[All of this] as justice from Thy decree
(Thou art not unjust in it!),
and equity from Thy judgement
(Thou dost not act wrongfully against him!).

21 Thou supported the arguments,
tested the excuses,
began with threats,
showed gentleness with encouragement,
struck similitudes,
made long the respite,
delayed,
while Thou art able to hurry,
and acted without haste,
while Thou art full of quick accomplishment!

22 Not because of
incapacity is Thy slowness,
feebleness Thy giving respite,
heedlessness Thy showing restraint,
dissemblance Thy waiting!
But that Thy argument be more conclusive,
Thy generosity more perfect,
Thy beneficence more exhaustive,
Thy favour more complete!
All of this has been and always was,

is and ever will be.

23 Thy argument is greater
than that its totality be described,
Thy glory more elevated
than that it be limited in its core,
Thy favour more abundant
than that its entirety be counted,
Thy beneficence more abundant
than that thanks be given for its least amount!

24 Speechlessness has made me fall short of praising Thee,
restraint has made me powerless to glorify Thee,
and the most I can do is admit to inability,
not out of desire, my God,
but out of incapacity.

25 So here I am:
I repair to Thee by coming forward,
and I ask from Thee good support
So bless Muḥammad and his Household,
hear my whispered words,
grant my supplication,
seal not my day with disappointment,
slap not my brow by rejecting my request,
and make noble my coming from Thee
and my going back to Thee!
Surely Thou art not constrained by what Thou desirest,
nor incapable of what Thou art asked!
Thou art powerful over everything,[197]
and 'There is no force and no strength save in God,
the All-high, the All-mighty!'[198]

47

His Supplication on the Day of 'Arafa[199]

1 *Praise belongs to God, Lord of the worlds!*[200]

2 O God,
to Thee belongs praise!
Originator of the heavens and the earth!
Possessor of majesty and munificence!
Lord of lords!
Object of worship of every worshiper!
Creator of every creature!
Inheritor of all things![201]
There is nothing like Him,[202]
knowledge of nothing escapes Him,[203]
He *encompasses everything,*[204]
and He is *watchful over everything.*[205]

3 Thou art God,
there is no god but Thou,
the Unique, the Alone,
the Single, the Isolated.

4 Thou art God,
there is no god but Thou,
the Generous, the Generously Bestowing,
the All-mighty, the Mightily Exalted,
the Magnificent, the Magnificently Magnified.

5 Thou art God,
there is no god but Thou,
the All-high, the Sublimely High,
the Strong in prowess.

6 Thou art God,
there is no god but Thou,
the All-merciful, the All-compassionate,
the All-knowing, the All-wise.

7 Thou art God,
there is no god but Thou,
the All-hearing, the All-seeing,

the Eternal, the All-aware.

8 Thou art God,
there is no god but Thou,
the Generous, the Most Generous,
the Everlasting, the Most Everlasting.

9 Thou art God,
there is no god but Thou,
the First before every one,
the Last after every number.

10 Thou art God,
there is no god but Thou,
the Close in His highness,
the High in His closeness.

11 Thou art God,
there is no god but Thou,
Possessor of radiance and glory,
magnificence and praise.

12 Thou art God,
there is no god but Thou.
Thou hast brought forth the things without root,
formed what Thou hast formed without exemplar,
and originated the originated things without limitation.

13 It is Thou
who hast ordained each thing with an ordination,[206]
eased each thing with an easing,[207]
and governed everything below Thyself with a governing.[208]

14 It is Thou
whom no associate helps with Thy creation
and no vizier aids in Thy command.
Thou hast no witness and no equal.

15 It is Thou
who willed,

and what Thou willed was unfailing,
who decreed,
and what Thou decreed was just,
who decided,
and what Thou decided was fair.

16 It is Thou
whom place does not contain,
before whose authority no authority stands up,
and whom no proof or explication can thwart.

17 It is Thou
who hast counted everything in numbers,[209]
appointed for everything a term,
and ordained everything with an ordination.

18 It is Thou
before whose selfness imaginations fall short,
before whose howness understandings have no incapacity,
and the place of whose whereness eyes perceive not.[210]

19 It is Thou
who hast no bounds,
lest Thou be bounded,
who art not exemplified,
lest Thou be found,
who dost not beget,
lest Thou be begotten.[211]

20 It is Thou
with whom there is no opposite,
lest it contend with Thee,
who hast no equal,
lest it vie with Thee,
who hast no rival,
lest it resist Thee.

21 It is Thou
who art He who began, devised,
brought forth, originated,

and made well all that He made.

22 Glory be to Thee!
How majestic is Thy station!
How high Thy place among the places!
How cleanly Thy Separator cleaves with the truth![212]

23 Glory be to Thee!
The Gentle - how gentle Thou art!
The Clement - how clement Thou art!
The Wise - how knowing Thou art!

24 Glory be to Thee!
The King - how invincible Thou art!
The Munificent - how full of plenty Thou art!
The Elevated - how elevated Thou art!
Possessor of radiance and glory,
magnificence and praise!

25 Glory be to Thee!
Thou hast stretched forth Thy hand with good things,
and from Thee guidance has come to be known,
so he who begs from Thee religion or this world
will find Thee.

26 Glory be to Thee!
Whatever passes in Thy knowledge is subjected to Thee,
all below Thy Throne are humbled before
Thy mightiness,
and every one of Thy creatures follows Thee
in submission.

27 Glory be to Thee!
Thou art not sensed, nor touched,
nor felt, nor beguiled,
nor held back, nor challenged,
nor kept up with, nor resisted,
nor deceived, nor circumvented.

28 Glory be to Thee!
Thy path is smooth ground,
Thy command right guidance,

and Thou art a living, eternal refuge.

29 Glory be to Thee!
Thy word is decisive,
Thy decree unfailing,
Thy will resolute.

30 Glory be to Thee!
None can reject Thy wish,
none can change Thy words.[213]

31 Glory be to Thee,
Outdazzling in signs,
Creator of the heavens,
Author of the spirits!

32 To Thee belongs praise,
a praise that will be permanent with Thy permanence!

33 To Thee belongs praise,
a praise everlasting through Thy favour!

34 To Thee belongs praise,
a praise that will parallel Thy benefaction!

35 To Thee belongs praise,
a praise that will increase Thy good pleasure!

36 To Thee belongs praise,
a praise along with the praise of every praiser
and a thanksgiving before which falls short
the thanksgiving of every thanksgiver;

37 a praise which is suitable for none but Thee
and through which nearness is sought to none but Thee;

38 a praise which will make permanent the first [bounty]
and call forth the permanence of the last;

39 a praise which will multiply through recurrence of times
and increase through successive doublings;

40 a praise which the guardians will not be able to number
and which exceeds what the writers number in
Thy Book;[214]

41 a praise which will counterbalance Thy glorious Throne
and equal Thy elevated Footstool;

42 a praise whose reward with Thee will be complete
and whose recompense will comprise every
recompense;

43 a praise whose outward conforms to its inward,
and whose inward conforms to correct intention;

44 a praise with whose like no creature has praised Thee
and whose excellence none knows but Thou;

45 a praise in which he who strives to multiply Thy praise
will be helped
and he who draws the bow to the utmost in fulfilling it
will be confirmed;

46 a praise which will
gather all the praise which Thou hast created
and tie together all which Thou wilt afterwards
create;

47 a praise than which no praise is nearer to Thy word
and than which none is greater from any who praise
Thee;

48 a praise whose fullness will obligate increase
through Thy generosity
and to which Thou wilt join increase after increase
as graciousness from Thee;

49 a praise that will befit the generosity of Thy face
and meet the might of Thy majesty!

50 My Lord,
bless Muḥammad and the Household of Muḥammad ,
the distinguished, the chosen,

the honoured, the brought nigh,
with the most excellent of Thy blessings,
benedict him
with the most complete of Thy benedictions,
and have mercy upon him
with the most enjoyable of Thy mercies!

51 My Lord,
bless Muḥammad and his Household
with a fruitful blessing,
more fruitful than which there is no blessing!
Bless him
with a growing blessing,
more growing than which there is no blessing!
And bless him
with a pleasing blessing,
beyond which there is no blessing!

52 My Lord,
bless Muḥammad and his Household
with a blessing
which will please him
and increase his good pleasure!
Bless him
with a blessing
which will please Thee
and increase Thy good pleasure toward him!
And bless him
with a blessing
through other than which Thou wilt not be pleased for him,
and for which Thou seest no one else worthy!

53 My Lord,
bless Muḥammad and his Household
with a blessing which will
pass beyond Thy good pleasure,
be continuous in its continuity
through Thy subsistence,
and never be spent,

just as Thy words will never be spent![215]

54 My Lord,
bless Muḥammad and his Household
with a blessing which will
tie together the blessings of
Thy angels, Thy prophets, Thy messengers,
and those who obey Thee,
comprise the blessings of Thy servants,
jinn or mankind,
and those worthy of Thy response,
and bring together the blessings
of every one of the kinds of Thy creatures
which Thou hast sown and authored!

55 My Lord,
bless Muḥammad and his Household
with a blessing
which will encompass every blessing,
bygone and new!
Bless him and his Household
with a blessing which
is pleasing to Thee
and everyone below Thee
and will bring forth with all that
a blessing
with which Thou wilt multiply those blessings
and increase them through the recurrence of days
with an increasing in multiples
which none can count but Thou!

56 My Lord,
bless the best of his Household,
those whom Thou hast
chosen for Thy command,
appointed the treasurers of Thy knowledge,
the guardians of Thy religion,
Thy vicegerents in Thy earth,
and Thy arguments against Thy servants,

purified from uncleanness and defilement
through a purification by Thy desire,[216]
and made the mediation to Thee[217]
and the road to Thy Garden!

57 My Lord,
bless Muḥammad and his Household
with a blessing which
makes plentiful Thy gifts and generosity,
perfects for them Thy bestowals and awards,
and fills out their share of Thy kindly acts and benefits!

58 My Lord,
bless him and his Household
with a blessing
whose first has no term,
whose term has no limit,
and whose last has no utmost end!

59 My Lord,
bless them to
the weight of Thy Throne and all below it,
the amount that fills the heavens and all above them,
the number of Thy earths and all below and between them,
a blessing that will bring them near to Thee in proximity,
please Thee and them,
and be joined to its likes forever!

60 O God,
surely Thou hast confirmed Thy religion in all times
with an Imam whom Thou hast set up
as a guidepost to Thy servants
and a lighthouse in Thy lands,
after his cord has been joined to Thy cord!
Thou hast appointed him the means to Thy good pleasure,
made obeying him obligatory,
cautioned against disobeying him,
and commanded
following his commands,

abandoning his prohibitions,
and that no forward-goer go ahead of him
or back-keeper keep back from him![218]
So he is the preservation of the shelter-seekers,
the cave of the faithful,
the handhold of the adherents,
and the radiance of the worlds!

61 O God,
so inspire Thy guardian[219] to give thanks
for that in which Thou hast favoured him,
inspire us with the like concerning him,
grant him an authority from Thee to help him,[220]
open for him an easy opening,[221]
aid him with Thy mightiest pillar,
brace up his back,[222]
strengthen his arm,[223]
guard him with Thy eye,
defend him with Thy safeguarding,
help him with Thy angels,
and assist him with Thy most victorious troops![224]

62 Through him
establish Thy Book, Thy bounds, Thy laws,
and the norms of Thy Messenger's *Sunna*
(Thy blessings, O God,
be upon him and his Household),
bring to life the guideposts of Thy religion,
deadened by the wrongdoers,
burnish the rust of injustice from Thy way,
sift the adversity from Thy road,
eliminate those who deviate from Thy path,
and erase those who seek crookedness in Thy straightness!

63 Make his side mild toward Thy friends,
stretch forth his hand over Thy enemies,
give us
his clemency, his mercy,
his tenderness, his sympathy,
and make us

his hearers and obeyers,
strivers toward his good pleasure,
assistants in helping him and defending him,
and brought near through that to Thee
and Thy Messenger
(Thy blessings, O God,
be upon him and his Household).

64 O God,
and bless
the friends [of the Imams],
the confessors of their station,
the keepers to their course,
the pursuers of their tracks,
the clingers to their handhold,
the adherents to their guardianship,[225]
the followers of their imamate,
the submitters to their command,
the strivers to obey them,
the awaiters of their days,
the directors of their eyes toward them,
with blessings blessed, pure, growing,
fresh, and fragrant!

65 Give them and their spirits peace,
bring together their affair in reverential fear,
set right their situations,
turn toward them,
Surely Thou art Ever-turning, All-compassionate[226]
and the Best of forgivers,
and place us with them in the Abode of Peace,[227]
through Thy mercy,
O Most Merciful of the merciful!

66 O God,
this is the Day of 'Arafa,
a day which Thou hast made noble, given honour, and magnified.
Within it Thou hast spread Thy mercy,
showed kindness through Thy pardon,

and made plentiful Thy giving,
and by it Thou hast been bounteous toward
Thy servants.

67 I am Thy servant whom Thou favoured before creating him
and after creating him.
Thou madest him one of those whom Thou
guided to Thy religion,
gavest success in fulfilling Thy right,
preserved through Thy cord,
included within Thy party,
and directed aright to befriend Thy friends
and show enmity to Thine enemies.

68 Then Thou commanded him,
but he did not follow Thy commands,
Thou restricted Him,
but he did not heed Thy restrictions,
Thou prohibited him from disobedience toward Thee,
but he broke Thy command by doing what Thou hadst
prohibited,
not in contention with Thee,
nor to display pride toward Thee;
on the contrary, his caprice[228] called him
to that which Thou hadst set apart and cautioned against,
and he was helped in that by Thy enemy and his enemy.
So he went ahead with it
knowing Thy threat,
hoping for Thy pardon,
and relying upon Thy forbearance,
though he was the most obligated of Thy servants
- given Thy kindness toward him -
not to do so.

69 Here I am, then, before Thee,
despised, lowly, humble, abject, fearful,
confessing the dreadful sins with which I am burdened
and the great offences that I have committed,
seeking sanctuary in Thy forgiveness,
asking shelter in Thy mercy,

and certain that
no sanctuary-giver will give me sanctuary from Thee
and no withholder will hold me back from Thee.

70 So act kindly toward me,
just as Thou actest kindly
by Thy shielding him who commits sins,
be munificent toward me,
just as Thou art munificent
by pardoning him who throws himself before Thee,
and show kindness to me,
just as it is nothing great for Thee to show kindness
by forgiving him who expectantly hopes in Thee!

71 Appoint for me in this day an allotment
through which I may attain
a share of Thy good pleasure,
and send me not back destitute
of that with which Thy worshipers return
from among Thy servants!

72 Though I have not forwarded
the righteous deeds
which they have forwarded,
I have forwarded the profession of Thy Unity
and the negation from Thee
of opposites, rivals, and likenesses,
I have come to Thee by the gateways
by which Thou hast commanded
that people come,
and I have sought nearness to Thee
through that without seeking nearness through which
none gains nearness to Thee.

73 Then I followed all this
with repeated turning toward Thee,
lowliness and abasement before Thee,
opinion of Thee,
and trust in what is with Thee;
and to that I coupled hope in Thee,
since the one who hopes in Thee

is seldom disappointed!

74 I asked Thee with the asking of one
vile, lowly,
pitiful, poor,
fearful, seeking sanctuary;
all that in fear and pleading
seeking refuge and asking shelter,
not presumptuous through the pride of the proud,
nor exalting myself with the boldness of the obedient,
nor presumptuous of the intercession of the interceders.

75 For I am still the least of the least
and the lowliest of the lowly,
like a dust mote or less!
O He who does not hurry the evildoers
nor restrain those living in ease![229]
O He who shows kindness through releasing the stumblers
and gratuitous bounty through respiting the offenders!

76 I am the evildoer, the confessor, the offender, the stumbler!

77 I am he who was audacious toward Thee as one insolent!

78 I am he who disobeyed Thee with forethought!

79 I am he who hid myself from Thy servants
and blatantly showed myself to Thee![230]

80 I am he who was awed by Thy servants
and felt secure from Thee!

81 I am he who dreaded not Thy penalty
and feared not Thy severity!

82 I am the offender against himself!

83 I am the hostage to his own affliction!

84 I am short in shame!

85 I am long in suffering!

86 By the right of him whom Thou hast distinguished
among Thy creation
and by him whom Thou hast chosen
for Thyself!
By the right of him whom Thou hast selected
from among Thy creatures
and by him whom Thou hast picked
for Thy task!
By the right of him the obeying of whom Thou hast joined
to obeying Thee,
and by him the disobeying of whom Thou hast made
like disobeying Thee!
And by the right of him whose friendship Thou hast bound
to Thy friendship
and by him whose enmity Thou hast linked
to Thine enmity!
Shield me in this day of mine,
by that through which Thou shieldest
him who prays fervently to Thee
while disavowing
and him who seeks refuge in Thy forgiveness
while repenting!

87 Attend to me
with that through which Thou attendest to the people of
obedience toward Thee,
proximity to Thee,
and rank with Thee!

88 Single me out,
as Thou singlest him out who
fulfils Thy covenant,
fatigues himself for Thy sake alone,
and exerts himself in Thy good pleasure!

89 Take me not to task for
my neglect in respect to Thee,
my transgressing the limit in Thy bounds,
and stepping outside Thy ordinances!

90 Draw me not on little by little by granting me a respite,[231]

like the drawing on little by little
of him who withholds from me the good he has
by not sharing with Thee in letting favour down upon me!

91 Arouse me from
the sleep of the heedless,
the slumber of the prodigal,
and the dozing of the forsaken!

92 Take my heart to that in which Thou hast
employed the devout,
enthralled the worshipers,
and rescued the remiss!

93 Give me refuge from that which will
keep me far from Thee,
come between me and my share from Thee,
and bar me from that which I strive for in Thee!

94 Make easy for me
the road of good deeds toward Thee,
racing to them from where Thou hast commanded,
and coveting them as Thou desirest!

95 Efface me not along with
those whom Thou effacest
for thinking lightly of what Thou hast promised!

96 Destroy me not with
those whom Thou destroyest
for exposing themselves to Thy hate!

97 Annihilate me not among
those whom Thou annihilatest
for deviating from Thy roads!

98 Deliver me from the floods of trial,
save me from the gullets of affliction,
and grant me sanctuary from being seized by respite![232]

99 Come between me and the enemy who misguides me,
the caprice which ruins me,

and the failing which overcomes me!

100 Turn not away from me
with the turning away in wrath
from one with whom Thou art not pleased!

101 Let me not lose heart in expecting from Thee,
lest I be overcome by despair of Thy mercy!

102 Grant me not that which I cannot endure,
lest Thou weighest me down
with the surplus of Thy love which Thou loadest
upon me!

103 Send me not from Thy hand,
the sending of him who possesses no good,
toward whom Thou hast no need,
and who turns not back [to Thee]!

104 Cast me not with the casting of him who has
fallen from the eye of Thy regard
and been wrapped in degradation from Thee!
Rather take my hand [and save me] from
the falling of the stumblers,
the disquiet of the deviators,
the slip of those deluded,
and the plight of the perishers!

105 Release me from that with which Thou hast afflicted
the ranks of Thy servants and handmaids
and make me reach the utmost degrees of him
about whom Thou art concerned,
towards whom Thou showest favour,
and with whom Thou art pleased,
so that Thou lettest him live as one praiseworthy
and takest him to Thee as one felicitous!

106 Collar me with the collar of abstaining from that which
makes good deeds fail
and takes away blessings!

107 Impart to my heart restraint before

ugly works of evil
and disgraceful misdeeds!

108 Divert me not
by that which I cannot reach except through Thee
from doing that which alone makes Thee pleased
with me![233]

109 Root out from my heart the love of this vile world,
which keeps from everything which is with Thee,
bars from seeking the mediation to Thee,[234]
and distracts from striving for nearness to Thee!

110 Embellish for me solitude
in prayer whispered to Thee
by night and by day!

111 Give me a preservation which will
bring me close to dread of Thee,
cut me off from committing things made unlawful by
Thee,
and spare me from captivation by dreadful sins!

112 Give me purification from the defilement of disobedience,
take away from me the filth of offences,
dress me in the dress of Thy well-being,
cloak me in the cloak of Thy release,
wrap me in Thy ample favours,
and clothe me in Thy bounty and Thy graciousness!

113 Strengthen me with Thy giving success
and Thy pointing the right way,
help me toward righteous intention,
pleasing words,
and approved works, and entrust me not to my force and
my strength
in place of Thy force and Thy strength!

114 Degrade me not on the day Thou raisest me up to meet Thee,
disgrace me not before Thy friends,
make me not forget remembering Thee,
take not away from me thanking Thee,

but enjoin it upon me in states of inattention
when the ignorant are heedless of Thy boons,
and inspire me to
laud what Thou hast done for me
and confess to what Thou hast conferred upon me!

115 Place my beseeching Thee above the beseeching of the beseechers
and my praise of Thee above the praise of the praisers!

116 Abandon me not with my neediness for Thee,
destroy me not for what I have done for Thee,[235]
and slap not my brow with that with which
Thou slappest the brow of those who contend with Thee,
for I am submitted to Thee.
I know
that the argument is Thine,
that Thou art closest to bounty,
most accustomed to beneficence,
worthy of reverent fear,
and worthy of forgiveness,[236]
that Thou art closer to pardoning
than to punishing,
and that Thou art nearer to covering over
than to making notorious!

117 Let me live an agreeable life
that will tie together what I want
and reach what I love
while I not bring what Thou dislikest
and not commit what Thou hast prohibited;
and make me die the death of him
whose light runs before him and on his right hand![237]

118 Abase me before Thyself
and exalt me before Thy creatures,
lower me when I am alone with Thee
and raise me among Thy servants,
free me from need for him who has no need of me
and increase me in neediness and poverty toward Thee!

119 Give me refuge from
the gloating of enemies,
the arrival of affliction,
lowliness and suffering!
Shield me in what Thou seest from me,
the shielding of him who
would have power over violence
had he no clemency,
and would seize for misdeeds
had he no lack of haste!

120 When Thou desirest for a people a trial or an evil,
deliver me from it, for I seek Thy shelter;
and since Thou hast not stood me in the station of disgrace
in this world of Thine,
stand me not in such a station
in the next world of Thine!

121 Couple for me the beginnings of Thy kindnesses with their ends
and the ancient of Thy benefits with the freshly risen!
Prolong not my term with a prolonging
through which my heart will harden![238]
Strike me not with a striking
that will take away my radiance![239]
Visit me not with
a meanness that will diminish my worth
or a decency that will keep my rank unknown!

122 Frighten me not
with a fright by which I will despair
or a terror through which I will dread,
but make me
stand in awe of Thy threat,
take precautions against Thy leaving no excuses[240]
and Thy warning,
and tremble at the recitation of Thy verses!

123 Fill my night with life by keeping me awake therein for
worshipping Thee,
solitude with vigil for Thee,
exclusive devotion to reliance upon Thee,

setting my needs before Thee,
and imploring that Thou wilt
set my neck free from the Fire
and grant me sanctuary from Thy chastisement,
within which its inhabitants dwell!

124 Leave me not
blindly wandering in my insolence[241]
or inattentive in my perplexity for a time,[242]
make me not
an admonition to him who takes admonishment,
a punishment exemplary for him who takes heed,
a trial for him who observes,
devise not against me along with those against whom Thou devisest,
replace me not with another,
change not my name,[243]
transform not my body,[244]
appoint me not
a mockery for Thy creatures,
a laughing-stock for Thyself,
a follower of anything but Thy good pleasure,
a menial servant for anything but avenging Thee!

125 Let me find
the coolness of Thy pardon
and the sweetness of
Thy mercy,
Thy repose,
Thy ease,
and the garden of Thy bliss![245]
Let me taste,
through some of Thy boundless plenty,
the flavour of
being free for what Thou lovest
and striving in what brings about proximity
with Thee and to Thee,
and give me a gift from among Thy gifts!

126 Make my commerce profitable[246]
and my return without loss,[247]
fill me with fear of Thy station,
make me yearn for the meeting with Thee,
and allow me to repent with an unswerving repentance
along with which Thou lettest no sins remain,
small or large,
and leavest no wrongs, open or secret!

127 Root out rancour toward the faithful from my breast,[248]
bend my heart toward the humble,
be toward me as Thou art toward the righteous,
adorn me with the adornment of the godfearing,
appoint for me
a goodly report[249] among those yet to come
and a growing remembrance among the later folk,
and take me to the plain of those who came first![250]

128 Complete the lavishness of Thy favour upon me,
clothe me in its repeated generosities,
fill my hand with Thy benefits,
drive Thy generous gifts to me,
make me the neighbour of the best of Thy friends
in the Gardens which Thou hast adorned for Thy chosen,
and wrap me in Thy noble presents
in the stations prepared for Thy beloveds!

129 Appoint for me
a resting place with Thee
where I may seek haven in serenity,
and a resort to which I may revert
and rest my eyes,
weigh not against me my dreadful misdeeds,
destroy me not on the day the secrets are tried,[251]
eliminate from me every doubt and uncertainty,
appoint for me a way in the truth from every mercy,
make plentiful for me the portions of gifts
from Thy granting of awards,
and fill out for me the shares of beneficence
from Thy bestowal of bounty!

130 Make my heart trust in what is with Thee
and my concern free for what is Thine,
employ me in that in which Thou employest Thy pure friends,
drench my heart with Thy obedience when intellects are distracted,
and combine within me
independence, continence,
ease, release,
health, plenty,
tranquillity, and well being!

131 Make not fail
my good deeds
through my disobedience that stains them
or my private times of worship
through the instigations of Thy trial!
Safeguard my face from asking
from anyone in the world,
and drive me far from begging
for that which is with the ungodly!

132 Make me not an aid to the wrongdoers,
nor their hand and helper in erasing Thy Book!
Defend me whence I know not with a defence
through which Thou protectest me!
Open toward me the gates of Thy repentance, Thy mercy,
Thy clemency, and Thy boundless provision!
Surely I am one of those who beseech Thee!
And complete Thy favour toward me!
Surely Thou art the best of those who show favour!

133 Place the rest of my life in the *hajj* and the *'umra*
seeking Thy face,
O Lord of the worlds!
And may God bless Muḥammad and his Household, the good, the pure,
and peace be upon him and them always and forever!

48

His Supplication on the Day of Sacrifice[252] and on Friday

1 O God,
this is a blessed and fortunate day,
within which the Muslims are gathered
in the quarters of Thy earth.
Among them are present the asker, the seeker,
the beseecher, the fearful,
while Thou art looking upon their needs.
So I ask Thee by Thy munificence and generosity
and easy upon Thee is what I ask Thee! -
that Thou blessest Muḥammad and his Household.

2 And I ask Thee, O God, our Lord -
for Thine is the kingdom and Thine is the praise;
there is no god but Thou,
the Clement, the Generous,
the All-loving, the All-kind,
Possessor of majesty and munificence,
Originator of the heavens and the earth -
whenever Thou apportionest among Thy faithful servants
good, well being,
blessing, guidance,
works in obedience to Thee,
or good through which
Thou art kind to them by guiding them to Thee,
or raisest them up a degree with Thee,
or givest them the good of this world or the next,
that Thou givest me amply my share and allotment of it.

3 And I ask Thee, O God -
for Thine is the kingdom and the praise;
there is no god but Thou -
that Thou blessest Muḥammad
Thy servant and Thy messenger,
Thy beloved and Thy selected friend,
Thy chosen from among Thy creation,
and the Household of Muḥammad
the pious, the pure, the chosen,

with a blessing no one has strength to count but Thou,
that Thou associatest us with
the most righteous of Thy faithful servants
who supplicate Thee today
- O Lord of the worlds!—
and that Thou forgivest us and them!
Surely Thou art powerful over everything.[253]

4 O God,
toward Thee I aim with my need
and before Thee I set my poverty, my neediness,
my misery,
for I have more trust in Thy forgiveness and Thy mercy
than in my own works.
Thy forgiveness and Thy mercy are vaster than my sins.
So bless Muḥammad and the Household of Muḥammad
and attend to the accomplishment of every need of mine
through
Thy power over it,
its easiness for Thee,
my poverty toward Thee,
and Thy freedom from need for me!
I will come upon no good whatsoever unless through Thee,
no one other than Thou will turn any evil away from me,
and I have hope in none but Thee for my affair
in the next world and in this world.

5 O God,
if anyone has ever
arranged,
made ready,
prepared,
and drawn himself up
to be received by a creature
in hope of his support and awards,
then today toward Thee, my Master, is
my arrangement,
my making ready,
my preparation,
and my drawing up,
in hope of Thy pardon and support
and in seeking to attain to Thee and Thy prize.

6 O God,
so bless Muḥammad and the Household of Muḥammad
and disappoint not my hope in that today!
O He who is not troubled by those who ask
and diminished by those who attain their desire!
I come not before Thee trusting
in a righteous work I have sent ahead,
nor in the intercession of any creature in whom
I have hope,
except the intercession of Muḥammad
and the Folk of his House
(upon him and upon them be Thy peace).

7 I come to Thee admitting sin and evildoing toward myself.
I come to Thee hoping for Thy abounding pardon
through which Thou hast pardoned the offenders,
while their long persistence in dreadful sin
did not prevent Thee
from returning toward them with mercy and forgiveness!

8 O He whose mercy is wide
and whose pardon is abounding!
O All-mighty!
O All-mighty!
O All-generous!
O All-generous!
Bless Muḥammad and the Household of Muḥammad
return toward me through Thy mercy,
be tender toward me through Thy bounty,
and spread out Thy forgiveness upon me!

9 O God,
this station belongs to Thy vicegerents, Thy chosen,
while the places of Thy trusted ones
in the elevated degree which Thou hast singled out
for them
have been forcibly stripped![254]
But Thou art the Ordainer of that -
Thy command is not overcome,
the inevitable in Thy governing is not overstepped!
However Thou willest and whenever Thou willest!
In that which Thou knowest best,

Thou art not accused for Thy creation or Thy will!
Then Thy selected friends, Thy vicegerents,
were overcome, vanquished, forcibly stripped;
they see Thy decree replaced,
Thy Book discarded,
Thy obligations distorted from the aims of Thy laws,
and the *Sunna* of Thy Prophet abandoned!

10 O God,
curse their enemies among those of old and the later folk,
and all those pleased with their acts,
and their adherents and followers!

11 O God,
bless Muḥammad and the Household of Muḥammad
(surely Thou art All-laudable, All-glorious)
like Thy blessing, benedictions, and salutations
upon Thy chosen Abraham and the people of Abraham!
And hasten for them relief,
ease,
help,
strengthening,
and confirmation!

12 O God,
and make me
one of the people who profess Thy Unity,
have faith in Thee,
and attest to Thy Messenger
and the Imams toward whom Thou hast enjoined obedience,
and one of those through whom and at whose hands
this takes place![255]
Amen, Lord of the worlds!

13 O God,
nothing repels Thy wrath but Thy clemency,
nothing repels Thy displeasure but Thy pardon,
nothing grants sanctuary from Thy punishment but Thy mercy,
and nothing will deliver me from Thee

except pleading to Thee before Thee,[256]
so bless Muḥammad and the Household of Muḥammad
and give us on Thy part, my God, relief by means of the power
through which Thou bringest the dead servants to life
and revivest the dead lands.[257]

14 Destroy me not through gloom, my God,
before Thou respondest to me
and givest me the knowledge of Thy response to
my supplication!
Let me taste the flavour of well-being to the end of my term!
And let not my enemy gloat over me,
place not my neck in his power,
and give him not authority over me!

15 My God,
if Thou raisest me up,
who is there to push me down?
If Thou pushest me down,
who is there to raise me up?
If Thou honourest me,
who is there to humiliate me?
If Thou humiliatest me,
who is there to honour me?
If Thou chastisest me,
who is there to have mercy upon me?
If Thou destroyest me,
who is there to stand up for Thy servant against
Thee
or ask Thee about his affair?
But I know that there is no wrong in Thy decree
and no hurry in Thy vengeance.
He alone hurries who fears to miss,
and only the weak needs to wrong.
But Thou art exalted, my God,
high indeed above all that!

16 O God,
bless Muḥammad and the Household of Muḥammad
make me not the target of affliction
nor the object of Thy vengeance,
respite me,

comfort me,
release me from my stumble,
and afflict me not with an affliction
in the wake of an affliction,
for Thou hast seen my frailty,
the paucity of my stratagems,
and my pleading to Thee!

17 I seek refuge in Thee today, my God, from Thy wrath,
so bless Muḥammad and his Household
and give me refuge!

18 I seek sanctuary in Thee today from Thy displeasure,
so bless Muḥammad and his Household,
and give me sanctuary!

19 I ask Thee security from Thy chastisement,
so bless Muḥammad and his Household,
and give me security!

20 I seek guidance from Thee,
so bless Muḥammad and his Household
and guide me!

21 I seek help from Thee,
so bless Muḥammad and his Household
and help me!

22 I ask Thee for mercy,
so bless Muḥammad and his Household
and have mercy upon me!

23 I seek sufficiency from Thee,
so bless Muḥammad and his Household
and suffice me!

24 I seek provision from Thee,
so bless Muḥammad and his Household
and provide for me!

25 I seek assistance from Thee,
so bless Muḥammad and his Household
and assist me!

26 I pray forgiveness for my past sins,
so bless Muḥammad and his Household
and forgive me!

27 I ask Thee to preserve me from sin,
so bless Muḥammad and his Household
and preserve me,
for I will not return to anything Thou dislikest from me,
if Thou willest that!

28 My Lord!
My Lord!
O All-loving!
O All-kind!
O Possessor of majesty and munificence!
Bless Muḥammad and his Household,
and grant me everything that I
ask from Thee,
seek from Thee,
and beseech from Thee!
Will it, ordain it, decree it, and accomplish it!
Give me good in that of it which Thou decreest!
Bless me in that,
be gratuitously bountiful toward me through it,
make me happy in that of it which Thou givest to me,
and increase me in Thy bounty
and the plenty of what is with Thee,
for Thou art Boundless, Generous!
And link that to the good and the bliss of the next world,
O Most Merciful of the merciful!

THEN YOU SUPPLICATE AS SEEMS PROPER TO YOU AND YOU CALL DOWN BLESSINGS ON MUḤAMMAD AND HIS HOUSEHOLD ONE THOUSAND TIMES. THIS IS WHAT HE USED TO DO (UPON HIM BE PEACE).

49

His Supplication in Repelling the Trickery of Enemies and Driving away their Severity

1 My God,
Thou guided me
but I diverted myself,
Thou admonished me
but my heart became hardened,
Thou tried me graciously
but I disobeyed.
Then, when Thou caused me to know it,
I came to know that from which Thou hadst turned [me] away,
so I prayed forgiveness
and Thou released,
and I returned
and Thou covered over.
So Thine, my God,
is the praise!

2 I plunged into the valleys of destruction
and settled in the ravines of ruin,
exposing myself to Thy chastisements
and the descent of Thy punishments!

3 My mediation with Thee is the profession of Unity,
my way of coming to Thee that I associate nothing with Thee,
nor do I take along with Thee a god;
I have fled to Thee with my soul -
in Thee is the place of flight
for the evildoer,
the place of escape
for him who has squandered the share of his soul
and seeks asylum.

4 How many an enemy has
unsheathed the sword of his enmity toward me,
honed the cutting edge of his knife for me,
sharpened the tip of his blade for me,

mixed his killing potions for me,
pointed toward me his straight-flying arrows,
not allowed the eye of his watchfulness to sleep toward me,
and secretly thought of
visiting me with something hateful
and making me gulp down the bitter water of his bile!

5 So Thou looked my God, at
my weakness in bearing oppressive burdens,
my inability to gain victory over him who aims to war against me,
and my being alone before the great numbers
of him who is hostile toward me
and lies in wait for me
with an affliction
about which I have not thought.

6 Thou set out at once to help me
and Thou braced up my back!
Thou blunted for me his blade,
made him, after a great multitude, solitary,
raised up my heel over him,
and turned back upon him what he had pointed straight.
So Thou sent him back,
his rage not calmed,
his burning thirst not quenched!
Biting his fingers,
he turned his back in flight,
his columns having been of no use.

7 How many an oppressor has oppressed me with his tricks,
set up for me the net of his snares,
appointed over me the inspection of his regard,
and lay in ambush for me,
the lying in ambush of a predator for its game,
waiting to take advantage of its prey,
while he showed me the smile of the flatterer
and looked at me with the intensity of fury!

8 So when Thou saw, my God,
(blessed art Thou and high exalted)
the depravity of his secret thoughts

and the ugliness of what he harboured,
Thou threw him on his head into his own pitfall
and dumped him into the hole of his own digging.
So he was brought down low, after his overbearing,
by the nooses of his own snare,
wherein he had thought he would see me;
and what came down upon his courtyard
- had it not been for Thy mercy -
was on the point of coming down upon me!

9 How many an evier has
choked upon me in his agony,
fumed over me in his rage,
cut me with the edge of his tongue,
showed malice toward me by accusing me of his own faults,
made my good repute the target of his shots,
collared me with his own constant defects,
showed malice toward me with his trickery,
and aimed at me with his tricks!

10 So I called upon Thee, my God,
seeking aid from Thee,
trusting in the speed of Thy response,
knowing that
he who seeks haven in the shadow of Thy wing
will not be mistreated,
and he who seeks asylum in the stronghold of
Thy victory
will not be frightened.
So Thou fortified me against his severity through Thy power.

11 How many
a cloud of detested things Thou hast dispelled from me,
a cloud of favour Thou hast made rain down upon me,
a stream of mercy Thou hast let flow,
a well-being in which Thou hast clothed me,
an eye of mishap Thou hast blinded,
and a wrap of distress Thou hast removed!

12 How many
a good opinion Thou hast verified,
a destitution Thou hast redressed,

an infirmity Thou hast restored to health,
and a misery Thou hast transformed!

13 All of that was favour and graciousness from Thee,
and in all of it I was occupied
with acts of disobeying Thee.
My evildoing did not hinder Thee
from completing Thy beneficence,
nor was I stopped
from committing acts displeasing to Thee.
Thou art not questioned as to what Thou dost![258]

14 Thou wert asked,
and Thou bestowed.
Thou wert not asked,
and Thou began.
Thy bounty was requested,
and Thou didst not skimp.
Thou refused, my Master, everything but
beneficence,
kindness,
graciousness,
and favour,
and I refused everything
but plunging into what Thou hast made unlawful,
transgressing Thy bounds,
and paying no heed to Thy threat!
So Thine is the praise, my God,
the All-powerful who is not overcome,
and the Possessor of patient waiting who does not hurry!

15 This is the station of one who confesses to lavishness of favours,
counters them with shortcomings,
and bears witness to his own negligence.

16 O God,
so I seek nearness to Thee through
the elevated rank of Muḥammad
and the radiant degree of ʿAlī,
and I turn to Thee through them
so that Thou wilt give me refuge
from the evil of [so and so],[259]

for that will not constrain Thee in Thy wealth,
nor trouble Thee in Thy power,
and *Thou art powerful over everything!*[260]

17 So give me, my God,
by Thy mercy and Thy lasting bestowal of success,
that which I may take as a ladder
with which to climb to Thy good pleasure
and be secure from Thy punishment,
O Most merciful of the merciful!

50

His Supplication in Fear

1 O God,
Thou created me without fault,
nurtured me when small,
and provided me with sufficiency.

2 O God,
I found in the Book
which Thou sent down
and through which Thou gave good news to
Thy servants,
that Thou said,
O My servants who hare been prodigal against yourselves,
do not despair of God's mercy,
surely God forgives all sins,[261]
but there has gone ahead from me what Thou knowest
(and of which Thou knowest more than I)!
O the shame of what Thy Book has counted against me![262]

3 Were it not for the places
where I expectantly hope for Thy pardon,
which enfolds all things,
I would have thrown myself down [in despair]!
Were anyone able to flee from his Lord,
I would be the most obligated to flee from
Thee!
But not a secret in earth and heaven is concealed from
Thee,
except that Thou bringest it.[263]
Thou sufficest as a recompenser!
Thou sufficest as a reckoner![264]

4 O God,
surely Thou wouldst seek me if I flee
and catch me if I run.
So here I am before Thee,
abject, lowly, abased.
If Thou chastisest me,
I am worthy of that,

and it would be, my Lord, an act of justice from Thee.
But if Thou pardonest me,
anciently has Thy pardon enfolded me
and Thy well-being garmented me!

5 So I ask Thee, O God,
by Thy names stored in Thy treasury[265]
and Thy splendour masked by the veils!
If Thou hast no mercy upon this anxious soul
and these uneasy, decaying bones -
he cannot endure the heat of Thy sun,
so how can he endure the heat of Thy Fire?
He cannot endure the sound of Thy thunder,
so how can he endure the sound of Thy wrath?

6 So have mercy upon me, O God,
for I am a vile man
and my worth is little.
Chastising me will not add the weight of a dust mote
to Thy kingdom.
Were chastising me something that would add to
Thy kingdom,
I would ask Thee for patience to bear it
and would love for it to belong to Thee;
but Thy authority, my God, is mightier,
and Thy kingdom more lasting,
than that the obedience of the obeyers should increase it
or the disobedience of the sinners diminish it!

7 So have mercy upon me,
O Most Merciful of the merciful!
Show me forbearance,
O Possessor of majesty and munificence!
And turn toward me,
Surely Thou art Ever-turning, All-compassionate![266]

51

His Supplication in Pleading and Abasement

1 My God,
I praise Thee,
- and Thou art worthy of praise -
for Thy benefaction toward me,
the lavishness of Thy favours toward me,
and Thy plentiful bestowal upon me,
and for showing bounty toward me through Thy mercy
and lavishing Thy favour upon me.
Thou hast done well toward me
and I am incapable of thanking Thee.

2 Were it not for Thy beneficence toward me
and the lavishness of Thy favours upon me,
I would not have reached the taking of my share
nor would my soul have been set right,
but Thou began with beneficence toward me,
provided me sufficiency in all my affairs,
turned away from me the toil of affliction,
and held back from me the feared decree.

3 My God,
how many a toilsome affliction
which Thou hast turned away from me!
How many a lavish favour
with which Thou hast gladdened my eye!
How many a generous benefaction of Thine
which is present with me!

4 It is Thou who
responded to my supplication at the time of distress,
released me from my slip in stumbling,
and took my enemies to task for doing wrong to me.

5 My God,
I did not find Thee a miser when I asked of Thee
nor a withholder when I desired from Thee.
No, 1 found Thee a hearer of my supplication
and a bestower of my requests;

I found Thy favours toward me lavish in my every situation
and in my every time.
So Thou art praised by me
and Thy benefaction honoured.

6 My soul, my tongue, and my intelligence praise Thee,
a praise that reaches fulfilment and the reality of thanksgiving,
a praise that attains to Thy good pleasure with me -
so deliver me from Thy displeasure!

7 O my cave when the ways thwart me!
O He who releases me from my stumble!
Were it not for Thy covering my shameful defects,
I would be one of the disgraced.
O my confirmer through help!
Were it not for Thy helping me,
I would be one of the overcome!
O He before whom kings place the yoke of lowliness
around their necks,
fearing His penalties!
O worthy of reverent fear!
O He *to whom belong the names most beautiful!*[267]
I ask Thee to pardon me
and to forgive me,
for I am not innocent
that I should offer excuses,
nor a possessor of strength
that I should gain victory,
nor have I any place of flight
that I should flee!

8 I ask Thee to release me from my stumbles,
and before Thee I disavow my sins,
which have laid me waste,
encompassed me,
and destroyed me!
I flee from them to Thee, my Lord,
turning repentantly,
so turn toward me,
seeking refuge,
so grant me refuge,
asking sanctuary,

so abandon me not,
requesting,
so deprive me not,
holding fast,
so leave me not,
supplicating,
so send me not back disappointed!

9 I have supplicated Thee, my Lord, as one
miserable, abased,
apprehensive, fearful,
quaking, poor,
driven to have recourse to Thee!

10 I complain to Thee, my God,
of my soul
- which is too weak
to hurry to
that which Thou hast promised Thy friends
or to avoid
that against which Thou hast cautioned
Thy enemies -
and of the multitude of my concerns,
and of my soul's confusing thoughts.

11 My God,
Thou hast not disgraced me through my secret thoughts
or destroyed me because of my misdeeds!
I call upon Thee,
and Thou respondest,
even if I am slow when Thou callest upon me.
I ask Thee everything I want of my needs,
and I deposit with Thee my secret
wherever I may be.
I supplicate no one besides Thee,
and I hope for no one other than Thee.

12 At Thy service! At Thy service!
Thou hearest him who complains to Thee!
Thou receivest him who has confidence in Thee!
Thou savest him who holds fast to Thee!
Thou givest relief to him who seeks shelter in Thee!

13 My God,

so deprive me not of the good
of the last world and the first
because of the paucity of my thanksgiving
and forgive me the sins of mine which Thou knowest!

14 If Thou chastisest,

I am the wrongdoer, the neglecter,
the negligent, the sinner,
the derelict, the sluggard,
the heedless of the share of my soul!

And if Thou forgivest -
Thou art the Most Merciful of the merciful!

52

His Supplication in Imploring God

1 O God, from whom nothing is concealed in earth or heaven!
How should what Thou hast created, my God,
be concealed from Thee?
How shouldst Thou not number
what Thou hast made?
How should what Thou governest
be absent from Thee?
How should one who has no life
except through Thy provision
have the ability to flee from Thee?
How should one who has no road
except in Thy kingdom
escape from Thee?

2 Glory be to Thee!
He among Thy creatures who fears Thee most
knows Thee best,[268]
he among them most bent in humility
is most active in obeying Thee,
and he among them whom Thou providest
while he worships another
is most contemptible before Thee!

3 Glory be to Thee!
He who associates others with Thee and denies
Thy messengers
diminishes not Thy authority.
He who dislikes Thy decree
cannot reject Thy command.
He who denies Thy power
keeps himself not away from Thee.
He who worships other than Thee
escapes Thee not.
He who dislikes meeting Thee
will not be given endless life in this world.

4 Glory be to Thee!
How mighty is Thy station,

overpowering Thy authority,
intense Thy strength,
penetrating Thy command!

5 Glory be to Thee!
Thou hast decreed death for all Thy creatures,
both him who professes Thy Unity
and him who disbelieves in Thee;
each one will taste death,[269]
each one will come home to Thee.
Blessed art Thou and high exalted!
There is no god but Thou, Thou alone,
who hast no associate.

6 I have faith in Thee,
I attest to Thy messengers,
I accept Thy Book,
I disbelieve in every object of worship other than Thee,
I am quit of anyone who worships another!

7 O God,
I rise in the morning and enter the evening
making little of my good works,
confessing my sins,
admitting my offences;
I am abased because of my prodigality against myself.
My works have destroyed me,
my caprice has ruined me,
my passions have deprived me.

8 So I ask Thee, my Master,
the asking of him
whose soul is diverted
by his drawn out expectations,
whose body is heedless
because of the stillness of his veins,[270]
whose heart is entranced
by the multitude of favours done for him,
whose reflection is little
concerning that to which he is coming home;

9 the asking of him whom
false expectation has overcome,

caprice has entranced,
and this world has mastered,
and over whom death has cast its shadow;
the asking of him who
makes much of his sins
and confesses his offence;
the asking of him who has
no Lord but Thou,
no friend besides Thee,
no one to deliver him from Thee,
and no asylum from Thee except in Thee.[271]

10 My God, I ask Thee
by Thy right incumbent upon all Thy creatures,
by Thy mighty name
with which Thou commanded Thy messenger to glorify Thee,
and by the majesty of Thy generous face,
which ages not,
nor changes,
nor alters,
nor passes away,
that Thou blessest Muḥammad and the Household of Muḥammad
that Thou freest me from need for all things
through worshipping Thee,
that Thou distractest my soul from this world
through fear of Thee,
and that Thou turnest me back toward Thy abundant generosity
through Thy mercy!

11 To Thee I flee,
Thee I fear,
from Thee I seek aid,
in Thee I hope,
Thee I supplicate,
in Thee I seek asylum,
in Thee I trust,
from Thee I ask help,
in Thee I have faith,
in Thee I have placed my confidence,

and upon Thy munificence and Thy generosity I rely.

53

His Supplication in Abasing himself before God (Mighty and Majestic is He)

1 My Lord,
my sins have silenced me,
and my words have been cut off.
I have no argument,
for I am the prisoner of my own affliction,
the hostage to my works,
the frequenter of my own offence,
the confused in my intended way,
the thwarted.

2 I have brought myself to a halt
in the halting place of the abased sinners,
the halting place of the wretched and insolent,
those who think lightly of Thy promise.

3 Glory be to Thee!
What insolence I have insolently shown toward Thee!
What delusion with which I have deluded myself!

4 My Master,
have mercy on
my falling flat on my face
the slipping of my foot,
grant me
my ignorance through Thy clemency,
and my evildoing through Thy beneficence,
for I admit my sin
and I confess my offence:
Here are my hand and my forelock!
I am resigned to retaliation against my soul!
Have mercy on
my white hair,
the depletion of my days,
the nearing of my term,

my frailty,
my misery,
and the paucity of my stratagems!

5 My Master,
and have mercy upon me when
my trace is cut off from this world,
my mention is effaced among the creatures,
and I join the forgotten, like the forgotten ones!

6 My Master,
and have mercy upon me at the change of my form and state when
my body decays,
my limbs are scattered,
and my joints are dismembered!
O my heedlessness toward what was wanted from me!

7 My Master,
have mercy upon me at my mustering and uprising
and on that day, appoint
my standing place
with Thy friends,
my place of emergence
with Thy beloveds,
and my dwelling
in Thy neighbourhood!
O Lord of the worlds!

54

His Supplication for the Removal of Worries

1 O Reliever of worry!
O Remover of grief!
O Merciful in this world and the next
and Compassionate in both!
Bless Muh□ ammad and his Household,
relieve my worry,
and remove my grief!

2 O One, O *Unique*, O *Eternal Refuge!*
O He *Who has not begotten,*
nor has been begotten,
and equal to Him is not any one![272]
Preserve me,
purify me,
and take away my affliction!

HERE YOU SHOULD RECITE THE THRONE VERSE (2:255), THE TWO SURAS OF TAKING REFUGE (113-114), AND UNITY (112). THEN SAY:

3 O God,
I ask Thee
with the asking of him
whose neediness is intense,
whose strength is frail,
whose sins are many,
the asking of one who finds
no helper in his neediness,
no strengthener in his frailty,
no forgiver of his sin
other than Thee,
O Possessor of majesty and munificence!
I ask of Thee
a work through which Thou wilt love him who works it
and a certainty by which Thou wilt profit him who is certain
with the truth of certainty
concerning the execution of Thy command!

4 O God,
bless Muḥammad and the Household of Muḥammad
take my soul while it is firm in sincerity,
cut off my need for this world,
make my desire for what is with Thee
become a yearning to meet Thee,
and give me true confidence in Thee!

5 I ask of Thee
the good of the writ that has been made
and I seek refuge with Thee
from the evil of the writ that has been made.[273]
I ask of Thee
the fear of The worshipers,
the worship of those humbly fearful of Thee,
the certainty of those who have confidence in Thee,
and the confidence of those who have faith in Thee.

6 O God, make
my desire in my asking
like the desire of Thy friends in their asking,
and my fear
like the fear of Thy friends!
Employ me in Thy good pleasure through works
in which I will not leave aside anything of Thy religion
fearing any of Thy creatures!

7 O God,
this is my need,
so make my desire for it great,
within it make manifest my excuse,
through it instil me with my argument,
and by means of it make well my body!

8 O God,
some rise in the morning
having trust or hope in other than Thee.
I rise in the morning,
and Thou art my trust and my hope in all affairs,
so decree for me those which are best in outcome
and deliver me from misguiding trials,

O Most Merciful of the merciful!

9 And God bless our chief,
Muḥammad the Messenger of God, the chosen,
and his Household, the pure!

The following are Appended to Some copies of the Sahifa

[55]

One of his Glorifications, that is, of Zayn al-'Ābidīn (upon him be peace)

1 Glory be to Thee, O God,
and I beg Thy loving care!

2 Glory be to Thee, O God,
and high art Thou exalted!

3 Glory be to Thee, O God,
and might is Thy loincloth![274]

4 Glory be to Thee, O God,
and mightiness is Thy cloak!

5 Glory be to Thee, O God,
and magnificence is Thy authority!

6 Glory be to Thee, All-Mighty!
How mighty Thou art!

7 Glory be to Thee!
Thou art glorified in the highest![275]
Thou hearest and seest what is under the soil![276]

8 Glory be to Thee!
Thou art witness over every whispered conversation![277]

9 Glory be to Thee,
the place where every complaint is put down!

10 Glory be to Thee,
present in every assembly!

11 Glory be to Thee,
object of great hopes!

12 Glory be to Thee!

Thou seest what is at the lowest depth of the water!

13 Glory be to Thee!
Thou hearest the breaths of the fish
in the lowest depths of the oceans!

14 Glory be to Thee!
Thou knowest the weight of the heavens!

15 Glory be to Thee!
Thou knowest the weight of the earths!

16 Glory be to Thee!
Thou knowest the weight of the sun and the moon!

17 Glory be to Thee!
Thou knowest the weight of the darkness and the light!

18 Glory be to Thee!
Thou knowest the weight of the shadow and the air!

19 Glory be to Thee!
Thou knowest the weight of the wind,
how many times it is greater than the weight of a dust mote!

20 Glory be to Thee,
All-holy, All-holy, All-holy!

21 Glory be to Thee!
I wonder how any who knows Thee could fear Thee not!

22 Glory be to Thee, O God,
and Thine is the praise!

23 Glory be to God, the All-high, the All-Mighty!

1,2 Al-Zuhrī related from Sa'īd ibn al-Musayyib.[278] He said: The people were not going out of Mecca until 'Alī ibn al-Ḥusayn, the chief of the worshippers (upon him be peace) went out.

3 So he went out, and they went out with him. He stopped in one of the waystations and prayed two *rak'as*. Then he glorified God - I mean with this glorification - during his prostration.

4 There was no tree and no clod of earth that did not glorify along with him, so we were frightened. He raised his head.

5 He said: O Saʿīd, are you frightened? I said: Yes, O son of the Messenger of God!

6 He said: This is the greatest glorification. It was related to me by my father from his grandfather from the Messenger of God (God bless him and his Household). No sins remain with this glorification. When God (majestic is His majesty) created Gabriel, He inspired him with this glorification. It is God's greatest name.

[56]

A Supplication and Magnification
by him (upon him be peace)

1 Praise belongs to God, who
disclosed Himself to hearts through mightiness,
veiled Himself from eyes through might,
and exercises power over the things through power!

2 Eyes are not firm enough to see Him
and imaginations reach not the core of His mightiness.

3 He displays His overwhelming power in mightiness and magnificence,
robes Himself in might, goodness, and majesty,
is far removed from imperfection through comeliness and beauty,
assumes His glory in pride and splendour,
puts on His majesty through glory and boons,
and has chosen for Himself light and radiance.

4 He is a Creator who has no equal,
a Unique who has no rival,
a One who has no opposite,
an Eternal Refuge who has no match,
a God who has no second,
an Initiator who has no partner,
a Provider who has no helper.

5 He is the First without disappearance,
the Everlasting without annihilation,
the Standing without difficulty,
the Security-giver without end,
the Originator without term,
the Maker without anything,
the Lord without partner,
the Initiator without discomfort,
the Accomplisher without incapacity.

6 He has no bound in space
and no limit in time;

He ever was,
He ever is,
He ever will be the same,
endlessly.
He is God,
the Living, the Self-subsistent,
the Everlasting, the Eternal,
the All-powerful, the All-wise.

7 My God,
Thy little slave is in Thy courtyard,
Thy beggar is in Thy courtyard,
Thy poor one is in Thy courtyard!

THIS VERSE SHOULD BE SAID THREE TIMES

8 My God,
before Thee tremble the pious tremblers,
to Thee devote themselves the lamenters,
in fear of Thee,
in hope of Thee!

9 O God of Truth,
have mercy upon the supplication
of those who cry for help!
Pardon the sins
of the heedless!
And increase beneficence
toward those who keep turning [to Thee]
on the Day they arrive before Thee,
O Generous God!

[57]

His Supplication (upon them be peace) in Mentioning the Household of Muḥammad (upon them be peace)

1 O God, O He who
singled out Muḥammad and his Household for honour,
showed favour toward them with messengerhood,
specified them for the mediation,[279]
appointed them the heirs to the prophets,
sealed with them the executors and the Imams,
taught them the knowledge of what has been
and what remains to be,
and made the hearts of the people incline toward them!

2 Bless Muḥammad and his Household, the pure,
and act toward us with that of which Thou art worthy
in religion, in this world, and in the next world!
Thou art powerful over everything.[280]

[58]

His Supplication in Calling down Blessings upon Adam

1 O God,
as for Adam,
the marvel of Thy creation,
the first made of clay to confess Thy Lordship,
the beginning of Thy argument
against Thy servants and creatures,
the guide to seeking sanctuary in Thy pardon
from Thy punishment,
the opener of the paths of repentance toward Thee,
the giver of the creatures access to knowledge of Thee,

2 the one concerning whom Thou hast conveyed Thy good pleasure
through Thy kindness and Thy mercy toward him,

3 the one who turned back and did not persist in disobeying Thee,
the forerunner
among the self-abasers,
who shaved his head in Thy sacred precinct,
and among the seekers of access to Thy pardon,
through obedience after disobedience,
and the father of the prophets,
who were made to suffer for Thy sake
and who strove more than all the earth's inhabitants
in obeying Thee -

4 bless him, Thou - O All-merciful -
Thy angels
and the inhabitants of Thy heavens
and Thy earth,
just as he magnified Thy inviolable commands
and guided us upon the path of Thy good pleasure,
O Most Merciful of the merciful!

[59]

His Supplication (upon them be peace) in Distress and Seeking Release

1 My God,
let not my enemy gloat over me
and torment not my dear kinsman or friend through me!

2 My God,
of Thy glances, give me one glance, and thereby
remove from me
that by which Thou hast afflicted me
and return me to
the best of Thy customs with me!
Respond to my supplication
and the supplication of him who devotes his supplication
sincerely to Thee,
for my power has become frail,
my stratagems few,
my situation severe,
and I despair of what is with Thy creatures,
so nothing remains for me but hope in Thee!

3 My God,
surely Thy power to remove
that in which I dwell
is like Thy power in
that with which Thou hast afflicted me!
And surely the remembrance of Thy acts of kindliness
comforts me
and hope in Thy showing favour and Thy bounty
strengthens me,
for I have not been without Thy favour
ever since Thou created me.

4 And Thou, my God, art
my place of flight,
my asylum,
my protector,
my defender,

5 the loving toward me,
the compassionate,
and the guarantor of my provision.
In Thy decree lay what has settled upon me
and in Thy knowledge that to which I have come home.

6 So, my Patron and Master,
place within that which Thou hast
ordained,
decreed,
and made unavoidable for me,
my well-being
and that wherein lies
my soundness
and my deliverance from that in which I am!

7 I hope for none to repel this other than Thee,
and I rely in it only upon Thee.

8 O Possessor of majesty and munificence,
be with my best opinion of Thee![281]

9 Have mercy upon my frailty and the paucity of my stratagems,
remove my distress,
grant my supplication,
ease me from my stumble,
and show kindness to me in that
and to everyone who supplicates Thee!
My Master, Thou hast commanded me to supplicate
and undertaken to respond,[282]
and Thy promise is the truth
in which there is no failing,
nor any change.[283]

10 So bless Muḥammad Thy prophet and servant,
and the pure, the Folk of his House,
and help me,
surely Thou art
the help of him who has no help
and the stronghold of him who has no stronghold,
while I am the distressed
the response to whom and the removal of evil

from whom
Thou hast made obligatory![284]

11 So respond to me,
remove my concern,
relieve my gloom,
return my state to the best it has been,
and repay me not according to what I deserve,
but according to Thy mercy
which *embracest all things,*[285]
O Possessor of majesty and munificence!
Bless Muḥammad and the Household of Muḥammad,
hear, and respond,
O All-mighty!

[60]

His Supplication against that which he Feared and Dreaded[286]

1 My God,
nothing repels Thy wrath but Thy clemency,
nothing delivers from Thy punishment but Thy pardon,
nothing rescues from Thee but Thy mercy and pleading to Thee![287]

2 So give me, my God, relief by means of the power
through which Thou bringest the dead lands to life
and revivest the spirits of the servants![288]
Destroy me not,
and give me the knowledge of Thy response,
my Lord!
Raise me up and push me not down,
help me,
provide for me,
and release me from every blight!

3 My Lord,
if Thou raisest me up,
who will push me down?
If Thou pushest me down,
who will raise me up?
But I know, my God, that there is no wrong in Thy decree,
and no hurry in Thy vengeance.
He alone hurries who fears to miss,
and only the weak needs to wrong.
But Thou art exalted, my Master,
high indeed above all that!

4 My Lord,
make me not the target of affliction
nor the object of Thy vengeance,
respite me,
comfort me,
release me from my stumble,
and send not affliction after me,
for Thou hast seen my frailty,
and the paucity of my stratagems.

So give me patience,
for I, my Lord, am weak,
and I plead to Thee, my Lord!

5 'I seek refuge in Thee from Thee',
so give me refuge![289]

6 I seek sanctuary in Thee from every affliction,
so grant me sanctuary!

7 I cover myself through Thee,
so cover me, my Master,
from what I fear and dread!

8 Thou art the All-mighty,
mightier than every mighty thing!

9 Through Thee,
through Thee,
through Thee,
I cover myself.

10 O God, O God, O God,
O God, O God, O God,
O God, O God, O God,
O God!

Bless Muḥammad and his Household,
the good, the pure!

[61]

His Supplication (upon them be peace) in Abasing himself

1 My Master, my Master!
Thou art the Master and I the servant!
Has anyone mercy upon the servant
but the master?

2 My Master, my Master!
Thou art the Exalted and I the abased!
Has anyone mercy upon the abased
but the exalted?

3 My Master, my Master!
Thou art the Creator and I the creature!
Has anyone mercy upon the creature
but the creator?

4 My Master, My Master!
Thou art the Giver and I the asker!
Has anyone mercy upon the asker
but the giver?

5 My Master, My Master!
Thou art the Helper and I the seeker of help!
Has anyone mercy upon the seeker of help
but the helper?

6 My Master, My Master!
Thou art the Subsistent and I the perishing!
Has anyone mercy upon the perishing
but the subsistent?

7 My Master, My Master!
Thou art the Everlasting and I the vanishing!
Has anyone mercy upon the vanishing
but the everlasting?

8 My Master, My Master!
Thou art the Living and I the dead!
Has anyone mercy upon the dead

but the living?

9 My Master, My Master!
Thou art the Strong and I the weak!
Has anyone mercy upon the weak
but the strong?

10 My Master, My Master!
Thou art the Rich and I the poor!
Has anyone mercy upon the poor
but the rich?

11 My Master, My Master!
Thou art the Great and I the small!
Has anyone mercy upon the small
but the great?

12 My Master, My Master!
Thou art the Owner and I the owned!
Has anyone mercy upon the owned
but the owner?

His Supplications for the Days of the Week

[62]

The Supplication for Sunday

In the Name of God, the All-merciful,
the All-compassionate

1 In the name of God,
from whom I hope for nothing but bounty,
and from whom I fear nothing but justice!
I rely only upon His word,
and I cling only to His cord!

2 In Thee I seek sanctuary
- O Possessor of pardon and good pleasure -
from wrong and enmity,
from the changes of time and the recurrence of sorrows,
from the striking of mishaps,
and from the expiration of my term
before preparation and readiness.

3 From Thee I seek guidance
to that wherein is righteousness and being set right.

4 From Thee I seek help
in that which is linked to success and favourable response.

5 Thee I beseech
for the garment of well-being
and its completion
and for the covering of health
and its permanence.
I seek refuge in Thee, my Lord,
from the goadings of the satans,
and I seek protection in Thy sovereignty
from the injustice of the sovereigns.
So accept my past prayers and fasting
and make my tomorrow and what is after
better than my present hour and my today!

Exalt me in my clan and my people
and protect me in my waking and my sleeping!
For Thou art *God, the Best Guardian,*
and Thou art *the Most Merciful of the merciful.*[290]

6 O God,
I am quit before Thee
on this day of mine
and on all Sundays that follow it
of associating others with Thee and of heresy,
and I devote my supplication sincerely to Thee,
addressing myself to Thy response.

7 So bless Muḥammad and the Household of Muḥammad
the best of Thy creation,
the summoner to Thy truth,
exalt me with Thy exaltation,
which is never made to suffer loss,
protect me with Thy eye,
which never sleeps,
and seal
my affairs by cutting me off from everything but Thee
and my life with forgiveness!
Surely Thou art the All-forgiving,
the All-compassionate!

[63]

The Supplication for Monday

In the Name of God, the All-Merciful,
the All-compassionate

1 Praise belongs to God,
who allowed none to witness
when He created the heavens and the earth,
and who took no helper
when He authored the spirits!

2 He has no associate in Divinity
and no support in Unity.

3 Tongues fall silent before the limit of describing Him,
intellects fail before the core of knowing Him,
tyrants fall low in awe of Him,
faces are humbled in fear of Him,[291]
and everything mighty
yields to His mightiness!

4 So to Thee belongs praise,
again and again, well-measured,
continually, methodically!

5 And may His blessings be upon His Messenger endlessly,
His salutation everlastingly, eternally!

6 O God, make
the beginning of this day of mine righteousness,
its middle prosperity,
and its end success!
I seek refuge in Thee
from a day whose beginning is fright,
whose middle is anxiety,
and whose end is pain!

7 O God,
I pray forgiveness from Thee
for every vow I have vowed,
every promise I have promised,

and every pledge I have pledged
and then failed to keep for Thee.

8 I ask Thee concerning the complaints of Thy servants against me:
If there is a servant from among Thy servants
or a handmaid from among Thy handmaids,
who has against me
a complaint because I have wronged him in respect to
himself,
his reputation,
his property,
his wife or his child,
evil words I have spoken about him in his absence,
an imposition upon him through inclination,
caprice,
scorn,
zeal,
false show,
bigotry,
whether he be absent or present,
alive or dead,
such that my hand has fallen short
and my capacity has been too narrow
to make restitution to him
or to annul my obligation to him,

9 I ask Thee,
O He who owns all objects of need
- which are granted by His will
and hasten to His desire -
that Thou blessest Muḥammad and the Household of
Muḥammad,
makest [the one I have wronged] satisfied with me
in the manner that Thou willest,
and givest me mercy from Thee!
Forgiveness decreases Thee not
and giving injures Thee not,
O Most Merciful of the merciful!

10 O God,
give me on every Monday two favours from Thee:
the felicity to obey Thee

at its beginning
and the favour of Thy forgiveness
at its end!
O He who is God
and none other than whom grants forgiveness for sins!

[64]

The Supplication for Tuesday

In the Name of God, the All-merciful,
the All-compassionate

1 Praise belongs to God
- and praise is His right, since He deserves it -
abundant praise!

2 I seek refuge in Him from the evil of my soul,
for surely the soul commands to evil
except as my Lord has mercy.[292]

3 I seek refuge in Him from the evil of Satan
who adds sins to my sin.

4 I seek protection with Him from every wicked tyrant,
unjust sovereign,
and conquering enemy.

5 O God,
place me among Thy troops,
for Thy *troops - they are the victors,*[293]
place me in Thy party,
for Thy *party - they are the ones who prosper,*[294]
and place me among Thy friends,
for Thy *friends - no fear shall be upon them,*
nor shall they sorrow.[295]

6 O God,
set right for me my religion,
for it is the preserving tie of my affair,
set right for me my hereafter,
for it is the abode of my permanent lodging
and to it I flee from the neighbourhood of the vile!
Make life an increase for me in every good
and death an ease for me from every evil!

7 O God, bless
Muḥammad the Seal of the Prophets
and the completion of the number of the envoys,

his Household, the good, the pure,
and his Companions, the distinguished,
and give me on the Tuesday three things:

8 Leave
no sin for me unless Thou forgivest it,
no grief unless Thou takest it away,
and no enemy unless Thou repellest him!
By means of 'in the name of "God"', the best of the Names,
in the name of God, Lord of earth and heaven,

9 I seek to repulse every hateful thing,
the first of which is His anger,
and I seek to attract every loveable thing,
the first of which is His good pleasure!

10 So seal me with forgiveness from Thee,
O Patron of beneficence!

[65]

The Supplication for Wednesday

In the Name of God, the All-merciful,
the All-compassionate

1 Praise belongs to God,
who appointed the night to be a garment,
and sleep for a rest,
and day He appointed for a rising![296]

2 To Thee belongs praise,
for Thou roused me from my sleep,
- and hadst Thou willed,
Thou wouldst have made it everlasting -
an everlasting praise that will never be cut off
and whose number the creatures will never count!

3 O God,
to Thee belongs praise,
for Thou created, then proportioned,
ordained and decreed,
gave death and bestowed life,
made sick and healed,
made well and afflicted,
sat upon the Throne and encompassed the Kingdom![297]

4 I supplicate Thee with the supplication of one
whose mediation is weak,
whose stratagems have been cut off,
whose term has drawn near,
whose expectation from this world has shrunk,
whose neediness for Thy mercy has intensified,
whose remorse for his neglect has become great,
whose slips and stumbles have become many,
and whose repentance is devoted sincerely to Thy face.

5 So bless Muḥammad the Seal of the Prophets,
and his Household, the good, the pure,
provide me with the intercession of Muḥammad
(God bless him and his Household)

and deprive me not of his companionship!
Surely *Thou art the Most Merciful of the merciful*![298]

6 O God,
decree for me on Wednesday four things:
Induce me
to be strong in obedience to Thee,
to be joyful in worshipping Thee,
to be desirous of Thy reward,
and to abstain from that which would make incumbent upon me
Thy painful punishment!
Thou art Gentle to whom Thou wilt!

[66]

The Supplication for Thursday

In the Name of God, the All-merciful,
the All-compassionate

1 Praise belongs to God,
who has taken away the shadowy night by His power
and brought the sight-giving day through His mercy.
He has clothed me in its brightness
and given me its favour.

2 O God,
just as Thou hast spared me for this day,
so also spare me for its likes,
bless the prophet Muḥammad and his Household,
torment me not in it and in other nights and days
by allowing me to commit unlawful acts
and to clothe myself in sins;
provide me with its good,
the good of all within it,
and the good of everything after it;
and turn away from me its evil,
the evil of all within it,
and the evil of everything after it!

3 O God,
by the protective compact of Islam,
I seek mediation with Thee!
By the inviolability of the Qur'an,
I rely upon Thee!
By Muḥammad the chosen (God bless him and his Household)
I seek intercession with Thee!
So recognize my protective compact
by which I hope my need will be granted,
O Most Merciful of the merciful!

4 O God,
decree for me on Thursday five things
which none embraces but Thy generosity

and none supports but Thy favours:
health through which I may have the strength to obey Thee,
worship by which I may deserve Thy plentiful reward,
plenty in my state through lawful provision,
and that Thou
makest me secure in the places of fear
through Thy security,
and placest me in Thy fortress
against the striking of worries and sorrows!
Bless Muḥammad and his Household,
and make my seeking his mediation as an intercessor
give profit on the Day of Resurrection!
Surely *Thou art the Most Merciful of the merciful*![299]

[67]

The Supplication for Friday

In the Name of God, the All-Merciful,
the All-compassionate

1 All Praise belongs to God,
the First before the bringing forth and the giving of life,
and the Last after the annihilation of all things,
the All-knowing who forgets not him who remembers Him,[300]
decreases not him who thanks Him,[301]
disappoints not him who supplicates Him,
and cuts not off the hope of him who hopes in Him!

2 O God,
I call Thee to witness
- and Thou art sufficient witness - and I call to witness
all Thy angels,
the inhabitants of Thy heavens,
the bearers of Thy Throne,
Thy prophets and Thy messengers whom Thou hast
sent out,
and the various kinds of creatures Thou hast
brought forth,
that I bear witness
that Thou art God;
there is no god but Thou, Thou alone,
who hast no associate nor any equal,
and Thy word has no failing,
nor any change;[302]
and that Muḥammad (God bless him and his Household)
is Thy servant and Thy messenger;
he delivered to the servants
that with which Thou charged him,
he struggled for God as is His due,[303]
he gave the good news of the truth of reward,
and he warned of the veracity of punishment.

3 O God,

make me firm in Thy religion
as long as Thou keepest me alive,
make not my *heart to swerve*
after *Thou hast guided* me,
and give me *mercy from Thee,*
surely Thou art the Giver.[304]

Bless Muḥammad and the Household of Muḥammad
make me one of his followers and his partisans,
muster me in his band,
and give me the success of
accomplishing the obligatory observance of Friday,
performing the acts of obedience
which Thou has made incumbent upon me
within it,
and [receiving] the bestowal
which Thou hast apportioned for its people
on the Day of Recompense!
Surely Thou art Mighty, All-wise![305]

[68]

The Supplication for Saturday

In the Name of God, the All-merciful
the All-compassionate

1 'In the name of God',
the word of those who hold fast to Him,
the speech of those who seek His protection!
I seek refuge in God (high exalted is He) from
the injustice of the unjust,
the trickery of the enviers,
and the oppression of the wrongdoers,
and I praise Him beyond the praise of the praisers!

2 O God,
Thou art the One without partner,
and the King without having been made sovereign;
no one opposes Thee in Thy decree
and no one contests Thee in Thy kingdom!

3 I ask Thee to
bless Muḥammad and his Household,
Thy servant and Thy messenger,
inspire me with a thanksgiving for Thy favours
which will take me to the utmost limit of Thy good pleasure,
help me through the gentleness of Thy solitude to obey Thee,
hold fast to worshipping Thee,
and deserve Thy reward,
have mercy upon me,
bar me from acts of disobedience toward Thee
as long as Thou keepest me alive,
give me success in what profits me
as long as Thou sparest me,
expand my breast through Thy Book,
lessen my burden through its recitation,
bestow upon me health in my religion and my soul,
estrange not my intimates from me,
and complete Thy beneficence in what is left of my lifetime,
just as Thou hast shown beneficence
in that of it which has passed!
O Most Merciful of the merciful!

Fifteen Whispered Prayers
From the Words of Sayyid al-Sājidīn

[69] I

The Whispered Prayer of the Repenters

In the Name of God, the All-merciful,
the All-compassionate

1 My God, offences have clothed me
in the garment of my lowliness,
separation from Thee has wrapped me
in the clothing of my misery!
My dreadful crimes have deadened my heart,
so bring it to life by a repentance from Thee!
O my hope and my aim!
O my wish and my want!
By Thy might,
I find no one but Thee to forgive my sins
and I see none but Thee to mend my brokenness!
I have subjected myself to Thee in repeated turning,
I have humbled myself to Thee in abasement.
If Thou castest me out from Thy door,
in whom shall I take shelter?
If Thou repellest me from Thy side,
in whom shall I seek refuge?
O my grief at my ignominy and disgrace!
O my sorrow at my evil works and what I have committed!

2 I ask Thee, O Forgiver of great sins,
O Mender of broken bones,
to overlook my ruinous misdeeds
and cover my disgraceful secret thoughts!
At the witnessing place of the Resurrection,
empty me not
of the coolness of Thy pardon and forgiveness,
and strip me not
of Thy beautiful forbearance and covering!

3 My God,
let the cloud of Thy mercy cast its shadow
upon my sins
and send the billow of Thy clemency
flowing over my faults!

4 [My God,
dost a runaway slave return to anyone
except his Master,
or dost anyone grant him refuge from His anger
other than his Master!]

5 My God,
if remorse for sins is a repentance,[306]
I - by Thy might - am one of the remorseful!
If praying forgiveness for offences is an alleviation,
I am one of those who pray forgiveness!
To Thee I return
that Thou may be well pleased!

6 My God,
through Thy power over me,
turn toward me,
through Thy clemency toward me,
pardon me,
and through Thy knowledge of me,
be gentle toward me!

7 My God,
Thou art He who hast opened a door to Thy pardon
and named it 'repentance',
for Thou said,
Repent to God with unswerving repentance.[307]
What is the excuse
of him who remains heedless of entering the door
after its opening?

8 My God,
though the sins of Thy servant are ugly,
Thy pardon is beautiful.

9 My God,
I am not the first

to have disobeyed Thee,
and Thou turned toward him,
or to have sought to attain Thy favour,
and Thou wert munificent toward him.
O Responder to the distressed!
O Remover of injury!
O Great in goodness!
O Knower of everything secret!
O Beautiful through covering over!
I seek Thy munificence and Thy generosity
to intercede with Thee,
I seek Thy side and Thy showing mercy
to mediate with Thee,
so grant my supplication,
disappoint not my hope in Thee,
accept my repentance,
and hide my offense,
through Thy kindness and mercy,
O Most Merciful of the merciful!

[70] II

The Whispered Prayer of the Complainers

In the Name of God, the All-merciful,
the All-compassionate

1 My God,
to Thee I complain of a soul
commanding to evil,[308]
rushing to offences,
eager to disobey Thee,
and exposing itself to Thy anger.
It takes me on the roads of disasters,
it makes me the easiest of perishers before Thee;
many its pretexts,
drawn out its expectations;
when evil touches it,
it is anxious,
when good touches it,
grudging;[309]
inclining to sport and diversion,
full of heedlessness and inattention,
it hurries me to misdeeds
and makes me delay repentance.

2 My God,
I complain to Thee
of an enemy who misguides me
and a satan who leads me astray.
He has filled my breast with tempting thoughts,
and his suggestions have encompassed my heart.
He supports caprice against me,
embellishes for me the love of this world,
and separates me from obedience and proximity!

3 My God,
to Thee I complain
of a heart that is hard,
turned this way and that by tempting thoughts,
clothed in rust and the seal,[310]

and of an eye
too indifferent to weep in fear of Thee
and eagerly seeking that which gladdens it!

4 My God,
there is no force and no strength
except in Thy power,
and no deliverance for me from the detested things
of this world
save through Thy preservation.
So I ask Thee
by Thy far-reaching wisdom
and Thy penetrating will
not to let me expose myself to other than Thy munificence
and not to turn me into a target for trials!
Be for me
a helper against enemies,
a coverer of shameful things and faults,
a protector against afflictions,
a preserver against acts of disobedience!
By Thy clemency and mercy,
O Most Merciful of the merciful!

[71] III

The Whispered Prayer of the Fearful

In the Name of God, the All-merciful,
the All-compassionate

1 My God,
what thinkest Thou?
Wilt Thou chastise me after my faith in Thee,
drive me far away after my love for Thee,
deprive me while I hope for Thy mercy and forgiveness,
forsake me while I seek sanctuary in Thy pardon?
How could Thy generous face disappoint me?!
Would that I knew - Did my mother bear me for
wretchedness?
Did she nurture me for suffering?
Would then that she had not borne me
and had not nurtured me!
Would that I had knowledge -
Hast Thou appointed me one of the people of felicity?
Hast Thou singled me out for Thy nearness and
neighbourhood?
Then would my eyes be gladdened,
and in that my soul reach serenity.

2 My God,
dost Thou blacken faces which fall down in prostration
before Thy mightiness?
Dost Thou strike dumb tongues which speak in laudation
of Thy glory and majesty?
Dost Thou seal hearts which harbour Thy love?
Dost Thou deafen ears which take pleasure in hearing
Thy remembrance according to Thy will?
Dost Thou manacle hands which expectations have raised to
Thee
in hope of Thy clemency?
Dost Thou punish bodies which worked to obey Thee
until they grew thin in struggling for Thee?
Dost Thou chastise legs which ran to worship Thee?

3 My God,
lock not toward those who profess Thy Unity
the doors of Thy mercy,
and veil not those who yearn for Thee
from looking upon the vision of Thy beauty!

4 My God,
a soul which Thou hast exalted by its professing Thy Unity -
how wilt Thou burn it in the heat of Thy fires?

5 My God,
give me sanctuary
from Thy painful wrath
and Thy mighty anger!
O All-loving, O All-kind!
O Compassionate, O Merciful!
O Compeller, O Subduer!
O All-forgiver, O All-covering!
Deliver me through Thy mercy
from the chastisement of the Fire
and the disgrace of shame
when the good are set apart from the evil,
forms are transformed,
terrors terrify,
the good-doers are brought near,
the evildoers taken far,
and every soul is paid in full what it has earned,
and they shall not be wronged![311]

[72] IV

The Whispered Prayer of the Hopeful

In the Name of God, the All-merciful,
the All-compassionate

1 O He who
gives to a servant
who asks from Him,
takes him to his wish
when he expectantly hopes for what is with Him,
brings him near and close
when he approaches Him,
covers over his sin and cloaks it
when he shows it openly,
and satisfies and suffices him
when he has confidence in Him!

2 My God,
who is the one who has come before Thee
seeking hospitality,
and whom Thou hast not received hospitably?
Who is the one who has dismounted at Thy door
hoping for magnanimity,
and to whom Thou hast not shown it?
Is it good that I come back from Thy door,
turned away in disappointment,
while I know of no patron qualified by beneficence but Thee?
How should I have hope in other than Thee,
when the good - all of it - is in Thy hand?[312]
How should I expect from others,
when Thine are the creation and the command?[313]
Should I cut off my hope for Thee,
when Thou hast shown me of Thy bounty
that for which I have not asked?
Wouldst Thou make me have need for my like?
But I hold fast to Thy cord!
O He through whose mercy
the strivers reach felicity

and through whose vengeance
the seekers of forgiveness are not made wretched!
How should I forget Thee,
while Thou never ceasest remembering me?
How should I be diverted from Thee
while Thou art my constant watcher?

3 My God,
I have fastened my hand
to the skirt of Thy generosity,
I have stretched forth my expectation
toward reaching Thy gifts,
so render me pure through the purest profession of
Thy Unity,
and appoint me one of Thy choice servants!
O He who is the asylum of every fleer,
the hope of every seeker!
O Best Object of hope!
O Most Generous Object of supplication!
O He who does not reject His asker
or disappoint the expectant!
O He whose door is open to His supplicators
and whose veil is lifted for those who hope in Him!
I ask Thee by Thy generosity to show kindness toward me
through Thy gifts,
with that which will gladden my eye,
through hope in Thee,
with that which will give serenity to my soul,
and through certainty
with that which
will make easy for me the afflictions of
this world
and lift from my insight the veils of blindness!
By Thy mercy,
O Most Merciful of the merciful!

[73] V

The Whispered Prayer of the Beseechers

In the Name of God, the All-merciful,
the All-compassionate

1 My God,
though my stores for travelling to Thee are few,
my confidence in Thee has given me a good opinion.[314]
Though my sin has made me fear Thy punishment,
my hope has let me feel secure from Thy vengeance.
Though my misdeed has exposed me to Thy penalty,
my excellent trust has apprised me of Thy reward.
Though heedlessness has put to sleep my readiness to meet Thee,
knowledge has awakened me to Thy generosity and boons.
Though excessive disobedience and rebellion
have estranged me from Thee,
the glad tidings of forgiveness and good pleasure
have made me feel intimate with Thee.
I ask Thee by
the splendours of Thy face
and the lights of Thy holiness,
and I implore Thee by
the tenderness of Thy mercy
and the gentleness of Thy goodness,
to verify my opinion in expecting
Thy great generosity
and Thy beautiful favour,
through nearness to Thee,
proximity with Thee,
and enjoyment of gazing upon Thee!
Here am I,
addressing myself to the breezes
of Thy freshness and tenderness,
having recourse to the rain
of Thy generosity and gentleness,
fleeing from Thy displeasure to Thy good pleasure
and from Thee to Thee,[315]

hoping for the best of what is with Thee,
relying upon Thy gifts,
utterly poor toward Thy guarding!

2 My God,
Thy bounty which Thou hast begun - complete it!
Thy generosity which Thou hast given me - strip it not away!
Thy cover over me through Thy clemency - tear it not away!
My ugly acts which Thou hast come to know - forgive them!

3 My God,
I seek intercession from Thee with Thee,
and I seek sanctuary in Thee from Thee!
I have come to Thee
craving Thy beneficence,
desiring Thy kindness,
seeking water from the deluge of Thy graciousness,
begging rain from the clouds of Thy bounty,
requesting Thy good pleasure,
going straight to Thy side,
arriving at the watering-place of Thy support,
seeking exalted good things from Thy quarter,
reaching for the presence of Thy beauty,
wanting Thy face,
knocking at Thy door,
abasing myself before Thy mightiness and majesty!
So act toward me with the forgiveness and mercy
of which Thou art worthy!
Act not toward me with the chastisement and vengeance
of which I am worthy!
By Thy mercy,
O Most Merciful of the merciful!

[74] VI

The Whispered Prayer of the Thankful

In the Name of God, the All-merciful,
the All-compassionate

1 My God,
the uninterrupted flow of Thy graciousness
hast distracted me from thanking Thee!
The flood of Thy bounty has rendered me incapable
of counting Thy praises!
The succession of Thy kind acts has diverted me
from mentioning Thee in laudation!
The continuous rush of Thy benefits has thwarted me
from spreading the news of Thy gentle favours!
This is the station of him who
confesses to the lavishness of favours,
meets them with shortcomings,
and witnesses to his own disregard and negligence.
Thou art the Clement, the Compassionate,
the Good, the Generous,
who does not disappoint those who aim for Him,
nor cast out from His courtyard those who expect from Him!
In Thy yard are put down the saddlebags of the hopeful
and in Thy plain stand the hopes of the help-seekers!
So meet not our hopes by disappointing and disheartening
and clothe us not in the shirt of despair and despondency!

2 My God,
my thanksgiving is small
before Thy great boons,
and my praise and news-spreading shrink
beside Thy generosity toward me!
Thy favours have wrapped me
in the robes of the lights of faith,
and the gentlenesses of Thy goodness have let down over me
delicate curtains of might!
Thy kindnesses

have collared me with collars not to be moved
and adorned me with neck-rings not to be broken!
Thy boons are abundant -
my tongue is too weak to count them!
Thy favours are many -
my understanding falls short of grasping them,
not to speak of exhausting them!
So how can I achieve thanksgiving?
For my thanking Thee requires thanksgiving.
Whenever I say, 'To Thee belongs praise!',
it becomes thereby incumbent upon me to say,
' To Thee belongs praise'!

3 My God,
as Thou hast fed us through Thy gentleness
and nurtured us through Thy benefaction,
so also complete for us lavish favours,
repel from us detested acts of vengeance,
and of the shares of the two abodes,
give us their most elevated and their greatest,
both the immediate and the deferred!
To Thee belongs praise
for Thy good trial and the lavishness of Thy favours,
a praise
conforming to Thy good pleasure
and attracting Thy great goodness and magnanimity.
O All-mighty,
O All-generous!
By Thy mercy,
O Most Merciful of the merciful!

[75] VII

The Whispered Prayer of the Obedient Toward God

In the Name of God, the All-merciful,
the All-compassionate

1 O God,
inspire us to obey Thee,
turn us aside from disobeying Thee,
make it easy for us to reach
the seeking of Thy good pleasure which we wish,
set us down in the midst of Thy Gardens,
dispel from our insights the clouds of misgiving,
uncover from our hearts the wrappings of doubt and the veil,
make falsehood vanish from our innermost minds,
and fix the truth in our secret thoughts,
for doubts and opinions fertilize temptations
and muddy the purity of gifts and kindnesses!

2 O God,
carry us in the ships of Thy deliverance,
give us to enjoy the pleasure of whispered prayer to Thee,
make us drink at the pools of Thy love,
let us taste the sweetness of Thy affection and nearness,
allow us to struggle in Thee,[316]
preoccupy us with obeying Thee,
and purify our intentions in devoting works to Thee,
for we exist through Thee and belong to Thee,
and we have no one to mediate with Thee but Thee!

3 My God,
place me among the chosen, the good,
Join me to
the righteous,
the pious,
the first to reach generous gifts,
the swift to come upon good things,
the workers of the abiding acts of righteousness,
the strivers after elevated degrees!
Thou art powerful over everything[317]
and disposed to respond!
By Thy mercy, O Most Merciful of the merciful!

[76] VIII

The Whispered Prayer of the Devotees

In the Name of God, the All-merciful,
the All-compassionate

1 Glory be to Thee!
How narrow are the paths
for him whom Thou hast not guided!
How plain the truth
for him whom Thou hast guided on his way!

2 My God,
so make us travel
on the roads that arrive at Thee
and set us into motion
on the paths nearest to reaching Thee!
Make near for us the far,
and make easy for us the hard and difficult!
Join us to Thy servants, those who
hurry to Thee swiftly,
knock constantly at Thy door,
and worship Thee by night and by day,
while they remain apprehensive in awe of Thee!
Thou hast purified their drinking places,
taken them to the objects of their desire,
granted their requests,
accomplished their wishes through Thy bounty,
filled their minds with Thy love,
and quenched their thirst with Thy pure drink.
Through Thee have they reached
the pleasure of whispered prayer to Thee,
and in Thee have they achieved
their furthest goals.
O He who
comes toward those who come toward Him
and grants gifts and bestows bounty upon them
through tenderness!
He is compassionate and clement toward those
heedless of His remembrance
and loving and tender in drawing them to His door!
I ask Thee to place me among those of them who have

the fullest share from Thee,
the highest station with Thee,
the most plentiful portion of Thy love,
and the most excellent allotment of Thy knowledge,
for my aspiration has been cut off from everything but Thee
and my desire has turned toward Thee alone.
Thou art my object, none other;
to Thee alone belongs my waking and my sleeplessness.
Meeting Thee is the gladness of my eye,
joining Thee the wish of my soul.
Toward Thee is my yearning,
in love for Thee my passionate longing,
in inclining toward Thee my fervent craving.
Thy good pleasure is the aim I seek,
vision of Thee my need,
Thy neighbourhood my request,
nearness to Thee the utmost object of my asking.
In whispered prayer to Thee
I find my repose and my ease.
With Thee lies the remedy of my illness,
the cure for my burning thirst,
the coolness of my ardour,
the removal of my distress.
Be my intimate in my loneliness,
the releaser of my stumble,
the forgiver of my slip,
the accepter of my repentance,
the responder to my supplication,
the patron of preserving me from sin,
the one who frees me from my neediness!
Cut me not off from Thee
and keep me not far from Thee!
O my bliss and my garden!
O my this world and my hereafter!
O Most Merciful of the merciful!

[77] IX

The Whispered Prayer of the Lovers

In the Name of God, the All-merciful,
the All-compassionate

1 My God,
who can have tasted the sweetness of Thy love,
then wanted another in place of Thee?
Who can have become intimate with Thy nearness,
then sought removal from Thee?

2 My God, place us with him
whom Thou hast
chosen for Thy nearness and Thy friendship,
purified through Thy affection and Thy love,
given yearning for the meeting with Thee,
made pleased with Thy decree,
granted gazing upon Thy face,
shown the favour of Thy good pleasure,
given refuge from separation from Thee and
Thy loathing,
settled in a sure sitting place in Thy neighbourhood,
singled out for true knowledge of Thee,
made worthy for worship of Thee,
whose heart Thou hast captivated with Thy will,
whom Thou hast picked for contemplating Thee,
whose look Thou hast made empty for Thee,
whose breast Thou hast freed for Thy love,
whom Thou hast made
desirous of what is with Thee,
inspired with Thy remembrance,
allotted thanksgiving to Thee,
occupied with obeying Thee,
turned into one of Thy righteous creatures,
chosen for whispered prayer to Thee,
and from whom Thou hast cut off all things
which cut him off from Thee!

3 O God,
place us among those
whose habit is rejoicing in Thee and yearning for Thee,
whose time is spent in sighing and moaning!
Their foreheads are bowed down before Thy mightiness,
their eyes wakeful in Thy service,
their tears flowing in dread of Thee,
their hearts fixed upon Thy love,
their cores shaken with awe of Thee.
O He
the lights of whose holiness
induce wonder in the eyes of His lovers,
the glories of whose face
arouse the longing of the hearts of His knowers!
O Furthest Wish of the hearts of the yearners!
O Utmost Limit of the hopes of the lovers!
I ask from Thee love for Thee,
love for those who love Thee,
love for every work which will join me to Thy nearness,
and that Thou makest Thyself more beloved to me
than anything other than Thee
and makest
my love for Thee
lead to Thy good pleasure,
and my yearning for Thee
protect against disobeying Thee!
Oblige me by allowing me to gaze upon Thee,
gaze upon me with the eye of affection and tenderness,
turn not Thy face away from me,
and make me one of the people of happiness with Thee
and favoured position!
O Responder,
O Most Merciful of the merciful!

[78] X

The Whispered Prayer of those Asking for Mediation

In the Name of God, the All-merciful,
the All-compassionate

1 My God,
I have no mediation with Thee
but the tender acts of Thy clemency,
nor any way to come to Thee
but the gentle favours of Thy mercy
and the intercession of Thy Prophet,
the prophet of mercy,
who rescued the community from confusion.
Make these two my tie to attaining Thy forgiveness
and let them take me to triumph through Thy good pleasure!
My hope has dismounted
in the sacred precinct of Thy generosity,
my craving has alighted
in the courtyard of Thy munificence.
So actualize my expectation from Thee,
seal my works with good,
and place me among Thy selected friends, those
whom Thou hast set down
in the midst of Thy Garden,
and settled in the abode of Thy honour,
whose eyes Thou hast gladdened
by gazing upon Thee
on the day of meeting Thee,
and whom Thou hast made heirs to
the sure stations in Thy neighbourhood!

2 O He
none more generous than whom is reached by the reachers
and none more merciful than whom is found by the aimers!
O Best of those with whom the lonely are alone,
O Tenderest of those with whom outcasts seek haven!
Toward the expanse of Thy pardon have I extended my hand,

upon the skirt of Thy generosity have I fastened my grasp!

Show me no deprivation
and afflict me not with disappointment and loss!

O Hearer of supplications!
O Most Merciful of the merciful!

[79] XI

The Whispered Prayer of the Utterly Poor

In the Name of God, the All-merciful,
the All-compassionate

1 My God,
nothing will
mend my fracture but Thy gentleness and loving care,
free me of my poverty but Thy affection and beneficence,
still my fright but Thy security,
exalt my abasement but Thy sovereignty,
take me to my hope but Thy bounty,
remedy my lack but Thy graciousness,
accomplish my need other than Thou,
relieve my distress other than Thy mercy,
remove my injury other than Thy clemency,
cool my burning thirst but reaching Thee,
quench my ardour but meeting Thee,
damp my yearning but gazing upon Thy face,
settle my settling place without closeness to Thee,
allay my worry but Thy repose,
cure my illness but Thy medicine,
eliminate my grief but Thy nearness,
heal my wound but Thy forgiveness,
remove the rust on my heart but Thy pardon,
banish the confusing thoughts from my breast but
Thy command!

2 O Utmost Hope of the hopers!
O Ultimate Demand of the askers!
O Furthest Request of the requesters!
O Highest Desire of the desirers!
O Patron of the righteous!
O Security of the fearful!
O Responder to the supplication of the distressed!
O Storehouse of the destitute!
O Treasure of the pitiful!
O Help of the help-seekers!
O Accomplisher of the needs of the poor and the miserable!

O Most Generous of the most generous!
O Most Merciful of the merciful!
To Thee is my humble subjection and request,
to Thee my pleading and imploring!
I ask Thee
to let me attain
the repose of Thy good pleasure,
and to make constant toward me
the favours of Thy kindness!
Here am I,
standing before the gate of Thy generosity,
opening myself up to the breezes of Thy goodness,
holding fast to Thy strong cord,
clinging to Thy firm handle!

3 My God,
have mercy upon Thy lowly slave
of silent tongue and few good works,
obligate him through Thy plentiful graciousness,
shelter him under Thy plenteous shade!
O Generous, O Beautiful,
O Most Merciful of the merciful!

[80] XII

The Whispered Prayer of the Knowers

In the Name of God, the All-merciful,
the All-compassionate

1 My God,
tongues fall short of attaining
praise of Thee proper to Thy majesty,
intellects are incapable of grasping
the core of Thy beauty,
eyes fail before gazing
upon the glories of Thy face,
and Thou hast assigned to Thy creatures
no way to know Thee
save incapacity to know Thee!

2 My God,
place us among those
within the gardens of whose breasts
the trees of yearning for Thee have taken firm root
and the assemblies of whose hearts
have been seized by the ardour of Thy love!
They seek shelter
in the nests of meditation,
feed upon the gardens
of nearness and disclosure,
drink from the pools of love
with the cup of gentle favour,
and enter into the watering-places
of warm affection.
The covering has been lifted
from their eyes,[318]
the darkness of disquiet has been dispelled
from their beliefs and their innermost minds,
the contention of doubt has been negated
from their hearts and their secret thoughts,
their breasts have expanded
through the verification of true knowledge,
their aspirations have ascended

through precedent good fortune in renunciation,
their drinking is sweet
from the spring of devotion to good works,
their secret thoughts are delicious
in the sitting-place of intimacy,
their minds are secure
in the place of terror,
their souls are serene
through the return to the Lord of lords,[319]
their spirits have reached certitude
through triumph and prosperity,
their eyes have been gladdened
through gazing upon their Beloved,
their settling place has been settled
through reaching the request and attaining the expectation,
and their commerce has profited
through the sale of this world for the next!

3 My God,
how agreeable for hearts are
the thoughts inspiring Thy remembrance,
how sweet
travelling to Thee through imagination
upon the roads of the unseen worlds,
how pleasant
the taste of Thy love,
how delightful
the drink of Thy nearness!
So give us refuge from Thy casting out and Thy sending far,
and place us among
the most elect of Thy knowers,
the most righteous of Thy servants,
the most truthful of Thy obeyers,
the most sincere of Thy worshipers!
O All-mighty, O Majestic,
O Generous, O Endower!
By Thy mercy and kindness,
O Most Merciful of the merciful!

[81] XIII

The Whispered Prayer of the Rememberers

In the Name of God, the All-merciful,
the All-compassionate

1 My God,
were it not incumbent to accept Thy command,
I would declare Thee far too exalted for me to remember Thee,
for I remember Thee in my measure,
not in Thy measure,
and my scope can hardly reach the point
where I may be a locus for calling Thee holy!
Among Thy greatest favours to us
is the running of Thy remembrance across our tongues
and Thy permission to us
to supplicate Thee,
declare Thee exalted,
and call Thee holy!

2 My God,
inspire us with Thy remembrance
alone and in assemblies,
by night and day,
publicly and secretly,
in prosperity and adversity!
Make us intimate with silent remembrance,
employ us in purified works and effort pleasing to Thee,
and reward us with the full balance!

3 My God,
love-mad hearts are enraptured by Thee,
disparate intellects are brought together by knowing Thee,
hearts find no serenity except in remembering Thee,[320]
souls find no rest except in seeing Thee.
Thou art the glorified in every place,
the worshipped at every time,
the found at every moment,
the called by every tongue,
the magnified in every heart!

I pray forgiveness from Thee for
every pleasure but remembering Thee,
every ease but intimacy with Thee,
every happiness but nearness to Thee,
every occupation but obeying Thee!

4 My God,
Thou hast said - and Thy word is true -
O you who have faith,
remember God with much remembrance
and glorify Him at dawn and in the evening![321]
Thou hast said - and Thy word is true -
Remember Me, and I will remember you![322]
Thou hast commanded us to remember Thee,
and promised us that Thou wilt remember us thereby,
in order to ennoble, respect, and honour us.
Here we are, remembering Thee as Thou hast commanded us!
So accomplish what Thou hast promised,
O Rememberer of the rememberers!
O Most Merciful of the merciful!

[82] XIV

The Whispered Prayer of those who Hold Fast

In the Name of God, the All-merciful,
the All-compassionate

1 O God,
O Shelter of the shelter-seekers!
O Refuge of the refuge-seekers!
O Deliverer of the perishing!
O Preserver of the pitiful!
O Merciful toward the miserable!
O Responder to the distressed!
O Treasure of the utterly poor!
O Mender of the broken!
O Haven of the cut off!
O Helper of the abased!
O Granter of sanctuary to the fearful!
O Aider of the troubled!
O Fortress of the refugees!
If I seek not refuge in Thy might,
in whom shall I seek refuge?
If I seek not shelter in Thy power,
in whom shall I seek shelter?
Sins have made me seek asylum in laying hold
on the skirts of Thy pardon,
offences have compelled me to beg the opening
of the doors of Thy forgiveness,
evildoing has summoned me to dismount
in the courtyard of Thy might,
fear of Thy vengeance has prompted me
to cling to the handhold of Thy tenderness!
It is not right for him who holds fast to Thy cord
to be abandoned,
nor proper for him who seeks the sanctuary of Thy might
to be surrendered or disregarded.
My God,
empty us not of Thy defending,
strip us not of Thy guarding,
and protect us from the roads of destruction,

for we are in Thy eye and under Thy wing!

I ask Thee

by those whom Thou hast singled out,

Thy angels and the righteous among Thy creatures,

to assign over us a protector through which Thou wilt

deliver us from destructions,

turn aside from us blights,

and hide us from the striking of great afflictions,

to send down upon us some of Thy tranquillity,

to wrap our faces in the lights of love for Thee,

to give us haven in Thy strong

pillar,[323] and to gather us under the wings of Thy preservation!

By Thy clemency and Thy mercy,

O Most Merciful of the merciful!

[83] XV

The Whispered Prayer of the Abstainers

In the Name of God, the All-merciful,
the All-compassionate

1 My God,
Thou hast settled us in an abode
which has dug for us pits of deception,
and Thou hast fastened us by the hands of death
in the snares of that abode's treachery!
In Thee we seek asylum
from the tricks of its guile,
and to Thee we hold fast, lest we be deluded
by the glitter of its ornaments!
It destroys its pursuers
and ruins its settlers,
it is stuffed with blights
and loaded with calamities.

2 My God,
induce us to renounce it
and keep us safe from it
by Thy giving success and Thy preservation from sin.
Strip from us
the robes of opposing Thee,
attend to our affairs
through Thy good sufficiency,
amplify our increase
from the boundless plenty of Thy mercy,
be liberal in our gifts
from the overflow of Thy grants,
plant in our hearts
the trees of Thy love,
complete for us
the lights of Thy knowledge,
give us to taste
the sweetness of Thy pardon
and the pleasure of Thy forgiveness,
gladden our eyes

on the day of meeting Thee
with the vision of Thee,
dislodge the love of this world
from our spirits,
just as Thou hast done for the righteous,
Thy selected friends,
and for the pious,
those whom Thou hast singled out!
O Most Merciful of the merciful,
O Most Generous of the most generous!

NOTES TO THE TRANSLATION

1.Sayyid Najm al-Dīn is not known other than in this text, but the commentators point out that this has no negative effect on the chain since the text is *mutawātir* and of unquestioned authority. This is a chain of permission and not of transmission; in other words, the text it self has reached us by many different routes, but permission the teach the present text itself has reached us by many different routes, but permission to teach the present text in this exact form was handed down by the figures being mentioned. The reason this particular chain is mentioned was suggested in the introduction. I would add that it is inconceivable that this is a deliberate forgery, since no forger can be so incompetent. Of the twelve mentioned (at the beginning and in the second chain to the end of the preface), five are unknown, four cannot be identified with certainty, and one is known to have unreliable.

2. There is some confusion as to the identity of the 'us' at the beginning of the chain, because it might be either of two scholars who figure in the various chains of transmission of the *Ṣaḥīfa.* Shaykh- i Bahā'ī one of the many authors of commentaries on the *Ṣaḥīfa* maintains that 'us' refers to 'Alī ibn al-Sukūn (that is, Abu I-Ḥasan 'Alī ibn Muḥammad ibn Muḥammad ibn 'Alī ibn Muḥammad ibn Muḥammad ibn al-Sukūn al- Ḥillī ' d *.c* 606/109). In his glosses on the *Ṣaḥīfa* , Mīr Dāmād writes that it is 'Amīd al-Ru'asā' Hibat Allāh ibn Ḥāmid ibn Aḥmad ibn Ayyūb al-Ḥillī (d. 610 / 1213-14). To prove this point he quotes manuscript of al-Shahīd al- Awwal, who had collated his copy with that of Ibn al-Sukūn, on which 'Amīd al- Ru'asā' has made certain annotations in the year 603/1206. Cf. Āqā Buzurg, *al-Dharī 'a s.v. Al-Ṣaḥīfat l-Sajjādiyya.*

3. He was the son-in-law of Shaykh al-Ṭā'ifa Abū Ja'far al-Ṭūsī (d. 460/1067-8) and an official shrine of 'Alī in Najaf.

4. Sayyid 'Alīkhān writes that al-'Ukbarī does not seem to be mentioned in the books of Shi'ite biographies, but al-Sam'ānī mentions in his *al-Ansāb (* adding al-Ḥusayn to his name after ibn Aḥmad) and gives his date of death as 472/1079-80.

5. Sayyid 'Alīkhān quotes four sources on Abū l-Mufaḍḍal as a *muḥaddith,* all of which question his reliability: Najāshī, Shaykh al-Ṭā' ifa al-Ṭūsī, Ibn al-Ghaḍā'irī, and Ibn Dāwūd.

6. Najāshī praises his reliability and mentions a number of works by him. He died in 308/921 at the age of more than ninety (Sayyid 'Alīkhān).

7. According to Sayyid 'Alīkhān, nothing is known about him. In his notes on his Persian translation, Sha'rānī suggests that here some of the authorities originally mentioned in the text may have been dropped, since only three figures are mentioned over a period of 251 years.

8. Najāshī mentions an 'Alī ibn al-Nu'mān al-A'lam al-Nakha'ī who was a companion of the eighth Imam, Riḍā (d. 203/818).

9. Neither 'Umayr ibn Mutawakkil nor his father Mutawakkil ibn Hārūn are known. However both Najāshī and Shaykh al-Ṭūsī speak of al-Mutawakkil ibn 'Umayr ibn al-Mutawakkil as the transmitter of the *Ṣaḥīfa* from Yaḥya ibn Zayd, and they provide a chain of authority leading from him to themselves different from that in the present text. As Sha'rānī points out (*Ṣaḥīfa*, p. 5), given their early dates and their agreement, the name they provide is to be preferred over the Present text.

10. This would have been in the year 122/740. As explained in the introduction, after the death of Zayn al-Ābidīn's son and successor, Muhammad al-Bāqir, his son Zayd revolted against the Umayyad authorities and was killed. According to the account being related here, Mutawakkil ibn Hārūn (or more properly, Mutawakkil ibn 'Umayr) met Zayd's son Yaḥya shortly before he was killed while continuing his father's revolt.

11. 13:39. According to Sayyid 'Alīkhān, by quoting this verse, Yaḥya is suggesting that even if this is the divine command known to al-Ṣādiq, God may change it. This is the Shi'ite doctrine of *badā'*, according to which God may appear to change His decree for His creatures. Imam Ja'far himself quotes this verse to prove the possibility of *badā'*.

12. As noted in the introduction, the use here of the expression *Al- Ṣaḥīfat al-kāmila* suggests that the *Ṣaḥīfa* was called by this term from earliest times. In explaining the expression, Sayyid 'Alīkhān quotes a passage employing it from *Ma'ālim al-'ulamā'* of Ibn Shahrāshūb (d. 588/1192).

13. In notes to his Persian translation, Sha'rānī tells us that the term meant a scroll wound around an iron rod, on the ends of which were placed iron locks, often sealed with wax.

14. Muhammad is better known as al-Nafs al-Zakiyya. He was designated as the Mahdī by his father and many swore allegiance to him, including al-Manṣūr, who later became the first Abbasid caliph. Muḥammad and Ibrāhīm revolted with a good deal of popular support when the 'Abbasids tried to make them accept their authority. Muḥammad, who was supported by the people of Medina, was killed in a fierce battle in 145/762, and Ibrāhīm, who was supported by the Zaydite and Mu'tazilite circles of Kufa and Basra, was killed a few months later. Cf. Ja'farī, *The Origins and Early Development*, pp. 269-71, 275-6.

15. Ismā'īl was the eldest son of Imam Ja'far and his designated successor. However, he died before his father, who then appointed his second son Mūsā as the Imam after himself. The Ismā'īlis follow Ismā'īl as Imam rather than Mūsā maintaining that the former's appointment was valid and that the imamate remained in his family.

16. 4:58.

17. An oft-repeated formula found in many *ḥadīth.*

18. 17:60. The Qur'ān commentators offer at least three possible interpretations for this vision. Concerning the third, Bayḍāwī writes 'It is also said that the Prophet saw a group of the Umayyads climbing his pulpit and jumping upon it like monkeys. So he said "This is their share of this world; they will be given it for accepting Islam". According to this interpretation, what is meant by *a trial for men* is what happened during their time' *(Anwār al-tanzīl,* commentary on 17:60). The Shī'ite commentator Ṭabarsi also offers this as a third possibility, providing two *ḥadīth* to support it *(Majma' al-bayān).* Sayyid 'Alīkhān quotes from Bayḍāwī and others to support this interpretation, while offering Ibn 'Abbās among others as authority for the statement that the 'accursed tree' refers to the Umayyads.

19. 97:1-3. Tirmidhī offers a *ḥadīth* going back to al-Ḥasan ibn 'Alī that supports this interpretation of one thousand months as referring to the Umayyads (Tafsīr sūra 97, 1).

20. 14:28-9.

21. i.e., the Twelfth Imam, he who will 'stand up' *(Qā'im)* in the Truth for the Truth and defeat the enemies of the Truth.

22. The speaker here is al-'Ukbarī (above, verse 3), who is now relating another chain through which he received the *Ṣaḥīfa* from Abū l-Mufaḍḍal (verse 3).

23. He is unknown in the books of biography.

24. He is also unknown.

25. In other words, the chapter headings as mentioned in the text, which are often slightly different from the chapter headings mentioned above, are in al-Ḥasanī's words (that is, al-Sharīf Abū 'Abd Allāh, mentioned in verse 4).

26. Here again by 'us' is meant al-'Ukbarī.

27. 53:31.

28. 21:23.

29. Allusion to 89:15: *As for man, whenever his Lord tries him, and honours him, and favours him....*

30. 25:46.

31. The interworld *(barzakh)* is the abode in which a person dwells between death and the Day of Resurrection.

32. The Witnesses, mentioned in 11: 20 and 40:54, are the angels, prophets, Imams, and faithful whom God appoints to give witness concerning the deeds of men at the Resurrection.

33. 45:21.

34. 44:41.

35. 'Illīyūn', mentioned in 83:18 and 19, and deriving from a root meaning 'high' or 'exalted', is said to be the highest level of paradise, or a book in paradise wherein the deeds of the righteous are recorded.

36. 83:20-21.

37. Cf. 75:7.

38. Cf. 3:106.

39. Several Qur'ānic verses mention the fact that God has subjected everything in the heavens and the earth to mankind, e.g., 14:33, 16:12, 31:20, 45:13.

40. Cf. 2:286: *Our Lord, charge us not with a load such as Thou didst lay upon those before us.*

41. 2:286.

42. Allusion to such passages as 2:286: *God charges no soul save to its capacity.*

43. Allusion to 9:33 and 61:9: *It is He who has sent His Messenger with the guidance and the religion of truth, that He may uplift it above every religion though the idolaters be averse.*

44. As Sayyid 'Alīkhān points out, there is an allusion here to the *ḥadīth* of 'mediation' *(wasīla)* according to one version of which the Prophet said: 'Mediation is a degree with God in the Garden, and there is no degree higher than it, so pray to God to give me the mediation' (Aḥmad III, 83). The fact that this is what the Imam has in mind is confirmed by his reference to 'intercession' in verse 25 (on the relationship between these two, cf. note 172).

45. On the Prophet's intercession, cf. Pad wick, *Muslim Devotions* pp. 37 ff. and *Encyclopaedia of Islam* (old edition), 'Shafā'a'. The commentator points out here that the Prophet's intercession alluded to in the Qur'ān as his 'praiseworthy station' (17:79) - will be of several types, including the raising of those who are already in paradise to higher degrees. Hence there is no contradiction between the sinlessness of the Imams on the one hand and the Prophet's interceding for them on the other.

46. Cf. 25:70: On Resurrection Day... *God will change the evil deeds [of those who repent, have faith, and do righteous works] into good deeds.*

47. The bearers of the Throne are said to be four angels, one on each corner of the Throne, who will be aided by four more on the Day of Resurrection. Hence the Qur'ān says: *Upon that day eight shall bear above them the Throne of thy Lord* (69: I7). On the various kinds of angels, see S. Murata, 'The Angels,' in S.H. Nasr (ed.), *Islamic Spirituality: Foundations* New York, 1987, pp. 324-44.

48. Cf. 81:20.

49. The veils meant here are those referred to in the *ḥadīth* often quoted in Sunni sources: 'God has seventy' - or 'seventy thousand' – 'veils of light and darkness; were they to be removed, the glories of His face would incinerate everything perceived by the creatures' eyes.' Shi'ite sources add several parallel *ḥadīth* from the Prophet and the Imams (see *Biḥār al-Anwār* v, 39-47, Bāb al-ḥūjūb wa l-astār wa l-surādiqāt). Cf. Supplication 50.5, where mention is made of God's 'splendour masked by the veils'.

50. Cf. 17:85.

51. Cf. 69:17.

52. Cf. 80:16.

53. i.e., the scribes and writers who record peoples' deeds in this world, cf. 82:11.

54. The two angels, mentioned in many *ḥadīth* who question the dead on the first night in the grave.

55. An angel who, according to some *ḥadīth* is the first to enter the grave with the dead person, telling him to write out his deeds on his shroud with his saliva as ink and his finger as pen.

56. A house in the celestial spheres mentioned in 52:4 and located directly above the Ka'ba.

57. The angel in charge of the Fire.

58. The angel in charge of paradise.

59. 66:6.

60. 13:24.

61. 69:30.

62. Cf. 16:85.

63. 50:21; the *driver* and *witness* are also angels.

64. 35:29.

65. 59:10.

66. The Qur'ān often mentions God's scheming and devising, usually in answer to the trickery and deception of the evildoers. For example: *They are scheming, and I am scheming. So respite the unbelievers; delay with them for a time* (86:15); *they devised, and God devised, and God is the best of devisers* (3:54).

67. God's protecting the servant from Himself is for Him to guard him against His wrath. 'Guidance to God' is guidance to His mercy, while being taken 'far from Him' is to be subjected to wrath. Cf. the introduction and passages such as 48.13 and 73.1.

68. 10:67.

69. 17:12.

70. Allusion to 47:31: We shall assuredly try you until we know those of you who struggle and are steadfast, and try your records.

71. 53:31.

72. Allusion to 6:96: *He splits the sky into dawn.*

73. Cf. above, 3.18.

74. Allusion to Satan's words in the Qur'ān (7:17): I shall come on them from before them and from behind them, from their rights hands and their left hands; Thou wilt not find most of them thankful.

75. 2:207.

76. 3:26.

77. The term 'caprice' denotes any desire that is opposed to the truth or turns man away from the divine guidance. *Who is further astray than he who follows his own caprice without guidance from God?* (28:50) *Obey not him whose heart We have made heedless of Our remembrance, so that he follows his own caprice* (18:28). God addresses David with the command: *Judge among men by the truth, and follow not caprice* (38:26).

78. Reference to 12:53: Surely the soul of man commands to evil, except inasmuch as my Lord has mercy.

79. Allusion to 30:54: *God is He who created you of frailty.*

80. 77:20.

81. Reference to 27:62: *He who responds to the distressed when he supplicates Him, and removes the evil.*

82. Allusion to the principle enunciated in the well known *ḥadīth:* 'God's mercy precedes His wrath', a constant theme of the *Ṣaḥīfa,* as pointed out in the introduction.

83. Allusion to such Qur'ānic verses as *Whosoever does evil, or wrongs himself, and then prays God's forgiveness, he shall find God is All-forgiving, All-compassionate* (4:110).

84. Reference to such Qur'ānic verses as *Supplicate Me and I will respond to you* (40:60), and *When My servants ask from Me, I am near: I respond to the supplication of the supplicate when he supplicates Me* (2:186).

85. Cf. the *ḥadīth* mentioned in the introduction: 'When one of you supplicates, he should not say: "O God, forgive me if You will", but he should be firm in his asking and make his desire great, for what God gives is nothing great for Him' (Muslim, Dhikr 8).

86. 74:56.

87. 3:26.

88. Reference to such Qur'ānic verses as: O *people, you are the poor toward God, and He is without need, praiseworthy* (35:15).

89. A case can be made for translating the word *ẓālim* (wrongdoer) in the context of the present supplication as 'oppressor' or 'tyrant', especially if we read the text as expressing the Imam's relationships with the Umayyad authorities. However, the word *ẓulm* along with its derivatives is an important and frequently used term in the Qur'ān, and only the Qur'ānic context can provide us with a reliable insight into the way the word must have been understood by Zayn al-'Ābidīn and his contemporaries. In the Qur'ān, it is obvious that terms like 'oppression' and 'tyranny', with their narrow political connotations, cannot begin to do justice to the wide range of meanings included in the primary Qur'ānic significance, since oppression is merely one of many forms of human 'wrongdoing', an English term which is sufficiently vague and concrete to render the Qur'ānic idea rather closely. According to the Qur'ān, the basic meaning of *dhūlm is* to deny the reality of God and the truth of His revelation and then to transgress the bounds, limits, laws, and statutes He has set down. This Qur'ānic concept can clearly be perceived in such typical verses as the following: *Who does greater wrong than he who bars God's places of worship, so that His Name be not rehearsed in them, and strives to destroy them?* (2:114); *Who does greater wrong than he who conceals a testimony received from God?* (2:140); *Whosoever transgresses the bounds of God - those are the wrongdoers* (2:229); *And the unbelievers - they are the wrongdoers* (2:254); *Whoso judges not accorDīng to what God has sent down - they are the wrongdoers* (5:45); *Who does greater wrong than he who forges against God a lie, or cries lies to His signs?* (7:37, 10:17); *Who does greater wrong than he who, being reminded of the signs of his Lord, turns away from them?* (18:57, 32:22); *None denies Our signs but the wrongdoers* (29:49); *Do not associate others with God; to associate others with God is a mighty wrong* (31:13); *And whoso repents not, those - they are the wrongdoers* (49:11); *Whoso trespasses the bounds of God has done wrong to himself* (65:1). In most of the cases in which the Imam employs the term in the *Ṣaḥīfa,* the Qur'ānic context is clear, and this is sufficient reason to maintain consistency of translation in the present supplication, where 'oppression' might also be a valid translation. (For uses of the term in obvious Qur'ānic contexts, cf. 1.12, 4.8, 8.4, 12.7, 12.11, 16.31, 24.11, 31.7, 37.8, 39.9, 42.16, 45.9, 45.47, 47.62, 47.132, 48.15, 51.14, 60.3, 63.8, 71.5; contexts which suggest 'oppression' as a valid rendering include 20.7, 51.4, 68.1). The term *ẓulm* is often used as the opposite of *'adl* or 'justice'; the *Ṣaḥīfa* also provides a few instances where 'injustice' would translate the term well, such as 22.13 (where it is used as a synonym for *jawr*, translated there as 'injustice'), 25.11, 44.10.

90. Some editions read *yuḥāḍiranī* for *yuḥāṣiranī.* The translation then becomes: 'and overcome me in my rights.'

91. Allusion to such Qur'ānic verses as: We shall surely destroy the wrongdoers (14:13); We have prepared for the wrongdoers a painful chastisement (25:37)

92. Again reference to 27:62: He who responds to the distressed when he supplicates Him, and removes the evil.

93. A believer who cannot perform the obligatory acts of worship because of illness is credited with them in any case. The commentator cites a number of *ḥadīth* to this effect, e.g.: 'When the believer becomes sick, God says to the angel charged with him: "Write for him what you used to write when he was healthy".'

94. 40:7.

95. 3:26.

96. The terms 'wretchedness' *(shiqā')* and 'felicity' *(sa'āda)* refer to heaven and hell, not to the misery or happiness of this world.

97. 3:26.

98. Reference to the principle enunciated in 2:264: *O believers void not your freewill offerings with obligation and harm, as one who expends of his substance to show off to men and believes not in God and the Last Day.*

99. i.e., 'Being gentle'. The expression is employed in 15:88 and 26:215.

100. That is, the return to God, alluded to with verbs from the same root in many Qur'ānic verses, such as *He originates creation, then He makes it return* (10:4). The word *ma'ād* becomes a standard term in Islamic thought for 'eschatology' and discussion of affairs having to do with the next world.

101. Allusion to 78: 21-23: *Behold, Gehenna has become an ambush, for the insolent a resort, therein to tarry for ages....*

102. Here the word 'guardianship' *(wilāya)* probably does not have a technical sense (on which, see note 219), but is employed in a more general sense as in the title to Supplication 5.

103. 2:201.

104. Cf. 11: 56: There is no creature that crawls, but He takes it by the forelock.

105. This sentence goes back to a prophetic saying (Aḥmad, 1, 391 and 402).

106. Allusion to 2:197: *Take provision, but the best provision is reverent fear.*

107. 3:26.

108. 6:122.

109. i.e., unaffected by my own good pleasure or wrath in a given situation.

110. That is, the lesser pilgrimage to Mecca made outside of the season of the *ḥajj.*

111. 22:3.

112. 11: 56.

113. This passage can be read in two ways: In the more general interpretation, the 'us' in 'ennobled us' and 'made incumbent upon us' refers to all Muslims,

while in the more specific interpretation, it refers to the Imams. In the first case, the 'rights' are those which all Muslims have in relationship to other Muslims, as explained, for example, in the Imam's 'Treatise on Rights'. In the second case, the rights are those of the Imams in respect to other Muslims. The commentator quotes among others the Prophet's *ḥadīth* of 'seven rights' (see the introduction to the 'Treatise on Rights') to illustrate the first interpretation. If we read it the second way, then 'the rights of the Imams are obvious, since all the rights which God has made obligatory upon the creatures for the Messenger of God are also obligatory for the Imams. Sufficient proof of this is provided by the Qur'ānic verse: *Obey God, and obey the Messenger and those in authority among you* (4:59)' (Sayyid 'Alīkhān).

114. Cf. note 46.

115. 45:22.

116. 7:151.

117. One is tempted to translate *shahawāt* as 'lusts', but the Qur'ānic context shows that the objects of desire in themselves are not necessarily negative; the Qur'ān blames only the fact that man allows himself to be occupied by them in lieu of God. For example, *Decked out fair to men is the love of passions - women, children, heaped-up heaps of gold and silver, horses of mark, cattle, and tillage. That is the enjoyment of the present life; but God - with Him is the fairest resort* (3:14). Arberry translates the term here as 'lusts', Pickthall as 'joys'.

118. Cf. 12.10.

119. These four lines refer to 2:186 and 40:60.

120. 2:201.

121. That is, those who recognize the Imamate of Zayn al-'Ābidīn and the other Imams. Cf. 47.64.

122. Sayyid 'Alīkhān explains the expression as meaning: 'Give them *lutf* (gracefulness, gentleness, subtlety) in their *makr* (guile, stratagem) so that their enemy will not become aware of their guile, for then it will be too subtle and fine to be perceived by the intellect and the understanding; so the meaning is that God should inspire them with careful watchfulness and excellence of artful stratagems.' He suggests that the text may also be interpreted to mean: Be kind and gentle to them in relation to the guile of their enemy, so that his guile will not harm them.

123. 8:57.

124. The commentator devotes a long discussion to the word *miḥāl,* which occurs in the Qur'ānic name of God, *shadīd al-miḥāl* (13:13). It may signify, among others, cunning, guile, stratagem, planning, managing, power, strength, dispute, enmity, punishment, vengeance, chastisement.

125. This victory of a small army of Muslims over a much larger contingent of unbelievers took place in the year 2/623. Many accounts are given of how the angels also took part in the fighting, and it is said to be in reference to Badr that God says in the Qur'ān, *When thy Lord was revealing to the angels: 'I am with you, so strengthen the faithful. I shall cast terror into the hearts of the unbelievers'* (8:12).

126. 51:22-3.

127. 40:60.

128. 9:104, 42:25.

129. 42:25.

130. 2:222.

131. Allusion to the well-known prophetic saying: 'Remorse is repentance' (Ibn Māja, Zūhd 30; Aḥmad I, 376, 423; VI, 264).

132. 2:128.

133. There is probably an allusion here to 3:103: *You were upon the brink of a pit of Fire, and He rescued you from it.*

134. 3:26.

135. Reference to the Qur'ānic account of Iblis, in which Iblis asks from God and is given permission to try to lead His servants astray until the Day of Resurrection (7:14-18, 15:36-43, 38:79-86).

136. Reference to 59:16: *Like Satan, when he said to man, 'Disbelieve!' Then, when he disbelieved, he said: 'Surely I am quit of you. Surely I fear God, the Lord of the worlds.'*

137. Reference to 32:7: *He originated the creation of man out of clay, then He fashioned his progeny of an extraction of mean water, then He shaped him and breathed His spirit into him.*

138. Reference to a number of Qur'ānic passages, especially 23:12-14: *We created man of an extraction of clay, then We set him, a drop, in a receptacle secure, then We created of the drop a clot, then We created of the clot a tissue, then We created of the tissue bones, then We garmented the bones with flesh; thereafter We produced him as another creature.*

139. As the commentators point out, this 'placing' is connected to the Qur'ānic doctrine of the transformation of evil deeds into good deeds, e.g.: *Whosoever does that shall meet the price of sin... save him who repents, has faith, and does righteous works - those, God will change their evil deeds into good deeds* (25:68-70).

140. This is part of a *ḥadīth;* cf. Lane, *Arabic-English Lexicon, s.v. ibqā'.*

141. 3:26.

142. 3:26.

143. Allusion to 4:59: *O you who have faith, obey God, and obey the Messenger and those in authority among you!*

144. 112.

145. Allusion to 25:40.

146. Literally, those who 'deviate' from the right way.

147. 2:285.

148. The commentator suggests that the expression *shakartahu,* 'for which Thou showest gratitude', which is found in most texts, means *qabaltahu,* 'which Thou acceptant'. He adds that another ancient text has *shukir bihi,* 'for which Thou art thanked', and that this is clearer and more appropriate in the context. Cf. the similar passages in 46.6-7.

149. Allusion to such Qur'ānic verses as Whoso brings a good deed shall have ten the like of it; and whoso brings an evil deed shall only be recompensed the like of it; they shall not be wronged Cf. 40:40.

150. Allusion to 2:222: *Truly God loves those who repent.*

151. The Persian translators read this as meaning, 'pardon me *(marā bibakhsh)* in spite of my wrongdoing against myself', and Mohani's English translation agrees:

152. Reference to several Qur'ānic names for the people of paradise. The Companions of the Right Hand are mentioned in 56:27, 38, 90, 91, and 74:39; the Secure in 27:89, 34:37, etc.; the Triumphant in 9:20, 23:111, 59:20; the Righteous in 2:130, 12:101, etc.

153. Allusion to 4:174: *We have sent down to you a manifest light.*

154. Allusion to 5:48: *We have sent down to thee the Book with the truth, confirming the Book that was before it and guarding over it.*

155. There are allusions here to several Qur'ānic verses, including 4:174, 5:48, and 39:23.

156. The Qur'ān calls itself a 'separator' in 2:185, 3:4, and 25:1.

157. Allusion to the title given to itself by the Qur'ān: 'the Arabic recitation' (12:2, 20:113, et al.). To 'make plain' *(I'rāb)* also means to 'express in Arabic'.

158. Cf. 41:3: *A book whose signs have been distinguished as an Arabic Qur'ān for a people having knowledge.*

159. Cf. 76:23: *Surely We have sent down the Qur'ān on thee, a sending down.*

160. *Cf. 14:1: A book We have sent down to thee that thou mayest bring forth mankind from the shadows to the light by the leave of their Lord; cf. also 57:9, 65:11.*

161. For the name 'healing', cf. 10:57 and 17:82.

162. Cf. 57:25.

163. According to Sayyid 'Alīkhān, by 'witnesses' the Imam means either those who bear witness to God's Unity and to the prophets, since the Qur'ān is their greatest proof, or the Prophet and his Household, who are (according to the Shi'ite interpretation) the witnesses referred to in the verse *Thus We appointed you a midmost nation that you might be witnesses to the people, and that the Messenger might be a witness to you* (2:143).

164. Here the prayer's specific reference to the Imam's own situation leads the commentators to suggest altering the text when it is recited. Sayyid 'Alīkhān suggests that one should make the following changes: *warrathtanā* -> *warrathta awṣiyā'ahū; faḍḍaltanā* -> *faḍḍaltahum; qawwaytanā* -> *qawwaytahum; tarfa'anā* -> *tarfa'ahum.* The meaning would then be: 'Thou madest his executors the heirs of its knowledge as interpreters, Thou preferred them over him who is ignorant of its knowledge, and Thou gavest them strength to lift them above...'

165. Allusion to 20:130: Proclaim thy Lord's praise.... in the watches of the night, and at the ends of the day.

166. Allusion to 59:21: If We had sent down the Qur'ān upon a mountain, thou wouldst have seen it humbled, split asunder out of the fear of God.

167. Allusion to two Qur'ānic verses: *They shall be secure from terror on that day* (27:89) and *The Greatest Terror shall not grieve them* (21:103).

168. Allusion to 8: 6: As though they were being driven into death with their eyes open and 50:21: And death's agony comes in truth.... And every soul will come, with it a driver and a witness.

169. 75:26-7.

170. Allusion to 17:13: And every man - We have fastened to him the bird of omen upon his neck.

171. Cf. 1.14 and 3:106.

172. The 'mediation' is mentioned in 5:35: *O you who have faith, fear God and seek the mediation to Him.* 'Mediation' may mean simply the means of access to God, defined in terms of any work of obedience or pious act. But most commentators point out the verse's connection to a well-known saying of the Prophet concerning 'mediation' as the highest station of Paradise and this in turn is normally defined as the permission God will give to the Prophet at the Resurrection to intercede for his community. The Prophet said: 'When you hear the muezzin, repeat what he says, then call down blessings upon me. If someone calls down a blessing upon me, God will call down ten upon him. Then ask that I be given the mediation, for it is a station in the Garden suited only for one of God's servants, and I hope to be that one. If anyone asks that I be given the mediation, my intercession for him will become lawful' (Muslim, Ṣalāt 11; Tirmidhī, Manāqib I; Abū Dāwūd, Ṣalāt 36; Aḥmad II, 168, 265; III 83). Pad wick discusses the connection between mediation and intercession in *Muslim Devotions,*

Ch. 2, 'The Prayer of Mediation' (the relationship between the two can be seen in the present work in 65.4-5, 66.3-4, and 78.1). On the mediation of the Imams, see note 217.

173. Allusion to the 'Pool of Abūndance' in Paradise, which, according to several *ḥadīth,* is the meaning of the 'Abundance' which God gave to the Prophet as mentioned in 108:1.

174. Allusion to 36:39: And the moon - We have determined it by mansions, till it returns like an aged palm-bough.

175. 2:185.

176. 97:4-5.

177. Sayyid 'Alīkhān offers four interpretations for this last clause, three given by earlier commentators and the fourth his own: (a) so that the acts of obedience and nearness-seeking of the angels will be less than ours; (b) so that none of the recording angels will bring the record of our sins except that they be less than the kinds of obedience and sorts of nearness seeking that we bring; (c) so that none of the angels will bring the works of the servants except that they be less than the kinds of obedience and sorts of nearness seeking that we bring; (d) so that none of the angels will bring our good works except that they be less than the good works that we ourselves bring. In support of the last reading he cites a *ḥadīth* from one of the Imams: 'The angel only writes down what it hears, but God has said, *Remember thy Lord in thyself, in pleading and fear* (7:205). So none knows the reward of the remembrance in the person's self except God.' He concludes that the best interpretation is to say that the passage includes all four of these meanings.

178. 23:11.

179. 23:60.

180. 23:61.

181. In other words, Thou art kind without the servants having done anything to deserve it. Cf. 12.3.

182. 66:8.

183. 6:160.

184. 2:261.

185. 2:245.

186. 2:152.

187. 14:7.

188. 40:60.

189. 97:3.

190. 97:3.

191. That is, the Ramadan of the year that has just passed and that of the coming year.

192. That is, we have been afflicted by the hardship of having to fast. This interpretation follows Sayyid 'Alīkhān's reading; the Persian translators interpret the sentence to mean: 'our being afflicted by grief at the passing of our month', a reading which Sayyid 'Alīkhān rejects.

193. i.e., that good pleasure and mercy.

194. Allusion to Qur'ānic verses such as *Truly God loves the repenters* (2:222) and *God is He who accepts repentance from His servants* (9:104; cf. 42:25).

195. 3:26.

196. Allusion to 8:53: *God would never change His favour that He conferred on a people until they changed what was within themselves.*

197. 3:26.

198. An oft-repeated formula found in many *ḥadīth.*

199. The ninth of Dhu l-Ḥijja, the last day of the *ḥajj,* when the pilgrims occupy themselves with prayer at Mount 'Arafa. Cf. Imam Ḥusayn's long supplication for the day, translated in Chittick, *A Shīʿite Anthology,* pp. 93-113.

200. 1:2.

201. Cf. 15: 21-23: *Naught is there, but its treasuries are with Us, and We send it not down but in a known measure... It is We who give life, and make to die, and it is We who are the inheritors.*

202. 42:11.

203. Reference to 10:61: *Not so much as the weight of an ant in earth or heaven escapes from thy Lord...*

204. 41:54.

205. 33:52.

206. Reference to 25:2: *He created everything, then He ordained it with an ordination.*

207. Allusion to 80:20: *He created him [man] and determined him then the way eased for him.*

208. Perhaps an allusion to 32:5: *He governs the affair from the heaven to the earth.*

209. Reference to 72:28: *He has counted everything in numbers.*

210. The terms 'howness' and 'whereness' are found already in *ḥadīth* attributed to the Prophet in Shīʿite sources, as well as to some of the Imams (cf. Chit tick, *A Shīʿite Anthology* index under *ayniyyah* and *kayfiyyah.* The term 'selfness' *(dhātiyya)* is certainly more rare. Lane in his *Lexicon* points out that it is a post-classical term used in philosophy, but in the present context it has no such philosophical sense and seems to be a coinage built on the analogy of the other two terms.

211. Reference to sura 112.

212. The 'Separator' is the Qur'ān (cf. Supplication 42.2). There is an allusion here to 15:94: *Therefore cleave [0 Muḥammad] by means of that which thou art commanded [i.e. the Qur'ānic injunctions] and turn away from the idolaters.*

213. Reference to 6:115.

214. The guardians or writers are the recording angels. Cf. Supplication 3.18. The 'book' mentioned here is referred to in such verses as: *The Book shall be set in place; and thou wilt see the sinners fearful at what is in it and saying: 'Alas for us! How is it with this Book that it leaves nothing behind, small or great but it has numbered it?'* (18:49).

215. Allusion to 18:109: *Say: 'If the sea were ink for the words of my Lord, the sea would be spent before the words of my Lord are spent.'*

216. Reference to 33:33: *Folk of the House God only desires to put away from you uncleanness and to purify you.*

217. Muslims hold that 'mediation' will be given to the Prophet (see note 172), while Shīʿite tradition adds that it will also belong to the Imams. Cf. the chapter in Majlisī's *Biḥār al-Anwār* 'The Mediation, and the station of the Prophet and the Folk of his House which will become manifest at the resurrection' (VII, 326-40). Among relevant sayings quoted in both Shīʿite and Sunni sources is that of 'Alī: 'In the Garden there are two pearls within the Throne, one of them white and the other yellow. In each there are 70,000 rooms whose gates and cups come from a single root. The white is the Mediation which belongs to Muḥammad and his Household, while the yellow belongs to Abraham and his household' (commentary on 5:35: al-Ṭabarsī, *Majma' al-bayān;* Maybudī, *Kashf al-asrār).*

218. Cf. Supplication 1.4.

219. The 'Friend' or *w'alī* is the Imam, who, in keeping with the various meanings of the root, is 'friend' of God, 'guardian' of the people under his care, and 'authority' in all matters of religious teaching. His function, known as *wilāya* (or *walāya*) and derived from the same Arabic root, is discussed in most books on Shīʿism; in the present text the word is mentioned, not always in the technical sense, in Supplications 5 (title); 8.3; 20.7, 22; 26.1; 47.64; and 77.2.

220. Allusion to 17:80: *And say [0 Muḥammad]: '... grant me authority from Thee to help me.'*

221. Cf. 48:1: *Surely We have given thee a manifest opening.*

222. Cf. Moses' supplication in 20:31: *Appoint for me of my folk a familiar, Aaron, my brother; by him brace up my back.*

223. Like the previous clause, this is an allusion to the story of Moses and Aaron in the Qur'ān, and more specifically, to God's words to Moses: *We shall strengthen thy arm by means of thy brother* (28:35).

224. Cf. 37:173: *Our troops - they are the victors.*

225. *Wilāya* - which may be translated as friendship, authority, guardianship, rule - is the office or function of the 'Friend' or *walī* mentioned above in note 219.

226. 2:128.

227. Cf. 10:25: *And God summons to the Abode of Peace.* Cf. also 6:127.

228. As indicated in note 77, 'caprice' denotes any desire opposed to the divine guidance.

229. This may be an allusion to 17:16.

230. Allusion to 4:108: *They hide themselves from men but hide themselves not from God.*

231. Allusion to 7:182: *We will draw them on little by little from whence they know not; and I grant them respite - surely My guile is firm.* Imam Ja'far al-Ṣādiq says: 'When God desires good for a servant who commits a sin, He causes the sin to be followed by a punishment so that he remembers to ask forgiveness. But when He desires evil for a servant who commits a sin, He causes the sin to be followed by a favour so that he forgets to ask forgiveness and persists in the sin. This is indicated by God's words *We draw them on little by little from whence they know not.*' (Sayyid 'Alīkhān)

232. Cf. above, 47.90.

233. In other words: Do not allow me to become diverted from the worship and obedience which please Thee by my seeking after the things of this world, which come only through Thee.

234. Allusion to 5:35: *O you who have faith fear God and seek the mediation to Him.* Cf. note 172.

235. The commentator suggests that this is an allusion to the principle enunciated in 18:103-104: *Say: 'Shall I tell you who will be the greatest losers in their works? Those whose striving goes astray in the present life while they think that they are working good deeds.'*

236. 75:56.

237. Reference to 66:8: *Upon the day when God will not degrade the Prophet and those who believe with him their light running before them and on their right hands.*

238. Allusion to 19:75: Say: *'Whoever is in error, let the All-merciful prolong his term for him!...'*

239. Cf. above, 47.60, where mention is made of the 'radiance' of the Imam.

240. Cf. the following *ḥadīth:* 'God has left no excuses for him who has reached sixty or seventy years of age. God has left him no excuses, no excuses!' (Aḥmad II, 275). See also Lane, *Arabic-English Lexicon s.v. i 'dhār.*

241. Reference to 7:186: *Whomsoever God leads astray no guide has he; He leaves them in their insolence blindly wandering.*

242. Reference to 23:54: *So leave them in their perplexity for a time.*

243. The commentator offers three possible interpretations: remove not my name from the register of the felicitous, writing it in the register of the wretched; change my name not for the worse, after it had been an elevated name; change not the name by which Thou hadst named us before (alluding to the Qur'ānic verse: *He named you Muslims a foretime and in this* [22:78]). The meaning thus becomes: Name me not an unbeliever after Thou hast named me a Muslim.

244. The commentator explains this to mean: Transform it not through an affliction in this world or through making it ugly in the next.

245. Reference to 56:88-9: *Then if he be of those brought nigh to the Throne, there shall be repose and ease, and a garden of bliss.*

246. Allusion to 2:16: *Those are they who have bought error at the price of guidance, and their commerce has not profited them.*

247. Reference to 79:6-12: *Upon the day when the first blast shivers... They shall say, 'what, are we being restored as we were before... That then is a return with loss!'*

248. Allusion to 15:47: *We shall root out all rancour that is in their breasts* (cf. 7:43).

249. 26:84, part of a prayer of Abraham.

250. The commentator sees this as a reference to the first Muslims, as in 9:100: *And the foremost, the first, who are the Emigrants and the Helpers, and those who followed them in good-doing - God will be well-pleased with them...; He has prepared for them gardens...* The 'plain' of the first is the place where they are brought together at the Resurrection.

251. 86:9.

252. That is, the tenth of Dhu l-Ḥijja, which marks the end of the *ḥajj* and is one of the two major festivals (along with the feast of fast breaking), celebrated universally throughout the Islamic world.

253. 3:26.

254. By 'this station' is meant the leading of the prayer of Friday and of the Day of Sacrifice. The latter of these prayers is obligatory according to the Shī'ites,

in contrast to the Sunnis. Zayn al-'Ābidīn alludes to the Shī'ite view that the Imams are the rightful leaders of these prayers for all Islam, not the Umayyad caliphs and their representatives. In explaining the meaning of this passage, Sayyid 'Alīkhān quotes a *ḥadīth* from Ja'far al-Ṣādiq: 'Both festivals of the Muslims, that of fast breaking and that of sacrifice, renew the sorrow of the Household of Muḥammad, for they see therein their right in the hands of others.'

255. i.e., those who actually put the profession of Unity, faith, and attestation into practice.

256. Allusion to the Prophet's supplication quoted in the introduction: 'I seek refuge in Thy good pleasure from Thy displeasure and in Thy pardon from Thy punishment. I seek refuge in Thee from Thee.'

257. Allusion to 43:11: *[We] sent down out of heaven water in measure; and We revived thereby a land that was dead; even so you shall be brought forth [on the Day of Resurrection].*

258. Allusion to 21:23: *He is not questioned as to what He does, but they shall be questioned.*

259. For 'so and so' the supplicant should supply words appropriate to his own situation.

260. 3:26.

261. 39:53.

262. This is the Book of Records on the Day of Judgement, mentioned, for example, in 18:49: *And the Book shall be set in place; and thou wilt see the sinners fearful at what is in it, saying: 'Alas for us! How is it with this Book, that it leaves nothing behind, small or great, but it has counted it?'* Cf. 17:13-14.

263. Allusion to such Qur'ānic verses as: *Not so much as the weight of an ant in heaven and earth escapes from Him neither is aught smaller than that, or greater, but it is in a Manifest Book (34:3).*

264. Allusion to 4:6, 33:39: *God suffices as a reckoner.*

265. Cf. the following sentence from a supplication of the Prophet: 'I ask Thee by every one of Thy names by which Thou hast named Thyself, which Thou hast taught to one of Thy creatures, which Thou hast sent down in Thy Book, or which Thou hast kept to Thyself in the knowledge of the Unseen' (Aḥmad I, 391, 402). A passage from the same *ḥadīth* is quoted in Supplication 21.6.

266. 2:128.

267. 20:8.

268. Allusion to 35:28: *Only those of His servants fear God who have knowledge.*

269. Reference to 29: 57: *Every soul shall taste death, then unto Us you shall be returned.*

270. The commentator suggests that the 'stillness of his veins' alludes to the health of his body, which in turn brings about comfort and ease, making him heedless of God and the next world.

271. Another allusion to the Prophet's supplication; cf. 48.13.

272. Sura 112.

273. Allusion to such verses as 8:68: *Had it not been for a prior writ from God, there had afflicted you, for what you took, a dreadful chastisement.*

274. This verse and the following allude to the well-known *ḥadīth qudsī:* 'Might is My loincloth and mightiness My cloak. If anyone contends with Me in either of these, I will cast him into Gehenna.' Cf. W. Graham, *Divine Word and Prophetic Word,* pp. 162-3.

275. This is probably an allusion to the Highest Assembly, the angels mentioned in 37:8 and 38:69.

276. Cf. 20:6.

277. Cf. 9:78: *Know they not that God knows their secret and their whispered conversation, and that God knows the things unseen?* See also 43:80, 58:7.

278. Ibn Shihāb al-Zuhrī (d. 124/742) was a well known jurist and traditionist and, as mentioned in the introduction, is credited with being the first to call the Imam by the title 'Zayn al-'Ābidīn'. Sa'īd ibn al-Musayyib (d. 94/712-713), one of the 'seven jurists' of Medina, was known as the 'Chief of the Followers' *(sayyid al-tābi'īn),* that is, those who followed the generation of the Prophet's Companions.

279. On the 'mediation' given to the Imams, see the note on 47.56.

280. 3:26.

281. Allusion to the *ḥadīth qudsī,* 'I am with My servant's opinion of Me'; in some versions, there occurs the phrase, 'so let him think about Me what he will' (Graham, *Divine Word,* pp. 127-130).

282. Again reference to 40:60: *Supplicate Me and I will respond to you.*

283. Allusion to Qur'ānic verses such as: *Surely God will not fail in His promise* (13:31), and *There is no change for the words of God* (10:64).

284. Allusion to 27:62. Cf. Supplication 10.4.

285. 7:156.

286. This supplication seems to be another version of 48.13 ff.

287. Cf. note 256.

288. Cf. note 257.

289. Part of the *ḥadīth* quoted in the introduction and note 256.

290. 12:64.

291. Allusion to 20:111: *Faces shall be humbled unto the Living, the Subsistent.*

292. 12:53.

293. 37:173.

294. 58:22.

295. 10:62.

296. 25:47.

297. There are a number of Qur'ānic allusions in this passage, including: *He created, then proportioned* (87:2), and *He sat upon the Throne* (7:54 etc.).

298. 7:151.

299. Ibid.

300. Allusion to such verses as: *They forgot God, so He forgot them (9:67); Today We forget you, just as you forgot the meeting on this your Day* (45:34; cf. 7:51).

301. Allusion to 14:7: *If you are thankful, surely I will increase you, but if you are thankless, My chastisement is surely terrible.*

302. Cf. 59.9 and note 283.

303. Reference to 22:78: *Struggle for God as is His due!*

304. 3:8.

305. 2:129.

306. Allusion to the saying of the Prophet: 'Remorse is repentance.' Cf. note 131.

307. 66:8.

308. Reference to 12:53.

309. Allusion to 70:19-21: *Surely man was created fretful, when evil touches him, anxious, when good visits him, grudging.*

310. Allusion to the Qur'ānic verse: *No indeed, but what they were earning has rusted upon the hearts* (83:14), as well as to the several instances where the Qur'ān refers to the sealing of the unbelievers' hearts, e.g.: *God has set a seal on their hearts, so they know not* (9:93).

311. 3:25.

312. Allusion to a well known formula found in many *ḥadīth*; in one version, the Prophet says in supplication: 'The good - all of it - is in Thy hands, and evil does not return to Thee' (Muslim, Musāfirīn 201; Nasā'ī, Iftitāḥ 17).

313. Allusion to 7:54: *Verily His are the creation and the command.*

314. Cf. 59.8 and note 281.

315. Cf. note 256.

316. Allusion to 29:69.

317. 3:26.

318. Allusion to the clarity of vision that the soul experiences at death: *Thou wast heedless of this; therefore We have now removed from thee thy covering, and so thy sight today is piercing* (50:22).

319. Allusion to 89:28: *O soul serene, return to thy Lord, well-pleased, well-pleasing!*

320. Allusion to 13:28: *In remembering God find serenity the hearts of those who have faith and do righteous deeds.*

321. 33:41.

322. 2:152.

323. Allusion to the words of Lot in 11:80, *Would that I had power against you, or might take shelter in a strong pillar!*

APPENDIX

THE TREATISE ON RIGHTS
RISĀLAT AL-ḤUQUQ

Zayn al-'Ābidīn 'Alī ibn al-Ḥusayn

INTRODUCTION

Imam Zayn al 'Ābidīn's 'Treatise on rights' is the only work attributed to him other than supplications or relatively short sayings and letters. The fact that it was a written document from the first may support the suggestion that at least some of the supplications were originally written compositions.

The 'Treatise on rights' elaborates on a well-known saying of the prophet, which has been transmitted in a rather larger number of versions, no doubt because he repeated it in many different contexts.

A typical version can be rendered as follows; 'Surely your Lord has a right against you, your self has a right against you, your wife has a right against you.' Other versions of the *ḥadīth* add guest, body, eye and friend to those who have rights. In some of the versions, another clause is added: 'So give to everyone who possesses a right (*kull dhī ḥaqq*) his right.'[1] Another *ḥadīth* tells us that 'God has given to everyone who possesses a right to his right.'[2]

Shi'ite sources provide many relevant *ḥadīth.* For example Prophet said;

> God has made seven rights incumbent upon the person of faith (*al-mu'min)* toward the person of faith: To respect him and his person, love him and his breast, share with him his property, consider backbiting against him unlawful, visit him in his illness, escort his coffin, and say nothing but good about him after his death.[3]

Zayn al-Ābidīn's 'Treatise on rights' seems to have been written at the request of a disciple, since, in one of its two versions, it is prefaced by the words: 'This is the treatise of 'Alī ibn al-Ḥusayn to one of his companions.' In it the Imam explains in more or less exhaustive fashion what is meant by 'everyone who possesses a right' as mentioned in the above *ḥadīth*. Throughout he provides specific examples, basing him self upon Qur'ān, the *sunna,* and the actions and sayings of the early Imams.

---

[1] Bukhāri Ṣawm 51. Cf Wensinck, Concordance, I, 487, under *inni 'alayka ḥaqqan.*

[2] Abū Dāwūd, Waṣāyā 6, Buyū 88; Tirmidhī, Waṣāyā 5; Ibn Māja, Waṣāyā 6, etc.

[3] Shaykh al-Ṣadūq, *Al-Khiṣāl,* 2, 6; and *Al-Amālī* , p. 20 (quoted in *Biḥār,* LXXI, 222). For other relevant *ḥadīth* , see *Biḥār,*, LXXI.

Though in the present context the word *ḥaqq* translates best as 'right', it has a number of closely related meanings which should be kept in mind, such as suitableness, justices, truth, realty, correctness, properness, appropriateness, necessity, incumbency, obligation, due, and duty. A glance at the 'Treatise on Rights' will quickly show the word 'rights' might better have been translated as duties, obligations, or responsibilities, since the treatise is not directly concerned with the rights of the individual, but rather with the rights of others which the individual must observe. Nevertheless, I think its important to preserve the term 'rights', if only to show that in considering human rights primarily in terms of responsibilities, Islam diverges profoundly from most modern western views, though it has deep kinships with other religious traditions of East and West.

Islam views the individual in his total context, which means that it considers first his relationships with God, then his relationships with God's creatures. What is important for the individual in his relationships with God is that he attain his salvation, or in other words, that he follow God's guidance, which is based upon mercy and directed toward his own best interest. In short, Islam devalues the individual's perspective, since human beings on there own can see no further then their immediate interests during life. But this devolution of individualism is not a devaluation of the individual; on the contrary, it raises him to the ultimate pinnacle of importance, since everything is directed toward his happiness in the next world. Islam merely recognizes the ignorance of human beings and their in ability to perceive there own ultimate good without divine guidance. Then it sets about to undermine and destroy individual ignorance, a process which involves deflating the ego and eliminating all self-centred desires. As a result, human self or soul (*nafs*) has

few 'rights', but many duties and responsibilities. Or rather, the soul has only one true right-the right to salvation.

The individual's right to salvation follows naturally upon God's right, which is to be worshiped without any partner (i.e., *tawḥīd*). The way to salvation is to obey God, and hence it is the soul's right to be employed in obedience toward Him. By His very nature-since 'His mercy precedes His wrath '-God displays compassion and guidance, and through obedience the servant opens himself up to the full range of this compassion. In other words, partaking of God's mercy and compassion depends upon following His guidance, and following His guidance means following the *Sharī'a* as revealed through the Qur'ān and the *sunna.* Hence the Imam speaks of 'being employed in obedience' as the self's key to right, since that can bring about its deliverances.

As soon as this wide context for attainting to the right of the self is envisaged, dozens of duties become obligatory upon the individual. The

Imam makes clear that the primary duties are toward the various organs and activities of the self, since these determine man's relationships to God. The organs have 'rights' because they share in the individual's destiny; the 'resurrection of the body' is taken for granted (cf. supplication 31.22). Activities have rights because they shaped the destiny of the soul. And other human beings have rights because they form the context within which activity occurs. Human actions can only be correct if the rights of all of God's creatures are observed. This, in short, is the theme of the 'Treatise on Rights ', a theme which is reinforced by many of the supplications of the *Ṣaḥīfa*, number 24 being a prime example.

The treatise has been transmitted in two versions, one in *Al-khiṣāl* and *Al-Amālī,* both by Shaykh al-Ṣadūq (d. 381/991), and the other in *Tuḥaf al-'uqūl,* by his contemporary Ibn Shu'ba. Perhaps one half of the text of the two versions is identical, but Ibn Shu'ba's version adds a good deal of material that shows it to be a later recession, perhaps by the Imam him self, or more likely by a later author trying to clarify the meaning. The translation follows

the earlier version, with a minor addition from the second version which seems to be demanded by the context.[4]

TEXT

INTRODUCTION

KNOW - God have mercy upon you - that God has rights against you and that these encompass you in every movement through which you move, every rest through which you rest, every waystation in which you reside, every limb which you employ, and every instrument which you put to work. Some of these rights are greater and some less.

[4] Both versions are provided in *Biḥār,* LXXI, 2-21 (where they have been collated against the printed versions in *Al-Khiṣāl* and *Tuḥaf al-'uqūl).* A far less satisfactory edition, with a number of errors and with a mixing of the two texts so that neither is complete nor clearly separated from the other, is given by al-Amīn in *A'yān al-shī 'a,* v, 215-30

[A] [1] The greatest of God's rights against you is the right which He has made incumbent upon you for Himself and which is the root of all rights, then [2] those which He has made incumbent upon you in yourself, from your crown to your foot, in keeping with the diversity of your organs. He has given [3] your tongue a right against you, [4] your hearing a right against you, [5] your sight a right against you, [6] your hand a right against you, [7] your leg a right against you, [8] your stomach a right against you, [9] and your private part a right against you. These are the seven organs through which acts (*af'āl*) take place.

[B] Then He gave your acts rights against you: He gave [10] your ritual prayer a right against you, [12] your fasting a right against you, [13] your charity a right against you, [14] your offering a right against you, and your acts a right against you.

[C] Then these rights extend out from you to others who have rights against you. The most incumbent of them against you are the rights toward your leaders (*a'imma*), then

the rights toward your subjects (*ra'iyya*), then the rights toward your womb [relatives] (*raḥim*).

From these rights branch out other rights. [C1] The rights of your leaders are three: The most incumbent upon you is [15] the right of him who trains you through authority, then [16] of him who trains you through knowledge, then [17] of him who trains you through property.

[C2] The rights of your subjects are three: The most incumbent upon you is [18] the right of those who are your subjects through authority, then [19] the right of those who are your subjects through knowledge for the man of ignorance is the subject of the man of knowledge then the right of those who are your subjects through property, such as [20] wives and [21] what is owned by the right hand.

[C3] The rights of your womb relatives are many; they are connected to you in the measure of the connection of the womb relationship. The most incumbent upon you is [22] the right of your mother, then [23] the right of your father, then [24] the right of your child, then [25] the right of your brother, then the next nearest, then the next nearest - the most worthy, then the next most worthy.

[D] Then there is [26] the right of your master who favours you [by freeing you from slavery], then [27] the right of the slave whose favours reach you [by the fact that you free him], then [28] the right of him who does a kindly act toward you, then [29] the right of the muezzin who calls you to the ritual prayer, then [30] the right of the imam who leads the prayer, then [31] the right of your sitting companion, then [32] the right of your neighbour, then [33] the right of your companion, then [34] the right of your partner, then [35] the right of your property, then the right of him who has a debt he must pay back to you, then [36] the right of him to whom you owe a debt, then [37] the right of your associate, then [38] the right of your adversary who has a claim against you, then [39] the right of your adversary against whom you have a claim, then [40] the right of him who asks you for advice, then [41] the right of him whom you ask for advice, then [42] the right of him who asks your counsel, then [43] the right of him who counsels you, then [44] the right of him who is older than you, then [45] the

right of him who is younger than you, then [46] the right of him who asks from you, then [47] the right of him from whom you ask, then the right of [48] him who does something evil to you through word or deed, or [49] him who makes you happy through word or deed, intentionally or unintentionally, then [50] the right of the people of your creed, then [51] the right of the people under your protection, then all rights in the measure of the causes of the states and the occurrence of events.

Therefore happy is he whom God aids in the rights which He has made incumbent upon him and whom He gives success therein and points in the proper direction!

[A. RIGHTS OF GOD AGAINST ONESELF]

[1] The greatest right of God against you is that you worship Him without associating anything with Him. When you do that with sincerity (*ikhlās*), He has made it binding upon Himself to give you sufficiency in the affair of this world and the next.[5]
[2] The right of your self (*nafs*) against you is that you employ it in obeying God; then you deliver to your tongue its right, to your hearing its right, to your sight its right, to your hand its right, to your leg its right, to your stomach its right, to your private part its right, and you seek help from God in all that.
[3] The right of the tongue is that you consider it too noble for obscenity, accustom it to good, refrain from any meddling in which there is nothing to be gained, express kindness to the people, and speak well concerning them.

[5] This phrase, seemingly demanded by the explanation below, is added from the other version of the treatise.

[4] The right of hearing is to keep it pure from listening to backbiting (*ghība*) and listening to that to which it is unlawful to listen.
[5] The right of sight is that you lower it before everything which is unlawful to you and that you take heed whenever you look at anything.[6]

[6] The right of your hand is that you stretch it not toward that which is unlawful to you.
[7] The right of your two legs is that you walk not with them toward that which is unlawful to you. You have no escape from standing upon the narrow bridge (*al-Ṣirāṭ* [over hell]), so you should see to it that your legs do not slip and cause you to fall into the Fire.
[8] The right of your stomach is that you make it not into a container for that which is unlawful to you and you eat no more than your fill (*shib'*).

[9] The right of your private part (*farj*) is that you protect it from fornication and guard it against being looked upon.

[B. RIGHT OF ACTS]

[10] The right of your ritual prayer (*ṣalāt*) is that you know that it is an arrival before God and that through it you are standing before Him. When you know that, then you will stand in the station of him who is lowly, vile, beseeching, trembling, hopeful, fearful, and abased, and you will magnify Him who is before you through stillness and dignity. You will approach the prayer with your heart and you will perform it according to its bounds and its rights.
[11] The right of the *ḥajj* is that you know it is an arrival before your Lord and a flight to Him from your sins; through it your repentance is accepted and you perform an obligation made incumbent upon you by God.
[12] The right of fasting is that you know it is a veil which God has set up over your tongue, your hearing, your sight, your stomach, and your private part to protect you from the Fire. If you abandon the fast, you will have torn God's protective covering away from yourself.
[13] The right of charity (*ṣadaqa*) is that you know it is a storing away with your Lord and a deposit for which you will have no need for witnesses. If you deposit it in secret, you will be more confident of it than if you deposit it in public.[7]

---

[6] Allusion to 59: 2: "*..therefore take heed you who have eyes*"
[7] it is related in most of the sources concerning Zayn al-'Ābidīn that people considered him stingy during his lifetime but at his death, provisions which used to be delivered at the doorsteps of many of the poor of medina by a man with a covered face stopped appearing,

You should know that it repels afflictions and illnesses from you in this world and it will repel the Fire from you in the next world.

[14] The right of the offering (*hady*)[8] is that through it you desire God and you not desire His creation; through it you desire only the exposure of your soul to God's mercy and the deliverance of your spirit on the day you encounter Him.

[C1. RIGHTS OF LEADERS]

[15] The right of the possessor of authority (*sulṭān*) is that you know that God has made you a trial (*fitna*) for him. God is testing him through the authority He has given him over you. You should not expose yourself to his displeasure, for thereby you cast yourself by your own hands into destruction[9] and become his partner in his sin when he brings evil down upon you. [10]

[16] The right of the one who trains you (*sā'is*) through knowledge is magnifying him, respecting his sessions, listening well to him, and attending to him with devotion. You should not raise your voice toward him. You should never answer anyone who asks him about something, in order that he may be the one who answers. You should not speak to anyone in his session nor speak ill of anyone with him. If anyone ever speaks ill of him in your presence, you should defend him. You should conceal his faults and make manifest his virtues. You should not sit with him in enmity or show hostility toward him in friendship. If you do all of this, God's angels will give witness for you that you went straight to him and learned his knowledge for God's sake, not for the sake of the people.

[17] The right of him who trains you through property is that you should obey him and not disobey him, unless obeying him would displease God, for there can be no obedience to a creature when it is disobedience to God.

---

and people realised that he had been giving alms in secret. Cf. Madelung, ' 'Alī ebn al-Ḥoseyn', p. 850.

[8] i.e, the animal sacrificed during the *ḥajj*

[9] Allusion to: 195: *cast not yourselves by your own hands into destruction.*

[10] Imam Zayn al-'Ābidīn's attitude of respect toward the Umayyad rulers was clearly based upon this principle.

[C2. RIGHTS OF SUBJECTS]

[18] The right of your subjects through authority is that you should know that they have been made subjects through their weakness and your strength. Hence it is incumbent upon you to act with justice toward them and to be like a compassionate father toward them. You should forgive them their ignorance and not hurry them to punishment and you should thank God for the power over them which He has given to you.
[19] The right of your subjects through knowledge is that you should know that God made you a caretaker over them only through the knowledge He has given you and His storehouses which He has opened up to you. If you do well in teaching the people, not treating them roughly or annoying them, then God will increase His bounty toward you. But if you withhold your knowledge from people or treat them roughly when they seek knowledge from you, then it will be God's right to deprive you of knowledge and its splendour and to make you fall from your place in people's hearts.
[20] The right of your wife (*zawja*) is that you know that God has made her a repose and a comfort for you; you should know that she is God's favour toward you, so you should honour her and treat her gently. Though her right toward you is more incumbent, you must treat her with compassion, since she is your prisoner (*asīr*) whom you feed and clothe. If she is ignorant, you should pardon her.

[21] The right of your slave (*mamlūk*) is that you should know that he is the creature of your Lord, the son of your father and mother, and your flesh and blood. You own him, but you did- not make him; God made him. You did not create any one of his limbs, nor do you provide him with his sustenance; on the contrary, God gives you the sufficiency for that. Then He subjugated him to you, entrusted him to

you, and deposited him with you so that you may be safeguarded by the good you give to him. So act well toward him, just as God has acted well toward you. If you dislike him, replace him, but do not torment a creature of God. And there is no strength save in God.[11]

[11] At this period in Islamic history, slavery was still common because of wars at the frontiers (slaves were invariably captured in battle; cf. Supplication 27, ' For the People of the Frontiers'). The sources indicate that the Imam often had slaves, most likely because people gave them to him as part of the alms (the family of the Prophet being entitled to these) and also because he used to purchase them in order to free them. It is said that he would never beat his slaves, but rather write down their misdeeds. Then. At the end of the month of

[C3. RIGHTS OF WOMB RELATIVES]

[22] The right of your mother is that you know that she carried you where no one carries anyone, she gave to you of the fruit of her heart that which no one gives to anyone, and she protected you with all her organs. She did not care if she went hungry as long as you ate, if she was thirsty as long as you drank, if she was naked as long as you were clothed, if she was in the sun as long as you were in the shade. She gave up sleep for your sake, she protected you from heat and cold, all in order that you might belong to her. You will not

be able to show her gratitude, unless through God's help and giving success. [12]

[23] The right of your father is that you know that he is your root. Without him, you would not be. Whenever you see anything in yourself which pleases you, know that your father is the root of its blessing upon you. So praise God and thank Him in that measure. And there is no strength save in God.

[24] The right of your child is that you should know that he is from you and will be ascribed to you, through both his good and his evil, in the immediate affairs of this world. You are responsible for what has been entrusted to

---

Ramadan, he would call them together and list their misdeeds, asking them to pray to God to forgive him just as he had forgiven them. Then he would free them with generous gifts. If he owned a slave at the beginning or the middle of the year, he would free him on the eve of the Feast of Fast-breaking and buy another slave. (*A'yān al-shī'a,*IV, 193-4). Once the Imam called his slave twice but he did not respond. When he answered the third time he said: 'Did you not hear my voice?' the slave answered: 'Yes, I did.' The Imam asked: 'Then why did you not answer me?' he replied: 'Because I am safe from you.' The Imam said: 'Praise belongs to God, who made my slave safe from me *(A'yān al-shī'a* ,IV, 200; *Biḥār,,* XLVI, 56). Once a slave girl poured water for the Imam while he was making the ablution for prayer. Suddenly the pot dropped from her hand and struck him in the face cutting him. He turned toward her and the slave girl said; 'God says *those who restrain their rage.'* He said: 'I have restrained my rage.' She said: '*and pardon the people.'* He said: 'God has pardoned you.' She said: '*and God loves the good-doers* (3: 134).' He said: 'Go. You are a free woman.' (*Biḥār,,* XLVI, 68; cf. 96)

[12] Cf. the well known *ḥadīth* in which the Prophet replied to a companion who asked him toward whom he should show familial devotion (*bir*): 'he answered: "your mother." He was asked: "Then to whom?" he replied: "your mother." Again he was asked: "Then to whom?" he replied: "your mother." Once again he was asked: "Then to whom?" he replied: "Then to your father, then to the next nearest, then to the next nearest".' (Tirmindhī, Birr I; Abū Dāwūd, Adab I20; Ibn Māja, Adab I; Aḥmad V, 3 and 5).

you, such as educating him in good conduct (*husn al-adab*), pointing him in the direction of his Lord, and helping him to obey Him. So act toward him with the action of one who knows that he will be rewarded for good doing toward him and punished for evildoing.

[25] The right of your brother is that you know that he is your hand, your might, and your strength. Take him not as a weapon with which to disobey God, nor as equipment with which to wrong God's creatures. Do not neglect to help him against his enemy or to give him good counsel. If he obeys God, well and good, but if not, you should honour God more than him. And there is no strength save in God.

[D. RIGHTS OF OTHERS]

[26] The right of your master (*mawlā*) who has favoured you [by freeing you from slavery] is that you know that he has spent his property for you and brought you out of the abasement and estrangement of bondage to the exaltation and comfort of freedom. He has freed you from the

captivity of possession and loosened the bonds of slavehood from you. He has brought you out of prison, given you ownership of yourself, and given you leisure to worship your Lord. You should know that he is the closest of God's creatures to you in your life and your death and that aiding him with your life and what he needs from you is incumbent upon you. And there is no strength save in God.

[27] The right of the slave (*mawlā*) whom you have favoured [by freeing him] is that you know that God has made your freeing him a means of access to Him and a veil against the Fire. Your immediate reward is to inherit from him-if he does not have any maternal relatives-as a compensation for the property you have spent for him, and your ultimate reward is the Garden.

[28] The right of him who does a kindly act (*dhu l-ma'rūf*) toward you is that you thank him and mention his kindness; you reward him with beautiful words and you supplicate for him sincerely in that which is between you and God. If you do that, you have thanked him secretly and openly. Then, if you are able to repay him one day, you repay him.

[29] The right of the muezzin is that you know that he is reminding you of your Lord, calling you to your good fortune, and helping you to accomplish what God has made obligatory upon you. So thank him for that just as you thank one who does good to you.

[30] The right of your imam in your ritual prayer is that you know that he has taken on the role of mediator between you and your Lord. He speaks

for you, but you do not speak for him; he supplicates for you, but you do not supplicate for him. He has spared you the terror of standing before God. If he performs the prayer imperfectly, that belongs to him and not to you; but if he performs it perfectly, you are his partner, and he has no excellence over you. So protect yourself through him, protect your prayer through his prayer, and thank him in that measure.

[31] The right of your sitting companion (*jalīs*) is that you treat him mildly, show fairness toward him while vying with him in discourse, and do not stand up from sitting with him without his permission. But it is permissible for him who sits with you to leave without asking your permission. You should forget his slips and remember his good qualities, and you should tell nothing about him but good.

[32] The right of your neighbour (*jār*) is that you guard him when he is absent, honour him when he is present, and aid him when he is wronged. You do not pursue anything of his that is shameful; if you know of any evil from him, you conceal it. If you know that he will accept your counsel, you counsel him in that which is between him and you. You do not forsake him in difficulty, you release him from his stumble, you forgive his sin, and you associate with him generously. And there is no strength save in God.

[33] The right of the companion (*ṣāḥib*) is that you act as his companion with bounty and in fairness. You honour him as he honours you and you do not let him be the first to act with generosity. If he is the first, you repay him. You wish for him as he wishes for you and you restrain him from any act of disobedience he might attempt. Be a mercy for him, not a chastisement. And there is no strength save in God.

[34] The right of the partner (*sharīk*) is that if he should be absent, you suffice him in his affairs, and if he should be present, you show regard for him. You make no decision without his decision and you do nothing on the basis of your own opinion, but you exchange views with him. You guard his property for him, and you do not betray him in that of his affair which is difficult or of little importance, for God's hand is above the hands of two partners as long as they do not betray each other. And there is no strength save in God.

[35] The right of your property (*māl*) is that you take it only from what is lawful and you spend it only in what is proper. Through it you should not prefer above yourself those who will not praise you. You should act with it in obedience to your Lord and not be miserly with it, lest you fall back into regret and remorse while suffering the ill consequence. And there is no strength save in God.

[36] The right of him to whom you owe a debt (*al-gharīm alladhī yuṭālibuka*) is that, if you have the means, you pay him back, and if you are in straitened

circumstances, you satisfy him with good words and you send him away with gentleness.

[37] The right of the associate (*khalīṭ*) is that you neither mislead him, nor act dishonestly toward him, nor deceive him, and you fear God in his affair.

[38] The right of the adversary (*khaṣm*) who has a claim against you is that, if what he claims against you is true, you give witness to it against yourself. You do not wrong him

and you give him his full due. If what he claims against you is false, you act with kindness toward him and you show nothing in his affair other than kindness; you do not displease your Lord in his affair. And there is no strength save in God. [13]

[39] The right of the adversary against whom you have a claim is that, if your claim against him is true, you maintain polite moderation in speaking to him and you do not deny his right. If your claim is false, you fear God, repent to Him, and abandon your claim.

[40] The right of him who asks you for advice (*mustashīr*) is that, if you consider that he has a correct opinion, you advise him to follow it, and if you do not consider it so, you direct him to someone who does consider it so.

[41] The right of him whom you ask for advice (*mushīr*) is that you do not make accusations against him for an opinion which does not conform to your own opinion. If it conforms to it, you praise God.

[42] The right of him who asks your counsel (*mustanṣiḥ*) is that you give him your counsel, but you conduct yourself toward him with compassion and kindness.

[43] The right of your counsellor (*nāṣiḥ*) is that you act gently toward him and give ear to him. If he presents you with the right course, you praise God, but if he does not agree with you, you show compassion toward him and make no accusations against him; you consider him to have made a mistake, and you do not take him to task for that, unless he should be deserving of accusation. Then attach no more importance to his affair. And there is no strength save in God.

[44] The right of him who is older than you (*kabīr*) is that you show reverence toward him because of his age and you honour him because he entered Islam before you. You leave off confronting him in a dispute, you do not precede him in a path, you do not go ahead of him, and you do not consider him foolish. If he should act foolishly toward you, you put

[13] Zayn al-ʿĀbidīn's personal qualitites of forbearance and pardon are often sighted in the sources. Once a man cursed him to his face but he ignored the man. Then the man shouted: 'I mean you!' the Imam replied: 'and from you I am turning away,' alluding the Qur 'ānic verse *bid to what is honourable. And turn away form the ignorant* (7: 199). If anyone reviled him, he would say: 'If I am as you say, I ask God to forgive me. And if I am not as you say, I ask God to forgive you.' (*A'yān,* pp. 194, 193).

up with him and you honour him because of the right of Islam and the respect due to it.

[45] The right of him who is younger (*saghīr*) is that you show compassion toward him through teaching him, pardoning him, covering his faults, kindness toward him, and helping him.

[46] The right of him who asks (*sā'il*) from you is that you give to him in the measure of his need.

[47] The right of him from whom you ask is that you accept from him with gratitude and recognition of his bounty if he gives, and you accept his excuse if he withholds.

[48] The right of him through whom God makes you happy (*surūr*) is that you first praise God, then you thank the person.

[49] The right of him who does evil to you is that you pardon him. But if you know that your pardon will harm him, you defend yourself. God says, *Whosoever defends himself after he has been wronged - against them there is no way* (42:41).

[50] The right of the people of your creed (*milla*) is harbouring safety for them, compassion toward them, kindness toward their evildoer, treating them with friendliness, seeking their well-being, thanking their good-doer, and keeping harm away from them. You should love for them what you love for yourself and dislike for them what you dislike for yourself. Their old men stand in the place of your father, their youths in the place of your brothers, their old women in the place of your mother, and their young ones in the place of your children.

[51] The right of the people under the protection [of Islam] (*dhimma*) is that you accept from them what God has accepted from them and you do no wrong to them as long as they fulfil God's covenant.

SELECT BIBLIOGRAPHY

(From the Arabic-English Edition - 2005)

THE ṢAḤĪFA

The Ṣaḥīfat=ul=Kamilah: 'The Psalms of the children of Muhammad', with preface and English translation by Syed Ahmad Ali Mohani, 1929, 2nd ed. Revised by M.A.H. Khan, Lucknow, 1969-70; the same work with many of the addenda appeared as *Saheefa -e-Kamelah*, 3rd ed., Karachi, 1971.

Al-Ṣaḥīfat al-kāmilat al-Sajjādiyya, with introductions by Sayyid Muḥammad Mishkāt and Sayyid Shihāb al-Dīn Mar'ashī (Āqā Najafī), Tehran, 1361/1942; same text with Persian translation by Ṣadr al-Dīn Balāghī, Tehran, 1369/1950.

Ṣaḥīfa-yi kāmila-yi Sajjādiyya, Arabic text with Persian trans. by Ḥājj Mīrzā Abu l-Ḥasan Sha'rānī, Tehran, n.d.

Ṣaḥīfa-yi kāmila-yi Sajjādiyya, in the hand of 'A. Miṣbāḥzāda, London, 1403/1983.

Al-Ṣaḥīfat al-Sajjādiyyat al-khāmisa, Muḥsin al-Amin al-'Āmilī, Damascus, 1330/1912.

Al-Ṣaḥīfat al-Sajjādiyyat al-rābi'a, Mīrzā Ḥusayn ibn Muḥammad Taqī Nūrī, [Iran], 1299/1881.

Al-Ṣaḥīfat al-Sajjādiyyat al-thālitha, Mīrzā 'Abd Allāh ibn 'Īsā Tabrīzī Afandī, Mashhad, 1287/1870.

Al-Ṣaḥīfat al-Sajjādiyyat al-thāniyya, Muḥammad ibn al-Ḥasan al-Ḥurr al-'Āmilī, Bombay, 1311/1893-4.

Sharḥ Al-Ṣaḥīfat al-Sajjādiyyat al-mawsūm bi-Riyāḍ al-Sālikīn, Sayyid 'Alīkhān Shīrāzī, Tehran, 1271/1854-5; a much shorter version of the same work was published in three volumes as *Talkhīṣ al-Riyāḍ*, Tehran, 1381/1961-2.

Tarjama wa sharḥ-i Ṣaḥīfa-yi kāmila-yi Sajjādiyya, Ḥājj Sayyid 'Alīnaqī Fayḍ al-Islām, Tehran, 1375/1955.

OTHER SOURCES

Abū Dāwūd, *Al-Sunan*, Cairo, 1371.

Aḥmad ibn Ḥanbal, *Al-Musnad*, Beirut, n.d.

al-Amīn al-'Āmilī, Muḥsin, *A'yān al-shī'a*, Damascus, 1935-.

Arberry, A.J., *The Koran Interpreted*, London 1962.

Al-Bukhārī, *al-Saḥiḥ*, Cairo, 1378/1958-9.

Chittick, W.C., 'Dhikr', *Encyclopedia of Religion*, New York, 1987, IV, 341-4.

-------, *A Shi'ite Anthology*, London, 1981.

Danner, V., and Thackston, W., *Ibn Ata'illah: The Book of wisdom/ Khwaja Abdullah Ansari: Intimate conversations*, New York, 1978.

Al-Dārimī, *Al-Sunan*, n.p., n.d.

Graham, W., *Divine Word and Prophetic Word in Early Islam*, The Hague, 1977.

BIBLIOGRAPHY

Ibn Māja, *Al-Sunan*, Cairo, 1372/1952-3.

Jafri, S.H.M., *The Origins and Early Development of Shi'a Islam*, Beirut, 1979.

Laine, E.W., *Arabic-English Lexicon*, reprinted Cambridge, 1984.

Laugier de Beaurecueil, S. de, *Les étapes des itinérants vers Dieu*, Cairo, 1962.

Madelung, W.F., "Ali ibn al-Hosayn', *Encyclopaedia Iranica*, London, 1982-, I, 849-50.

Majlisī, Muḥammad Bāqir, *Biḥār al-anwār*, reprinted Beirut, 1983.

Al-Maybudī, *Kashf al-asrār*, edited 'A. A. Ḥikmat, Tehran, 1338-9/1959-60.

Murata, S., 'The Angels', in S.H. Nasr (ed.), *Islamic Spirituality: foundations*, New York, 1987, pp. 324-44.

Muslim, *Al-Saḥīḥ*, Cairo, 1334/1914-15.

Nakamura, K., *Ghazali on prayer*, Tokyo, 1973.

Al-Nasā'ī, *Al-Sunan*, Beirut, 1348/1929-30.

Nurbakhsh, J., *Sufism IV: Repentance, Abstinence, Renunciation, Wariness,Humility, Humbleness, Sincerity, Constancy, Courtesy*, London, 1987.

Padwick, Constance E., *Muslim Devotions: A Study of Prayer-manuals in Common Use*, London, 1961.

Robson, J. (trans.), *Mishkat al-masabih*, Lahore, 1962-6.

Smith, J.I., and Haddad, Y.Y, *The Islamic Understanding of Death and Resurrection*, Albany, 1981.

Al-Ṭabarsī, *Majma' al-bayān*, Tehran, 1379/1959-60.

Al-Ṭihrānī, Āqā Buzurg, *Al-Dharī'a ilā taṣānīf al-shī'a*, Najaf, 1355-/1936-.

Al-Tirmidhī, *Al-Sunan*, Cairo, 1357/1938.

Wensinck, A.J., et al., *Concordance et indices de la tradition musulmane*, Leiden, 1936-69.

Wensinck, A.J., 'Shafā'a', *Encyclopedia of Islam* (old edition), London and Leiden, 1908-36.